REINVENTING PHILANTHROPY

RELATED TITLES FROM POTOMAC BOOKS

Business Behaving Well:
Social Responsibility, from Learning to Doing
Ron Elsdon, ed.

American Poverty:
Presidential Failures and a Call to Action
Woody Klein

Warfare Welfare: The Not-So-Hidden Costs
of America's Permanent War Economy
Marcus G. Raskin and Gregory D. Squires, eds.

Reinventing Philanthropy

A Framework for More Effective Giving

ERIC FRIEDMAN

Potomac Books / Washington, D.C.

Potomac Books is an imprint of the
University of Nebraska Press.

Library of Congress Cataloging-
in-Publication Data
Friedman, Eric, 1977–
Reinventing philanthropy: a framework for more effective giving /
Eric Friedman. — First edition.
pages cm
Includes bibliographical references and index.
ISBN 978-1-61234-572-7 (hardcover: alk.
paper) — ISBN 978-1-61234-573-4 (electronic
edition) 1. Charities. 2. Charities—Moral
and ethical aspects. 3. Nonprofit organizations. 4. Voluntarism. I. Title.
HV41.F686 2013
361.7—dc23
2013019243

Printed in the United States of
America on acid-free paper that meets
the American National Standards
Institute Z39-48 Standard.

Potomac Books
22841 Quicksilver Drive
Dulles, Virginia 20166

First Edition

10 9 8 7 6 5 4 3 2 1

For those donating to make
the world a better place: may
your philanthropic success drive
your personal fulfillment.

And for my daughter, who,
as I write this, is growing and
kicking in utero: may the future
always improve on the past.

Contents

Preface

> To give money away is an easy matter and in any man's power. But to decide to whom to give it, and how large, and when, and for what purpose and how, is neither in every man's power nor an easy matter.
>
> —attributed to Aristotle

Philanthropy is broken and almost everyone involved knows it. Fundraisers know that the causes that get the most donations are not necessarily the ones that make the greatest impact. Many donors recognize that they do not know how to define what "high-performing" nonprofits are, let alone how to identify them. Nonprofit program staff members know that tremendous resources—both time and money—are diverted from their programs in order to engage and solicit donors. Longtime observers of the philanthropic world know that the personal whims and preferences of donors determine where dollars flow regardless of need or impact. Philanthropy isn't working as it should, and it needs to be reinvented.

Donors share the blame. No one holds donors accountable; it's their money, so they can do with it as they choose. Donors control the money, so charities adapt to their behavior, regardless of whether it is good or bad. Rarely do donors receive critical feedback: organizations they donate to (or consider donating to) are reluctant to say anything that might reduce potential donations, and organizations they don't (or won't) consider donating to have no reason to interact with them. Most donors get plenty of appreciation from the recipient organizations, but no substantive feedback.

Unfortunately, today's dominant paradigm of philanthropy presents as axiomatic the idea that donors should give to the causes they care about and have personal ties to, rather than trying to make the biggest dent in the causes most effective at helping others.

Is philanthropy about helping those in need or pursuing the personal passions of those with enough money to give away? If it is the former, then shouldn't a central tenet be to try to provide the most help possible? Is there an alternative framework that focuses on the recipients, assessing who is most in need of help and how donors can make the most impact?

Changing donors' behavior must start with the donors. Donors should critically analyze their own motivations and actions. Are their motivations more selfish than altruistic? How can donors know when their personal biases impede their ability to give effectively? What conditions, if any, should donors attach to their gifts to ensure the highest and greatest use for the donation? Which behaviors impose undue burdens on the organizations they work with?

As a donor, I've struggled with many of these issues myself. This book is the culmination of my thinking, and it challenges many commonly accepted views about philanthropy. It is written by a donor, about donors, and for donors who want to look critically at what they can do to improve their philanthropy. Although effective philanthropy can bring donors benefits such as tax breaks, public recognition, and emotional fulfillment, this book is not written for people who treat these items as more important than maximizing the positive impacts of their giving.

Within the philanthropic community, there is an extreme fear of being judgmental. The social rules of order are that almost anyone who is trying to do "good" is beyond criticism. A donor who chooses to give to a well-endowed art museum instead of helping those in extreme poverty who are dying of preventable diseases cannot be criticized, as that donor is doing more good than the person who doesn't give to either cause. And any donor who is also a critic—myself included—delivers his or her critique from an equally vulnerable glass house. The resulting code of silence suffocates constructive discourse, harming the philanthropic community and the world it is trying to serve.

In the spirit of helping others, I will break the social rules of order and state my opinions in this book. With respect to the donor who gives to a well-endowed art museum instead of helping those in extreme poverty who are dying of diseases that are easily preventable or curable, I believe that person is doing more good than the person who gives nothing. But not much more good—at least, not relative to the amount of good they could be doing with an equal-value donation to other causes. And I don't think that my position is unreasonable, unfair, or inappropriately judgmental.

I think the relative merits of supporting art museums versus saving people dying of diseases that are easily preventable or curable are pretty clear. Both are "good" causes, but one is likely to do a lot more good than the other. However, there is a slippery slope with this type of critique. Where do we draw the line between constructive commentary and inflammatory rhetoric?

This book includes many stories about real philanthropists. The examples incorporate role models, ineffective donors, and donors who meet objectives based more on their own personal preferences than on what would help others most. These stories help illustrate not only the type of philanthropy that I'm advocating, but also differentiate it from the typical philanthropy that needs to be reinvented. These "anti–role models" are not dishonest or corrupt; in most cases, they engage in fairly common philanthropic behavior. But certain aspects of this behavior reduce its capacity for improving the world. My intention is not to personally attack these donors. Rather, I want to challenge broader cultural beliefs in the philanthropic sector, and the approaches of these donors are symptomatic of common practice. They are generous people trying to do good things, and for that they should be commended. But this book is not about effort or intent; it is about impact. While writing it, there were times when I felt like a bit of a jerk, as I criticized well-intentioned, compassionate people. And though you, too, may perceive some of the illustrations to be meanspirited or inappropriate, that is not my goal. Instead, I ask you to take the book in the manner it is intended: to illustrate points to make the world better by improving philanthropy.

Although not all good causes are equally good, it is difficult to compare diverse causes. Individual judgments on the relative merits of different causes will surely vary, as will perceptions of the effectiveness of different organizations. So a dozen thoughtful philanthropists, all trying to maximize their impact on global welfare, may produce a dozen different philanthropic approaches with a meaningful level of diversity. This book will not present a one-size-fits-all solution, but there are broad principles for thinking about the core issues.

I've gone through this thought process for my own philanthropy. I am not a trained expert in philanthropy, but I have found that nearly all of the experts fail to honestly and adequately address these issues. They are too entrenched in a flawed system that doesn't sufficiently differentiate between donating and donating effectively. They are too unwilling to acknowledge that donating to some causes, although beneficial, does not have the same impact as donating to others. And they are too unwilling to pass judgment on the giving patterns of others.

Giving can go a long way to improving the world, and I hope that this book will help you through the self-reflection and analysis necessary to reinvent your philanthropy. Donors who understand and embrace the process of making their giving more impactful will not only do more good, but also get more satisfaction.

Acknowledgments

There are few things more helpful to an author than people willing to give their honest opinions, especially when they disagree. I am tremendously thankful to have had that in spades. The constructive criticism provided throughout this process was instrumental in helping clarify my thinking and writing. Each person shared their own unique perspective, making this book much better.

Hilary Claggett, my acquisitions editor, was the first person at Potomac Books who believed in me and the idea of this book. The guidance she provided during the initial stages of publication was critical. Laura Briggs, Elizabeth Demers, Sam Dorrance, and Liz Norris provided assistance that has been important for the book. Julie Gutin combed through every word in the manuscript and suggested a tremendous number of ways to improve it. And Kathryn Owens managed the production process, answering all of my questions along the way and taking care at each step to add value to the ultimate product for readers.

I am lucky to have several close friends who spent a lot of time and effort helping me. I cannot do justice to the amount of thanks I owe to Chad Brooker, Chanita Chantaplin-Mclelland, Fred Hyland, and Matt Mclelland. Each of them reviewed the book, often the early drafts when it was in its roughest form, and gave detailed suggestions on how to make it better. I had several hour-plus-long conversations with each of them over evenings and weekends to help refine my thinking and writing, and I learned so much from each of them. They sometimes re-reviewed later drafts to make sure

I got it. And while critiquing so many areas that needed work, they also provided extraordinary amounts of encouragement throughout the process.

Chris Dunford, the retired president of Freedom from Hunger, is someone I am proud to consider a friend and role model. He has dedicated his life to helping others. Every time we talk, Chris impresses me with his thoughtfulness, expertise, and integrity. He reviewed the manuscript in detail and shared valuable insights from his perspective as a leader of a nonprofit.

Elie Hassenfeld and his colleagues at GiveWell took huge risks, both personal and career-related, to fill a void in the charitable sector. They have influenced my giving and advanced my thinking. I am certain that countless others would say the same thing, and the charitable sector is better because of them. Elie also provided important feedback to help improve several aspects of the book.

Anastasia P. Sibano Austin-Friedman and Vladimir P. Sibano Austin-Friedman are my furry feline friends, who not only encouraged me to stay home as often as possible to work on the book, but also kept me company much of the time.

Renee and Mike Slade and Ryan Weddle reviewed portions of the book and provided guidance on how I could make it better. Corinne Liccketto provided advice and help that has been critical for a successful launch.

I owe great thanks to my parents, not only for raising me to be the person I am, but also for helping me with the book. They are usually agreeable individuals, but when I asked them to tell me everything about the manuscript that they disagreed with, they both delivered. The book includes dozens of major improvements to reflect their feedback.

Most important, my wonderful wife, Jenny, has provided support in so many different ways. How can I say enough to thank the person who has been my best friend and partner in life throughout this process? I made her read every word of the book multiple times, and she has influenced so many key changes. She was often the first person to read what I wrote and helped me bring it to a more suitable form. She took care of family chores while I wrote, and she tolerated me being a lousy companion when I holed up to write. And now she is carrying our child. She supports the things that are important to me and is a wonderful wife. I won the lottery the day we got married.

Although I could not have written this book without assistance from so many people, all flaws remain my own.

REINVENTING PHILANTHROPY

1

THE PHILOSOPHY OF PHILANTHROPY

1

A Tale of Two Children

It's very easy to want to support all good causes,
but in the real world this is just not possible.
—Bjørn Lomborg[1]

A few years ago, the following story was highlighted on St. Jude Children's Research Hospital's website as an inspiring testament to the hospital's work:

> Sabrina developed bruises on her arms and legs that didn't go away, even after a few weeks. Then one night, during bath time, Sabrina's mom, Vicky, was startled to see a rash across her little girl's chest. When she noticed that her usually sunny daughter was becoming more and more lethargic, mother's intuition kicked in. This was something serious, Vicky felt. The next day, she took Sabrina to the pediatrician.
>
> At the doctor's office, Sabrina underwent an ultrasound and blood work. When Sabrina's doctor referred the family to the local St. Jude Children's Research Hospital affiliate, Vicky felt her dread rising. At the affiliate, Sabrina underwent more tests. The results were devastating: Sabrina suffered from t-cell acute lymphoblastic leukemia.
>
> The next day, Sabrina and Vicky arrived at St. Jude, where Sabrina quickly started chemotherapy on a two-and-a-half-year treatment plan....
>
> "Something like this puts life in perspective," Vicky said. "We thank St. Jude every day for saving Sabrina." Sabrina is able to do her weekly chemotherapy at the local St. Jude affiliate. She takes oral chemotherapy

> each day, and returns to Memphis once a month for intense chemotherapy. Happily, she is responding well to treatment.
>
> Vicky and her husband are grateful for the donors who support St. Jude. . . . "Never receiving a bill from St. Jude . . . that is a true blessing," said Vicky.[2]

Sabrina is lucky to be alive, thanks to St. Jude and the donors who help maintain its high standards of care. According to St. Jude's National Director of Outreach, Marlo Thomas, "When a family comes through the door here . . . the first thing we say is 'We're going to try everything to save your child.' We're the pioneers. We're the cutting edge of science. We take sick children that have no place else to go."[3] And a look at St. Jude's financials makes it very believable that the organization does everything possible for its patients. The daily operating cost for St. Jude is nearly $1.8 million, which supports its research and treatment of about 260 patients each day.[4] Most of St. Jude's revenue comes from donations. Every patient St. Jude accepts is treated without regard to the family's ability to pay. St. Jude pays for all the costs of treatment not covered by third-party insurers, even if a patient has no insurance.

There can be no doubt that St. Jude saves lives, and its donors play a critical role.

Halfway around the world, in Malanje, Angola, Domingos Antonic struggled with a different illness. He was sick with malaria for several days before being brought to the Malanje Provincial Hospital, already underweight for an eight-month-old. Domingos suffered from acute anemia and had difficulty breathing. He needed oxygen, but the hospital did not have an oxygen tank. His veins were so small that the staff was unsuccessful at giving him the transfusion he needed; a surgeon could have cut to find a vein, but there was no surgeon available. A $10 mosquito net probably would have prevented his illness, but the hospital received only 300,000 of the 1.2 million needed to cover everyone in the area.[5]

Domingos died.

Two innocent children got sick. One received the best treatment in the world. Another barely received any treatment. One lived; one died.

In a perfect world, neither would have died. But that's not the world we live in. We live in a world with limited resources, and bad things happen that more resources could prevent. That fact drives many philanthropists to donate their wealth to make the world a better place, and for most of them, giving feels good.

But there's a dark side to giving that is rarely discussed in the world of philanthropy. For every person a donor helps, countless others are not helped. It isn't the donor's fault—it's impossible to help everyone—but it is reality. Donors who chose St. Jude over Malanje Provincial implicitly chose Sabrina over Domingos. Just as every donor to St. Jude deserves credit for saving Sabrina's life, they also made a decision that influenced the ultimate outcome for Domingos. They certainly didn't kill Domingos, but the choices that helped save Sabrina's life also influenced Domingos's death. Many find this way of thinking offensive—and it is—but it is also reality. It makes giving seem less fun. Some donors might respond by splitting their gift among many different organizations to help both children, but spreading resources around doesn't effectively tackle the broader issue: scarce resources prevent them from helping everyone in need. Choices must be made.

Some might argue that giving to St. Jude doesn't necessarily change the amount a donor would give to Malanje Provincial; that may be true in practice today, but it is the result of the decisions donors make and can reconsider. Most donors ignore these issues and move on, helping a lucky few and not others, because they can't help everyone. They may rationalize this because by helping one, they are doing more than those who helped neither.

When the stakes are so high, doesn't Domingos deserve more consideration? Shouldn't donors think about their options more carefully? Maybe you believe that it is more important to save Sabrina's life than Domingos's because you're American and "charity begins at home." But the decision isn't as simple as Sabrina versus Domingos: one child here versus one there. Considering the $1.8M daily operating costs of St. Jude, it is fair to ask: Would a donation to Malanje Provincial Hospital have saved more lives? If there ever has been a question whose answer affected life-and-death situations, this is it. Even without perfectly reliable "cost-per-life-saved" measures from each institution, we can still make comparisons. This is not about criticizing one institution and taking money away from it to promote another, but about trying to do the most good with limited resources to balance the needs of the world's Sabrinas and Domingoses.

If I had a child with cancer, I'd want her to get the best care in the world. I'd do my best to get her the best doctors, nurses, and hospital I could find. I'd spare no expense to do anything that might help. I'd probably take her to a place like St. Jude. And I'd be eternally thankful for all the donors who made the institution available to help my child.

If I lived in Malanje and had a child dying of malaria, I'd take my child to the only place I knew with skilled medical professionals: the Malanje Provincial Hospital. I'd ask for the best doctors and nurses they have and would empty my life savings—probably not much if I lived in Malanje—to do whatever I could to get care for my child. I'd be eternally thankful for any donors that supported the hospital.

I probably wouldn't know that a place like St. Jude existed halfway around the world for children with different illnesses. I wouldn't know that American hospitals cannot refuse patients in need of emergency care, regardless of their ability to pay. I wouldn't know that in America, all hospitals have oxygen and surgeons. I wouldn't know that in an American hospital, it would be routine to save my child. I would have never known the difference between hospitals in America and those in Malanje.

If I knew those things, I'd be confused and disillusioned that donors gave so much to help those children, but left mine with a shell of a facility that can hardly be called a "hospital." I'd probably also be very angry at the donors who are continuously funding St. Jude and leaving Malanje Provincial woefully under-resourced. Why are those children so much more worthy of life than mine?

We can sympathize with the perspectives of either of these parents. We know that we would probably feel the same as them if we were in their shoes. But as a donor, we are neither. While the desperation of these parents is real, it is not ours. We are not trying to save our own children. Our choice is about helping others. We are somewhat removed from the situation. This is the perspective we have when we make our giving decisions. Who will we help, how, and why?

Many donors "adopt" the perspective of one set of parents over the other. They can imagine themselves having a family member with cancer, but not malaria. They can see themselves going to a hospital like St. Jude, but not Malanje Provincial. They are geographically and culturally closer to families at St. Jude. So donating to St. Jude seems more like helping their own children. The children helped by Malanje Provincial are strangers.

The psychological aspects of this line of thinking are very real. They definitely affect how many donors decide where to give, but should they?

Whether they acknowledge it or not, donors to St. Jude made a decision that affected children like Sabrina as well as those like Domingos. Many of them will feel good simply because their donation helped some children. This is not unreasonable, but it also doesn't capture the depth of the situation.

Can St. Jude do more with the donation than the Malanje Provincial Hospital, or another organization? Most people would expect someone from Malanje to donate to their local hospital and someone who has had a child with cancer to donate to St. Jude, but a better approach to philanthropy would be to consider either hospital regardless of the donor's personal background.

This is a moral issue. What are our obligations to help others? How should we think about the ethical consequences of choosing between helping Sabrina, Domingos, and anyone else who is in need? What about a decision to spend money on ourselves instead of using it to help others? These are undoubtedly important issues. The people who have tried to build frameworks for thinking about them range from religious leaders, politicians, philosophers, and even ordinary individuals deciding how to live their own lives. This topic is very meaty and could easily fill up an entire book. Nevertheless, this book will not focus on the moral aspects of philanthropy.[6] Instead, *Reinventing Philanthropy* is intended for those who have already decided to dedicate their charitable budgets to do the most good possible, regardless of whether this decision was made due to a moral obligation or a practical desire to get the most bang for each charitable buck. It addresses the following question: How can donors make the biggest impact with their donations?

This question is not easy and doesn't have an objective answer. I hope this book encourages you to think about philanthropy differently and gives you more knowledge on how to increase the impact of your gifts. If maximizing the impact of your gift is not your primary concern—maybe you seek public recognition, tax breaks, or emotional fulfillment—then this book may not be for you. But I believe that most donors are deeply concerned about helping others and I have written this book for them. Donors who are more confident in their decisions will ultimately give better and maybe even more, resulting in greater and greater positive impacts.

2

Failings of Philanthropy

Billions are wasted on ineffective philanthropy.
Philanthropy is decades behind business in applying
rigorous thinking to the use of money.
—Michael Porter[1]

Answering the question of Sabrina versus Domingos is no easy task, and it is worthwhile to start by stepping back and considering why people give. There are as many reasons as there are donors, but many say they are motivated by a desire to "give back." Everyone seems to know what this means, but it is difficult to define. Let's explore this concept further because of its centrality to many of the failings of philanthropy.

What differentiates "giving back" from other forms of giving? Is it defined so literally that the donation must be to the specific people, community, or institution that helped the donor or made the donor who he is today? Is the purpose of giving back primarily to repay an obligation or to help others? Do these questions even matter?

I graduated from Stanford University, and the university has reminded me about the importance of giving back since my freshman year. Stanford focuses on a very specific form of giving back: donating to Stanford. At the same time, Stanford prides itself in teaching critical thinking, which helps me evaluate the merits of giving back by donating to my alma mater.

I enjoyed my college years and gained a lot from them; however, I can't actually give back to those who helped me. The university's founders have long since passed away, so I cannot give back to them for building many of the classrooms I studied in or for seeding the endowment that helped fund much of the cost of my education. My fellow students are also long gone from the university and dispersed around the globe, so it is impractical to repay them for enriching my collegiate experience. Some of the professors and administrators who helped me are still there, though many are retired or deceased. I simply can't give back to the people who gave to me, but many people might not be concerned about that, as it may be too literal an interpretation of "giving back."

What about other definitions of giving back? Maybe giving back is about a quasi-debt obligation to the institution or community that helped the donor. When I came to Stanford, did I enter into an implicit agreement with the university to donate to it in the future, especially if I made money because of the education I was provided? I certainly wasn't aware of this at the time I accepted Stanford's offer of admission, though maybe it is an implied obligation. But again, most people would not view "giving back" as such a formal obligation.

Many people believe that "giving back" is not so much about repaying the specific people who helped me, but reciprocating the favors of prior generations by giving to future generations. If I want to give back, do I have to reciprocate the exact same favor given to me, or can I provide a different favor instead? Do I have to give to the same institution that helped me? After all, Stanford has a $17 billion endowment,[2] and I find it hard to believe that it needs my donation as much as other organizations.[3]

A slightly different view is that the goal of giving back may be to repay the advantages that a person received by providing similar advantages to others, in which case I might consider donating to a different university, possibly Stanford's cross-town rival, the University of California at Berkeley. A less fortunate university, UC Berkeley could use the help—its endowment is only $3 billion.[4] Never in a million years would I root for its basketball team, but philanthropy should extend beyond such rivalries, and it might be worth considering whether UC Berkeley could do more good with my donation than my alma mater.

A more expansive purpose of giving back would be to help future generations because past generations have helped me: "paying it forward." Then it would be more important to find the most effective way to help others than to give to the same institution or type of institution that helped me.

The organizations that helped me aren't necessarily the most effective at helping others. Even if they used to be, the world changes so quickly that, for most adults, donating to the exact same types of institutions that helped us years ago is unlikely to be the most effective way to help others. Although Leland and Jane Stanford's decision to found a university in 1891 may (or may not) have been the most impactful thing they could have done with their philanthropy at that time, what helped me isn't necessarily what others need most. Though some people may view donating to their alma maters as an expression of loyalty and gratitude to the institutions that helped them in the past, isn't the primary purpose of philanthropy to help others rather than express loyalty and gratitude?

Maybe I should give to a cause unrelated to higher education, even though higher education is what I benefited from. Perhaps I have an obligation to consider "giving back" to other causes that might do more good than any university. Can I "receive" from higher education and still "give back" to poverty elimination, environmental causes, or medical research?

Some donors will tell you that they have two-pronged goals, both to help others and to support the institutions that helped them. While it is reasonable to have multiple goals, it is naïve to believe that both goals can exist without impairing the effectiveness of either, and it is fair to ask about the size of the impairment, though the question might be difficult to answer.

When a donation is for an amount around $100, then it might be reasonable to give to an organization that the donor knows is good without spending a lot of time trying to figure out if there is something better. But if the figure increases to $10,000 or $1 million, then it absolutely has to be worth the extra effort to choose wisely. Giving back is a major justification for philanthropy, and understanding the dysfunctions of doing it blindly could give the Domingoses of the world a better chance.

The American Cancer Society's magazine, *Triumph,* includes a full-page donor profile of Larry. He made a donation in the name of his late wife, who lost her battle with cancer.

> Larry gave a $720,000 "pay if" donation to support research into breast cancer metastasis. . . . Important research projects that the Society has approved for funding are identified as "pay-if" when insufficient funds are available—unless generous donors like Larry step forward.

> "This fit my wife's situation," recalls Larry. "If it was another type of research, I probably wouldn't have been interested."[5]

It is unfortunate that Larry's wife passed away and noble that he is using the experience as motivation to help others. But even he acknowledged that he was more focused on addressing the disease that impacted his wife, rather than looking for the area where his donation could help others the most. The project Larry's donation went to was not even among the highest priorities for the American Cancer Society's research budget. They categorized it as a second-tier "pay if" project, meaning that they were not planning on funding it with their unrestricted budget for research. Although they consider it a worthwhile project, the second-tier pay-if categorization suggests that it is less important than projects funded with unrestricted donations.

It is not fair to present Larry in a bad light. Most people don't donate as generously as he did, and his generosity should be lauded. He made his choice of charity in the same way as most donors: focused on his own life experiences. But it is important to shine light on the consequences of this common type of giving so other donors can better understand the implications if they are considering something similar.

Not only is this method of charitable giving common, but it is encouraged and often held out in print as if it were a "best practice." Larry's situation is interesting because he presented it as if the alternative to this donation was not to donate at all. If the choice truly was between a significantly constrained donation and nothing, then one could certainly ask whether the purpose of the donation is designed more to help others or to express his feelings for his late wife.

I wonder if donors like Larry would give differently if they were explicitly told that their initial direction was viewed by objective experts as having inferior prospects for impact. As a more clear-cut example, what if a donor originally wanted to donate $100,000 to fund a stranger's life-saving medical treatment for kidney disease—possibly the donor knew about this treatment because a family member's life was saved by a similar treatment. Then the donor found out that for a donation of the same amount, two lives could be saved by focusing on treatment for a different illness—maybe a specific type of heart disease—though the donor has never known anybody with the illness. What would the donor do in that situation?

It appears that many, if not most, people supporting medical charities choose charities that have provided treatment for someone they know or specialize in a disease that someone close to them has suffered from. Do those people prefer to save one life instead of two, or have they simply not thought about the question?

One could certainly ask why I am so presumptuous as to think I have the right to comment on choices that other donors make. They are making decisions that literally affect who lives and who dies. These are serious decisions, and they should be made with more focused consideration for impact. In Larry's case, his donation made the world a better place, but probably could have gone a lot further toward that end if it had been done differently. And I believe the stakes are high enough to be presumptuous and comment.

Too many donors give to charities that affect them emotionally rather than to charities where their money will do the most good. They excuse themselves from effective giving under the rubric of "giving back." Further, the fact that Larry was profiled in a philanthropic publication serves as evidence that the philanthropic community does not object—and even encourages—less effective giving based on the emotional gratification the donor receives. Giving is too often about making the donor feel better and too infrequently about making those in need better. But should we criticize donors for giving to causes that touch their hearts?

Let's revisit our example of the person whose family was affected by kidney disease and was inspired to donate $100,000 to provide someone else with treatment for the same illness. Recall that there was a different medical condition—a type of heart disease—for which two lives could be saved for the same donation. Should we applaud the donor for saving one life or criticize him for not saving two? Does the donor deserve to feel good for saving one life or feel bad for not saving two? Although the donor could have allocated the $100,000 differently to save more lives, if the donor didn't donate to a cause he had personal experience with—in this case, kidney disease—maybe he wouldn't have given anything. This is not unlike Larry's situation—although he probably wasn't explicitly aware of the trade-off—and there is no simple answer.

In effect, both the donor to kidney disease as well as Larry chose to save one life instead of two by focusing on an area that is close to their hearts without considering other areas with greater potential impact. Donors need a connection to the recipients to get the emotional warm glow that inspires more giving.

One way of thinking about this issue is to classify giving as being either expressive or instrumental.[6] The purpose of an expressive gift is to express the donor's feelings. Examples include:

- Donating in memory of someone who recently passed away.
- Giving to the donor's alma mater as a gesture of gratitude, to repay the support given, or to help someone in similar circumstances to the donor.
- Giving to a medical cause or facility because its particular area of focus is something that has personally touched the donor's life.
- Donating within a particular geographic region because the donor has lived there and wants to help those near home.

Although most expressive donors hope their gifts help others, it is important to realize that their focus in selecting the gift's recipient is largely based on expressing personal emotions rather than having an impact.

Instrumental gifts, on the other hand, are designed to create positive social change. Instrumental gifts are much less likely to be specifically directed at meeting the emotional needs of the donor. They are also much more likely to meet the needs of the recipients.

To give in a way that is fully instrumental, the donor must be focused on impact in making decisions about which philanthropic goals to pursue as well as how to pursue those goals. For example, consider a donor who focuses on increasing the public's appreciation of sousaphone music. The donor extensively researches the many different ways to accomplish this goal and funds the program he believes will be most effective at accomplishing his goal. This donor could be considered very instrumental in one aspect of his giving because of his research into the most effective ways to increase the public's awareness of sousaphone music. However, he probably was not instrumental in choosing to focus on promoting sousaphone music; more likely, he chose this area because of a personal passion he wanted to express.

Many experts in philanthropy do not make a distinction between instrumental and expressive choices in terms of the donors' goals, only in how the donors pursue those goals. As an example, Philanthropedia, an organization that provides information to help guide donors, tells donors on its "Guide to Better Giving" webpage, "Wondering where to begin? Think about what you care about most. Our motto is: Pick a cause with your heart and then an organization with your mind."[7] They appear to believe that if a donor who cares about sousaphone music picks the best organization to increase its public appreciation, the gift would be extremely instrumental. But this logic is drawing a bright line where none should exist. The key difference between philanthropy and spending money on oneself is that philanthropy helps others, so all decisions about philanthropy should be considered in terms of how instrumental they are at helping others. In that respect, the importance to the world of having slightly greater public appreciation of sousaphone music should be a factor in considering how instrumental this donor is, just as the donor's effectiveness in pursuing this goal is.

Most giving tends to be a combination of expressive and instrumental. Even the most expressive donor would be unlikely to make a gift without believing it would do some good. And even the most instrumental donor is unlikely to write a large check without feeling some passion for the cause. However, there is a spectrum, and some philanthropy is closer to the expressive side while some is closer to instrumental.

Unfortunately, much of today's philanthropy is too far on the expressive end of the spectrum. Although expressive philanthropy should not be dismissed, as donors do need some motivation, serious philanthropy should be primarily instrumental. Donors should attempt to make a strong, positive impact when selecting the goals as well as when pursuing them. The irony is that donors often feel good because they are helping others, so logic suggests that instrumental donors should feel better about their giving than expressive donors. But logic doesn't always hold in the emotional world.

Within what is often considered "best practice" in today's institutional giving, there is significant room for improvement in balancing expressive and instrumental giving. About 90 percent of all foundations in the United States are restricted by their donors to specific geographic regions, usually to the city, county, or state in which the donors live.[8] While they may see many things around them that could be improved, most American donors remain insulated from many of the world's problems because we live in a wealthy country. So the most impactful causes are often not what most donors know best. Although geographic focus can be useful when it helps donors gain knowledge that improves giving patterns, a donor is unlikely to live in the region where a donation will have the most impact. Of course, a donor, likely more familiar with his hometown, probably knows how to make his contribution more effective there. This is especially true for small donors, for whom the difficulty of researching the merits of other geographies may not be worth the benefit of improved impact. Despite these possible rationalizations, it is unrealistic to expect that most donors have done the calculus and made an instrumental decision that "home" is the best place to give. They've probably just donated to express their desire to give back.

There is nothing wrong with having *some* expressive component of giving, but most philanthropists don't even seem to be aware of the inherent tensions between satisfying their own needs and those of the recipients. This dysfunction of philanthropy can only be addressed by donors developing more self-awareness to make more intentional decisions about what they should do and why.

There is no requirement for donors to do thorough research or give thoughtful consideration on whether there are other areas that should be of higher priority. It's their money, so donors are in control. In a free society, this is okay people can do whatever they want with their money, and certainly doing something good for others is better than being completely selfish, even if that "something good" isn't attempting to do the most good for others. Some donors may not care, though they probably won't admit it. It's their money and they're in control, so they certainly don't have to care. But one of the major reasons philanthropy is failing is because of the imbalance in focus on what will make donors feel good to the detriment of what will do the most good—it is hard to characterize philanthropy as "successful" if donations are not directed primarily to help others as much as possible.[9]

This is not the only failure of philanthropy, as many donors do care about the effectiveness of their donation. Another major reason for philanthropy's failure to get close to its potential is the lack of critical analysis regarding how donors can make the most impact. There is very little willingness to explicitly acknowledge that some good causes are better than others. This results in a severe lack of constructive criticism for donors. It is socially taboo to do anything other than enthusiastically praise donors or those working for good causes, with rare exceptions in the case of politically motivated charities and outright corruption. For example, while writing this book, many of my friends warned me that my reputation could be damaged for criticizing philanthropic practice—even though my intention is to make the world better with constructive criticism. How can philanthropy be effective if donors generally don't know how to improve and refuse to critically analyze ways to get better? It can't. It's time for philanthropy to be reinvented.

3

Do-Gooders and Do-Besters

> Sometimes, even when we have all the good intentions in the world, we don't find the most effective or most efficient way to act on them. . . . What we really need to know is: How can we act with more than good intentions? How can we find the best solutions?
>
> —Dean Karlan and Jacob Appel[1]

Sometimes people who are passionate about charitable causes are called "do-gooders." Merriam-Webster's dictionary defines a "do-gooder" as "an earnest often naive humanitarian or reformer."[2] Being called a do-gooder is simultaneously receiving a compliment and a slap in the face, and in many cases, both are well deserved. Many do-gooders act with more heart than head, and unfortunately, their good deeds often don't do as much good as possible.

It doesn't have to be that way. There are "do-besters," which I define as earnest, yet practical humanitarians or reformers whose actions attempt to maximize positive impacts. In philanthropy, these are the people who have great compassion, but who, when determining how to express their compassion, use robust, logical thought processes to figure out how best to improve the world. Their philanthropy is not just well intentioned, but well executed.

Fundamental to the concept of the do-bester is the notion that although there are many good causes and organizations to support, they are not all equally good. Some are more efficient and effective. Some do more great things with every dollar given. Some are, simply put, more deserving of financial support than others. These are the ones do-besters seek out. There is neither a single "best" cause or organization, nor is there a well-defined, objective way to identify the most promising ones. In that sense, the "best" in "do-bester" represents making a best possible effort to direct giving to the most fruitful areas.

Making a best effort to identify the most deserving causes and organizations is not easy. So many have compelling missions, often carefully crafted to appeal to donors' generosity, and most of the information about charitable causes is positive, not critical or objective. How often do you see an editorial criticizing someone for donating a million dollars to any good cause, even if the recipient charities are not doing much good by most people's standards? You see such criticisms occasionally in incidents of outright fraud and in reference to highly politicized nonprofits, but in general, there is a scarcity of critical viewpoints about philanthropy. It's hard to criticize those who are doing good for not doing "enough good." And in many cases, it seems equally hard to reserve greater praise for those doing the most good. Society doesn't differentiate between do-gooders and do-besters or help do-gooders become do-besters.

Ineffective philanthropy has very damaging consequences. With so many good causes and not enough critical analysis to identify the most effective ways to give, insufficient accountability is the norm in philanthropy, resulting in gifts that don't reach their potential and social needs that aren't fully met. The world would be a better place if do-gooders became do-besters. Unfortunately, given a philanthropic culture that largely fails to differentiate between the two, donors have difficultly identifying publicly recognized do-besters to emulate and seek advice from. Further, information helping donors transform from do-gooders to do-besters is limited and hard to find. As a result, it is more difficult than it should be for donors to approach their philanthropy from a do-bester perspective.

Numerous books on giving have been written to help donors. I read many of them to help sort through my own thoughts about philanthropy. While each provided some valuable insights, I found that nearly all were inadequate. They generally suggest that donors start by thinking about their own philanthropic interests and then find the best ways to address social needs in those areas. As a typical example, in their book on effective philanthropy, *Money Well Spent*, Hal Harvey and Paul Brest advise:

> We do not presume to tell you . . . what passions to pursue. *Those are personal choices*. . . . You may wish to promote the arts, religion, social

> services, education, health and medicine, or world peace; or protect the environment; or support the search for extraterrestrial life. . . . [S]uch issues are outside the scope of this book. The subjects considered here are relevant to all philanthropic goals.[3]

In practice, this might mean that a donor decides that helping the homeless in his or her community is an area of interest based on a personal choice, then use more analytical means to identify and fund the best ways to help the homeless. This is a very common approach, and it causes philanthropy to be much less effective than it could be.

An alternative approach is to start by trying to understand social needs, rather than the donor's own interests, and then find ways to address those needs. In this approach, the donor would be agnostic about who to help or how to help them, only caring that the help is as effective as possible at improving welfare. The starting point of this approach is very high-level, even a bit abstract. It requires asking questions such as these: What is the most effective way to improve social welfare? Is helping the homeless the best way to make the world a better place? Or is it promoting the arts, education, health, the environment, animal rights, or something else? Where are needs greatest? Where are solutions most effective? The difference between this approach and the traditional approach is whether philanthropy should start with donor-centric interests or with society's needs.

The difference can be huge. Everybody has a limited set of life experiences, and our interests tend to stem from them. It is no coincidence that many of the neediest causes in the world are those that (often wealthy) donors have no exposure to, so donors who focus their giving on areas they have personal experience with are stacking the deck against maximizing impact. Let's look more deeply at some examples discussed earlier:

- Many donors like Larry give to health-related organizations focused on areas that have touched their lives. When a family member suffers from cancer, the natural thing may be to give to a cancer-focused organization to alleviate the suffering of others with similar illnesses. But there are many illnesses like tuberculosis, malaria, and river blindness that are almost exclusively diseases for the poor. Those with enough money to donate will rarely have life experiences with these illnesses, so they are neglected by philanthropists. It is precisely because of this neglect that there are so many untapped opportunities for donors to make an impact—these diseases of poverty are often among the most curable with donor help. But donors like Larry, who focus on their own life experiences, typically exclude themselves from areas where their gifts can be stretched farthest to alleviate the most suffering for most people.

- It is well known that most people who donate to universities "give back" to the ones they attended. The schools donors attended tend to be those that are well resourced enough to train business and social leaders, which results in the best and wealthiest schools getting better and wealthier. Such inequality doesn't necessarily mean that donor money is used ineffectively—these schools could produce successful alumni precisely because they effectively use donations. But it is valid to question this practice when you consider that Stanford has an endowment of over $1 million per student and Princeton's is over $2 million,[4] despite so many other educational institutions being under-resourced. It seems likely that the culture of alumni contributions causes the neediest schools to be least likely to get the help they could use effectively.
- Though many people believe that "charity begins at home," our world is much more global now than when that cliché was first uttered. The needs in countries and neighborhoods near donors are likely to be very different from those in areas far away. There are different philanthropic merits to helping the neediest people in a wealthy country versus those in a poor country.

These are all issues do-besters think about. Do-besters will approach these issues from different perspectives, and they will come to different conclusions. It is not my goal to convince you that my favorite causes are the only ones that do-besters should give to. Rather, the common denominator of do-bester philanthropy is using a logical framework for filtering through all of the options and doing what the donor expects to generate the greatest positive impact. The best efforts of do-besters will not yield a single "best" cause or organization, and donors will find it difficult to define and measure impact. Different philanthropists will have different judgments about what types of things will make the greatest impact and which impacts will be most valuable to society. There is no formula for being a do-bester. But that doesn't mean the do-bester concept is useless or flawed; rather, it means that it is nuanced and subjective. Simply put, do-besters must be thoughtful.

When thinking about the do-bester idea, many wonder about the implications of everyone becoming a do-bester. While this is a theoretical exercise because the scenario is unlikely, it is worth exploring some of the concerns that people may have. I've heard others say that this would result in outcomes like the following:

- All donors would give their money to charities working overseas, and many nonprofits focused on local issues would have to close their doors as donations dry up.
- Funding for the arts would vanish.
- Funding advanced research for many diseases such as cancer would be eliminated in favor of other diseases like malaria.
- Donors would no longer be able to choose where to give. Instead, donors would give to a central (maybe even government-run) body of experts responsible for allocating resources.
- Research into new solutions might stop in favor of implementing existing solutions, as the benefits of research are much less certain and short-term than most existing solutions.
- The diversification of nonprofit goals would be drastically reduced, as donors only seek the "best" causes, and many needs would go unmet with fewer causes being addressed.

These conclusions reflect oversimplified views on do-besters. While each has some truth, they are all too extreme to be accurate expressions of what a do-bester world of philanthropy would look like.

What *would* such a world look like? Although do-besters, by definition, focus their giving decisions on maximizing expected impact, "impact" means different things to different people and evaluating it is subjective. So a do-bester world would be extremely diverse. Just as people have extremely different views in areas like politics, religion, and business, they also have different views in philanthropy. Some might favor saving lives while others might focus on improving the quality of life. Among those focused on improving the quality of life, some might focus on reducing suffering while others might focus on increasing pleasure. Some might think that global climate change is a problem in urgent need of being addressed, while others might not share that concern. Some might favor research that could either create a major breakthrough or fail to produce anything, while others might favor implementing a known solution. A world where all donors were do-besters would be very pluralistic, as donors would give according to their unique world views on how to best help others.

Each individual do-bester would look for the single perceived "best" place to give. And variations in views would create diversity in the causes and organizations supported. Do-besters further create diversity by gravitating toward opportunities that are underserved relative to their perceived potential impact. The tendency toward underserved areas would make it unlikely for any single cause to be flooded with donations beyond its capacity to be effective. In practice, a philanthropic world of do-besters would have an extremely broad reach.

To some extent, this is similar to the current system. The difference is that donors would evaluate options based not on their personal interests, but on attempts to assess what areas have the greatest potential impact on the recipients. A donor's life experiences would certainly color their philanthropic judgments—similar to how their political views are formed—but their judgments would be based on a more utilitarian set of criteria. Donors wouldn't just pursue whatever tugs on their emotions. The difference is subtle but very real.

Donors would probably give more to geographic areas with high concentrations of extreme poverty. Funds for health-related causes would tend to be directed less to the causes that affect the most people (in countries with donors with deep pockets), and more to those causes with the most promising opportunities for researching and implementing solutions. Donations to education would be made less frequently to the schools donors attended and more frequently to schools where resources could be best used. Donations to the arts might decrease, as donors might have a harder time justifying them when compared to the full opportunity set of alternative causes—though it is certainly possible that some do-besters believe that certain gifts to the arts uplift the human spirit enough to make them more worthy than any other form of giving. These changes would not be beneficial to everyone, as funds would be diverted from some programs. But the world collectively would see a much greater benefit.

But more practically, everyone won't adopt these views. This book is an attempt to gradually and incrementally change the philanthropic community's thinking and behavior. While its ideas may be threatening to those organizations that benefit from the mind-sets of most donors—U.S.-focused causes, nonprofits in the arts, and alumni-relations departments of elite universities—these organizations will all continue to survive even if this book has a meaningful impact. Donors should not be as concerned with a massive shift in the philanthropic equilibrium. Instead, if they want to be do-besters, they should focus on incremental improvements, and as a first step, making sure their individual contributions have the greatest impact.

For the future of philanthropy, do-gooders should take the challenge to transform into do-besters.

4

The Role of Emotional Giving

A benefit consists not in what is done or given,
but in the intention of the giver or doer.
—Seneca[1]

Once I was talking with a professional who advises family foundations, and she mentioned a recent assignment she had, helping a client select a grantee for a $1 million donation for diabetes research. Hinting that I knew something she didn't, I asked her what she would do if I showed her a credible scientific study finding that cancer research is three times more effective than diabetes research, dollar-for-dollar, toward reducing human suffering and death.

She immediately got very defensive and was reluctant to entertain the question, claiming that no such study exists. It was probably rude of me to probe further, but I did, and I was fascinated when she explicitly told me that she would not even *inform* her client about such a study. She explained that this particular donor had several family members with diabetes and simply wouldn't donate to other causes, so it was pointless to inform him of alternatives.

To the best of my knowledge, she was right when she said that no such study exists. Although the hypothetical situation was oversimplified, I believe that it is valid to ask about the relative effectiveness of alternative uses of a donation. Further, this situation is not that far from reality, as there is substantial evidence that philanthropy directed toward developing-world health issues like malaria, tuberculosis, and water-borne illnesses is far more than three times as effective at reducing illness and death as health-related causes in the developed world.

She knows her client, and I find her explanation partially persuasive. The reason I find it only partially persuasive is because it strikes me as extreme to not even inform him of the (hypothetical) study about the relative effectiveness of different types of grants. Apparently she categorized the donor's decision to focus on diabetes as strongly expressive giving—impact appeared to be of secondary concern.

I presented this situation to another philanthropy consultant who advises donors professionally to see what she would do. She also said that she would not tell the client about the (hypothetical) study suggesting that cancer research is more effective; she explained that the study is "irrelevant" if the donor's mission was to focus on diabetes. Again, there was a strong acceptance of a largely expressive mission.

While I understood the reasoning, both of these answers left me feeling empty. So for a totally different perspective, I asked a close friend how she would advise her client if she were the philanthropy consultant. She agreed with the others, noting that the donation was "personal" and not "business," so the rational case for information about investing in the (hypothetically) more effective cancer research was not as persuasive as the fact that diabetes had personally touched the donor.

I struggled with the fact that my perspective was clearly in the minority. If I were the donor, I'd certainly want the information so I could make my own decision about whether or how to react. But clearly other people would not. This disregard for impact and unwillingness to engage in critical thinking are prime examples of philanthropy failing to meet its potential to improve the world.

The approach seems fundamentally backward because it is focused on what the donor wants to do. Isn't donating supposed to be about helping others? If so, then shouldn't a central tenet be to try to provide the most help possible? I wondered if an alternative was to start by focusing on the recipients. Who is most in need of help? Where could donors make the most impact? What is the best way to improve the world? Clearly, this approach would be much more challenging, as it would be harder to search the world for the best causes (and develop criteria for which causes are best) as opposed to just thinking about the causes that have touched the donor's life most.

Despite the additional challenge, this seems like a much more recipient-focused method for giving, which should be more effective. Shouldn't it?

Donor-focused giving happens more often than not, and it troubles me because philanthropy is supposed to be for the benefit of others. While research focused on either cancer or diabetes would benefit the public, it feels less philanthropic when the donor decides which research to fund for reasons that are based more on personal preference than public benefit.

Unfortunately, giving purely based on recipient-focused criteria has a huge downside. When potential donors don't feel inspired or connected to a cause, they don't donate. For many donors, their emotional needs must be met in order to open their wallets. Giving must satisfy the donor's needs or it will never happen. Is it realistic for a donor to want to adopt a do-bester approach? Do pure do-besters actually exist? If not—if helping people is not the primary purpose of philanthropy—what are the implications? Is donating about satisfying the needs of the recipient or the donor?

Thinking about the relative importance of satisfying the needs of donors and recipients made me start exploring gradations of altruism. As an example, if I bought a really nice birthday present for a close friend, he would probably thank me and tell me that giving the gift was "generous," but he probably would not call it "altruistic."

What differentiates this generous gift from a gift that is both generous and altruistic? Although the birthday present is for the good of someone else, it is not based on an assessment of need. There might be a homeless person who needs my help much more, but I wanted to give the gift to my close friend. Even though the gift benefits someone else, it is too donor-focused to be altruistic.

Alternatively, if I did give a few dollars to a homeless person I walked past, some people may call it altruistic, or at least charitable. That action would probably be considered more altruistic than the birthday present for my friend because it is based on some consideration of social need. But it is not based on a very robust consideration of need; in fact, it is a relatively thoughtless act, making an arbitrary choice of which needy person to help (the one I saw) and not addressing any of the underlying causes of his homelessness or ensuring that the gift is spent wisely (e.g., not on harmful things like drugs and alcohol). As the cliché tells us, buying a man a fish is not as good as teaching him to fish. So giving to the homeless person might be altruistic, but it isn't the most altruistic act.

To be more altruistic, a donor might consider giving to a homeless shelter, assuming the donor believes homeless shelters are better able to identify needy people and assist them more effectively. Giving to homeless shelters requires a bit more thought and effort, which hopefully makes the gift more impactful at helping the homeless.

To be even more altruistic, one might choose the homeless shelter to donate to by doing research to determine which homeless shelter could use the donation to have the greatest impact. Or a donor could even research whether there are organizations other than homeless shelters that can more effectively reduce poverty or other forms of suffering. Perhaps giving to cancer research might have greater social benefits; certainly it is difficult to compare the relative impacts of homeless shelters and cancer research, but in a world with limited giving resources, the question is extremely important nevertheless.

Just as most people would consider it more meaningful to put a lot of thought into buying a friend a birthday present that he'd really appreciate rather than simply buying something arbitrary at the local mall, it is more altruistic to make a donation that is based on thoughtful consideration of what would have the greatest positive impact on the recipient. As a practical example, suppose a corporation gives a large grant to build and operate a homeless shelter, but insists that the homeless shelter be named after the company, then advertises this to make sure everyone in the community knows about the grant. Maybe their budget for publicizing the grant is bigger than the grant itself. While many people may still benefit from the homeless shelter, the cynic would point out that the company appears to have selfish interests in promoting its good deeds. That doesn't necessarily imply that the shelter's work has less benefit to the community, but it might make one wonder whether the company designed its philanthropic pursuits around what it could publicize best, rather than pursuing some other (possibly more effective) type of philanthropy. We might question its altruism.

Altruism is a spectrum with many shades of gray, and it is worthwhile to build on these examples to understand it better. The "Axis of Altruism" in figure 4.1 is helpful in laying the groundwork for understanding the merits of different philanthropic objectives and strategies. It can help donors understand

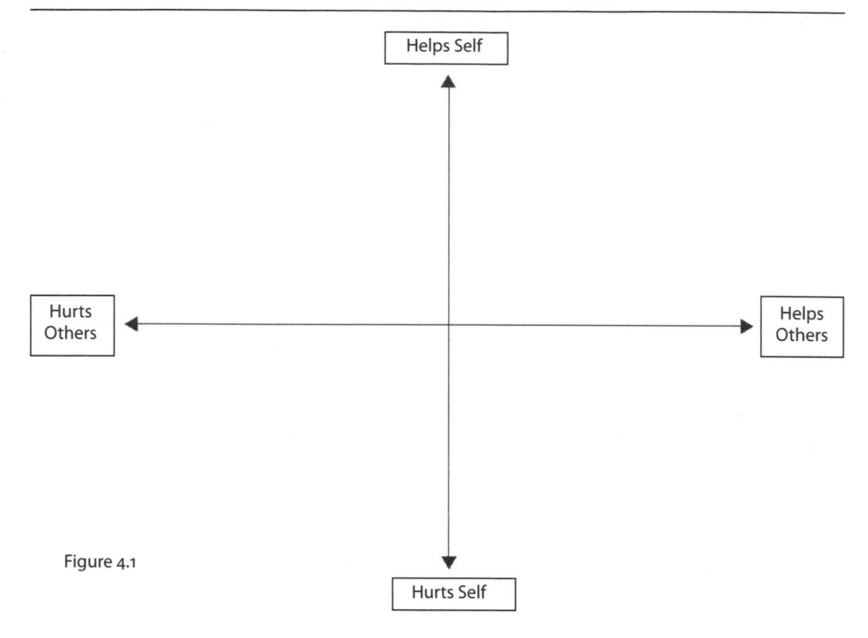

Figure 4.1

how their own preferences impact their philanthropic effectiveness, thus helping them uncover personal biases and improve their philanthropy.

Every action can be considered on the Axis of Altruism based on how it affects oneself and others. The center position on the graph is for something that is neutral: neither hurting nor helping anyone. Actions that help others are right of center, and hurting others is to the left. Moving up and down on the Axis of Altruism represents helping and hurting oneself. What constitutes "helping" and "hurting" can include both tangible and intangible effects. I will not define these terms more specifically, though, as what constitutes helping and hurting must be determined using your own judgment on a case-by-case basis.

Let's look at a simple example not related to philanthropy: going out for a drink. Suppose I enjoy a few drinks at my favorite bar, tip the bartender generously, then take a taxi home. Since I had fun and the bartender appreciated the tip, this is a win-win situation for all and belongs in the northeast quadrant. Alternatively, suppose I stiffed the bartender, drove myself home drunk (risking the safety of others), and woke up the next morning hung over. Everyone was hurt by my actions, including myself, so this would be in the southwest quadrant. We can similarly describe scenarios in the other two remaining quadrants, as illustrated in figure 4.2.

Philanthropy generally falls in the northeast quadrant. The notion that

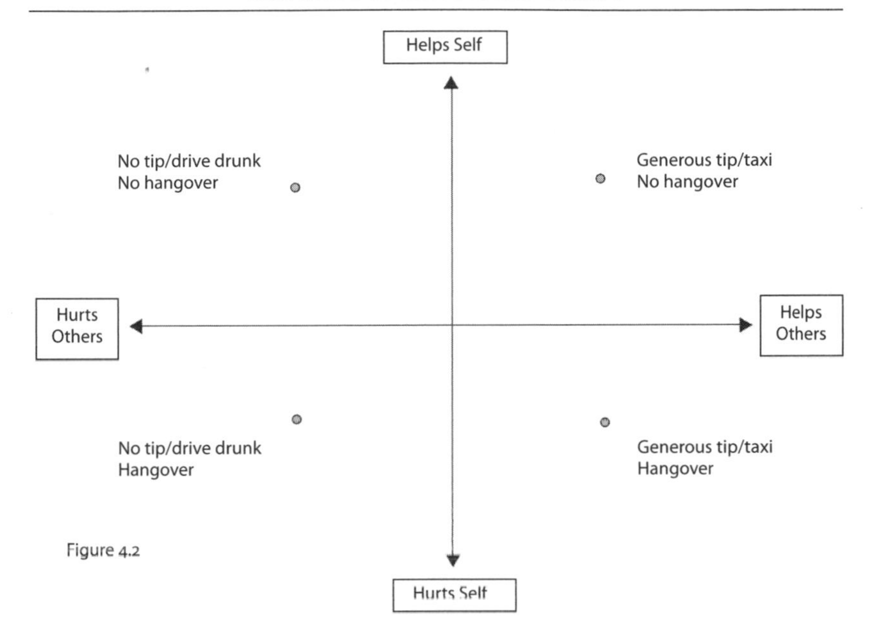

Figure 4.2

philanthropy typically benefits others is clear. And because philanthropy is a voluntary action on the part of the donor, the personal/emotional benefits to the donor must exceed the financial sacrifice made—otherwise the donor wouldn't have made the gift.

Where within the northeast quadrant does a particular donation fall? Let's revisit our prior example of gifts to research either diabetes or cancer, plotting each relative to the other in figure 4.3. For cancer research, there are two possible locations plotted.

Giving to diabetes research provides more emotional benefits to the donor because the cause has directly touched his family, though giving to cancer research would have helped others more. So the gift supporting diabetes is to the northwest of the gift to cancer research. Alternative 1 shows the gift to cancer research as still providing some positive benefits to the donor, just not as much as the gift to diabetes research. Alternative 2 is more extreme—that the gift to cancer research would actually make the donor worse off because the emotional benefit is not great enough to offset the financial cost. This is the scenario that the donor's adviser stated was more realistic, and it implies that the person would not make any donation to cancer research. Regardless of how much more effective the donation to cancer research (or any other cause) might be, the donor's choice was a gift to diabetes research, rather than not donating at all.

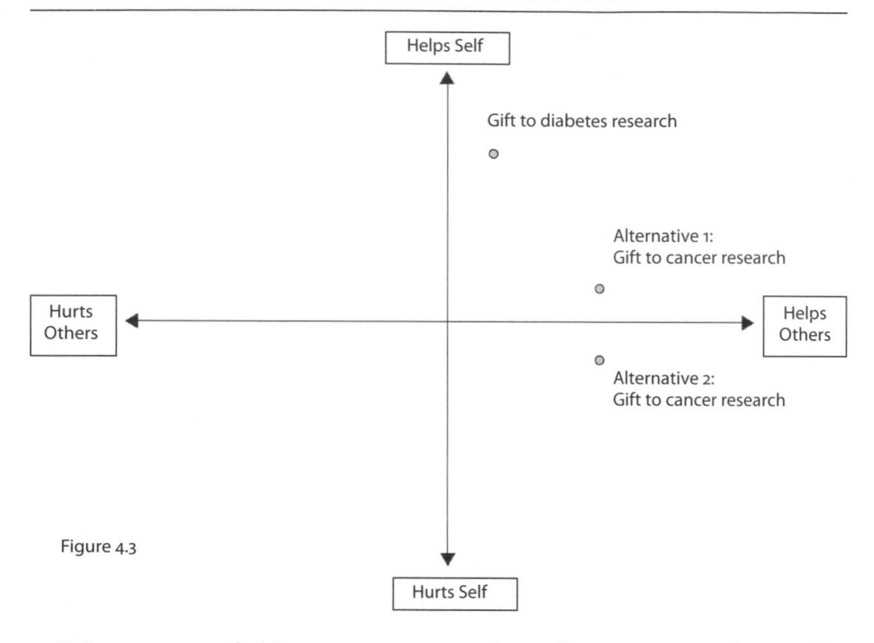

Figure 4.3

We can expand this concept to more broadly encompass do-gooder and do-bester giving in figure 4.4. The do-gooders are all in the northern portion of the figure, as they donate to make sure they get the most emotional benefits. The do-besters, however, are in the far eastern portion of the figure. There appears to be tension between donors giving for personal (emotional) gain versus those giving to help others. But what about the small area in the northeasternmost portion of the figure, where the do-gooders and do-besters seem to overlap? Who are these donors and how do they get the best of both worlds?

Peter Frumkin tries to address a related issue in his book *Strategic Giving*:

> Philanthropy can be both a potent vehicle through which public needs are met and an instrument for the expression of private beliefs and commitments. Finding a way to maximize both the public benefits of giving and the private fulfillment of donors is critical not just to securing the continued flow of funds into philanthropy, but also to ensuring that private giving in all its many idiosyncratic forms continues to play a vital role in supporting pluralism in society.[2]

Frumkin is right that more giving happens when it meets the donor's emotional needs, and giving wouldn't do any good if it didn't help others. But does he understate the challenge of simultaneously maximizing both

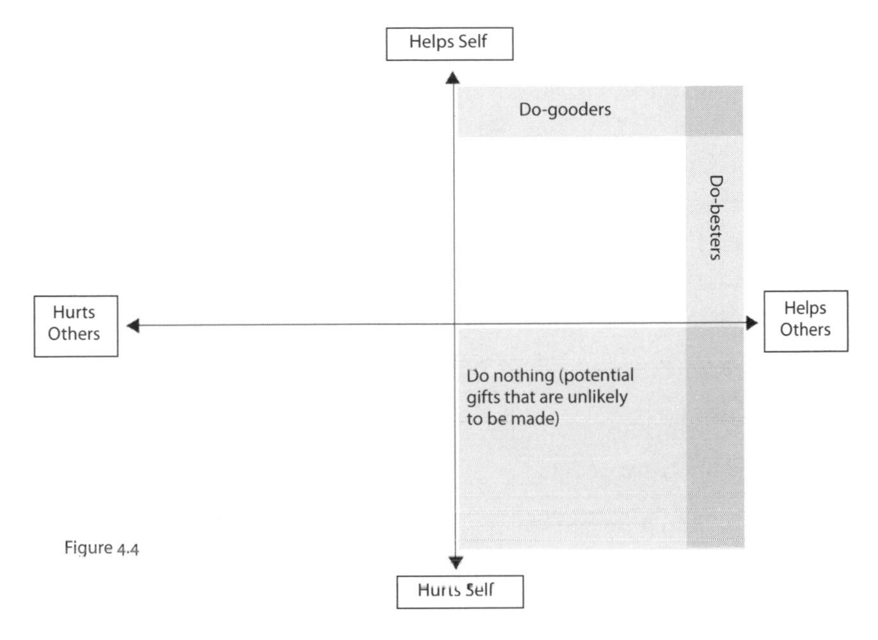

Figure 4.4

the public benefits of giving and the personal fulfillment of donors? If you only feel genuine passion for diabetes research (or whatever other narrow cause you have personal experience with), then it may not be possible to simultaneously maximize benefits for yourself and others.

So who are the do-besters? How do they muster the willpower to give to the most impactful causes, even when they don't feel personally passionate about them? Do they not have strong emotions? Do they think more like heartless computers than ordinary people? Is it realistic for someone to try to adopt a do-bester approach? Do do-besters even exist?

Some academic research is raising challenging questions about whether the human brain is hardwired to favor being a do-gooder rather than a do-bester. There is some research that people who think about giving effectively tend to give less than those who give emotionally. "Caring" and "thinking" might be done by different parts of the brain, so donors who try to be do-besters will tend to donate less, or maybe nothing at all, according to this research.

A study published in the journal *Organizational Behavior and Human Decision Processes* is a frequently cited example of such research.[3] The researchers offered university students $5 to take a short survey about their use of various technological products—a topic unrelated to the true purpose of the study. Upon completion of the survey, the respondents were given an envelope with the $5 as well as a receipt and a charity request letter for the nonprofit Save the Children. For some participants, the charity request letter was designed to appeal to their feelings, including a picture of an impoverished seven-year-old girl, Rokia, from Mali, Africa, and a description of her. The appeal stated that any money you give would go to help Rokia. Other participants had a different letter in their envelope, designed to appeal to their analytical side by focusing more on the broader problem of the drought in Africa affecting millions of people, rather than on individual victims. The letter stated that any money given would go to Save the Children to help those affected by the drought. All survey participants were then given final instructions:

> Now that you have had the opportunity to learn about how any money you donate will be used, please fill out the following page and include it with any money you donate in the envelope you have been given. Even if you choose not to donate, please fill out the form and return it to us with the envelope.[4]

The survey results showed that participants receiving the emotional appeal were significantly more generous than those given the analytical appeal. Some participants were given a letter with both the emotional and analytical appeals, and even the inclusion of both reduced the generosity of participants relative to those given just the emotional appeal. The authors of the study suggest that this supports the notion that when people think analytically, they give less.

One could certainly challenge the robustness of the conclusions based solely on the survey. Perhaps the emotional appeal was very well written, whereas the analytical appeal may not have been written persuasively. Further, the analytical appeal only described the scope of the problems, not the efficacy of the solutions, so do-besters would find it insufficient.

However, these potential criticisms do not apply to a follow-up study performed by the same researchers, which appears to more clearly reject the notion that people think analytically when they give. In the new study, some participants got a survey asking analytical questions such as, "If an object travels at five feet per minute, then by your calculations how many feet will it travel in 360 seconds?" The other survey asked participants to answer questions more oriented to their feelings, such as, "When you hear the word 'baby' what do you feel?" After each survey, they received identical requests to donate to charity.

The researchers found that even though both surveys were unrelated to the charity request, the participants who were primed to think analytically were significantly less generous. This research suggests that not only do people give with their hearts, but they don't give with their heads. If this is really true, what are the implications?

The answer is fairly clear for charities trying to fundraise: appeal to the emotions of most potential donors without barraging them with statistics and "rational" arguments. But the answer for donors is not as obvious. The assertion that "caring" and "thinking" are disjointed mental processes, with one reducing the other, is not that different from stating that caring, generous philanthropists must be thoughtless, and possibly even stupid. Offensive? Yes. True? I hope not. One potential implication is that people who want to be philanthropists shouldn't think too much—that just gets in the way of writing checks. But with this approach, they are unlikely to give to the best causes and organizations. To feel good about giving, they can't acknowledge to themselves that they are giving to inferior causes and organizations, but such delusion shouldn't be hard for people who are not thinking much. Their gifts will not have as much of a positive impact on others, but at least they're donating. While this potential implication for donors is consistent with the research, it is far from being an appealing argument or a practical way to make philanthropy better. It is also unappealing for me, as a donor, when I think about how to approach my own giving.

The research presented so far suggests that our brains may be hardwired against being do-besters. How much truth does this have?

While it may explain a lot of do-gooder philanthropy, the research may not be as valid for "major" giving as for "casual" giving (by whatever standard you want to define the terms). The study was conducted on random university students, who are not likely to be deeply invested in their decision of whether to give the $5. In contrast, major donors cutting large checks are more likely to spend time and effort considering where to give. It is harder for many major givers to delude themselves, because they are considering their choices more. The argument that generous donors must be full of "caring feelings" and void of "analytical thought" isn't consistent with what goes through the minds of many major donors (especially those who read books about philanthropy).

That doesn't mean that purely analytical arguments for a charity are necessarily appealing to major donors, but it does mean that they have a harder time remaining ignorant about a lack of impact from giving to mediocre causes. As they become more experienced donors, they will only get the emotional benefits from giving by having conviction that the charities they support will make good use of their donations. In my own experience, many of the major donors I know started with the emotional side for wanting to give, and as they began to deeply consider where and how to donate, they transitioned to more thinking behaviors. The academic research could be interpreted to suggest that some people become less generous as this happens. To the extent that this occurs—and I'm sure it has—it is an open question whether it is better for the world to have a larger amount of less effective giving or a smaller amount of more effective giving. There appears to be a strong tension between giving more and giving better. Is this tension truly irreconcilable? If so, do-besters may only be people who coincidentally have their passions stirred by the areas of greatest impact. But is that really the case?

There are very few, if any, people who actually donate to causes other than those they get the most emotional benefit from. However, do-besters exist due to more than just coincidental alignment of their passions and the areas of greatest impact. They are people who get more emotional fulfillment when they know their donations have greater positive impact. Do-besters may simply be a special type of do-gooders who wouldn't *feel* good about donating to support diabetes research if they knew that cancer research would help others more. Do-besters have a very strong connection between "heart" and "head." In fact, do-besters may get *more* happiness from their donations because they are satisfying their emotional side as well as their analytical side. Being a do-bester is not an extreme form of self-sacrifice (giving money without getting emotional benefit), but a natural consequence of how some people think.

In that sense, a more accurate variation of figure 4.4 is presented in figure 4.5, which only allows do-besters to be far to the northeast.

This should provide optimism for those who want to become do-besters or hope the philanthropic sector as a whole will shift to have greater emphasis on do-bester approaches. There is not an inherent conflict between helping

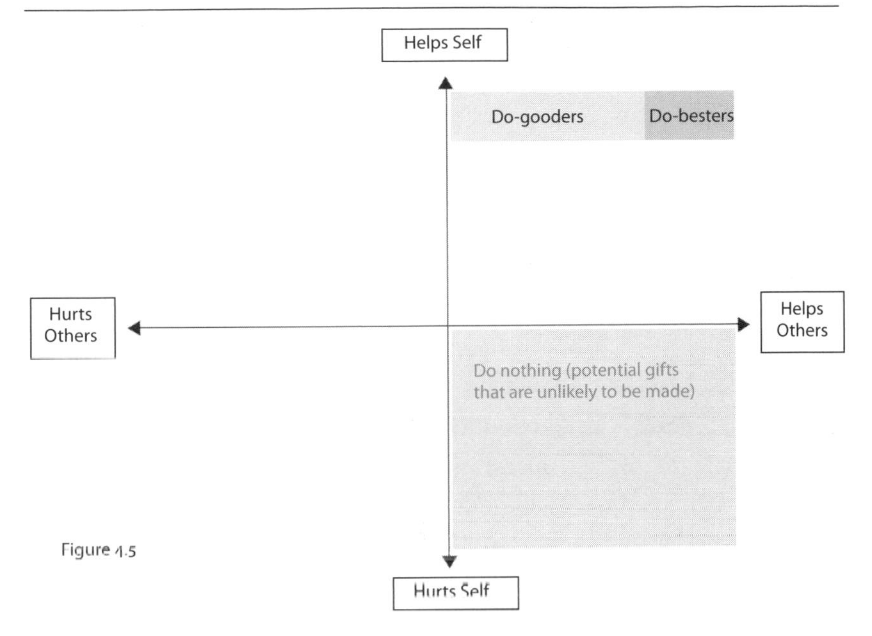

Figure 1.5

others and feeling good. Being a do-bester doesn't necessarily require tremendous amounts of self-discipline or unnatural behaviors. For those who want to be do-besters—which probably includes you if you're reading this book—it may only be a matter of learning how.

For some do-besters, getting a high emotional benefit from a high-impact donation may require only knowing the impact. That is, a reliable research report from the nonprofit is enough to give them a warm, emotional glow from their gift. But most people's heads and hearts are not that closely linked—they need more than just a research report. They may need the pictures and anecdotes of those the nonprofit has helped. They may require a site visit to where the nonprofit works, to actually see them in action. They may need some or even all of the things that fundraisers do to keep donors feeling good about giving. This is simply recognizing your own natural tendencies and incorporating them into your behaviors, combining the "thinking" and "caring" sides of your brain into the giving process. For example, deciding where to give based on rational criteria for what will have the greatest impact, then immersing yourself in emotional triggers to help maintain do-bester giving. This may be the ultimate takeaway donors should get from the academic research.

Donors who want to be do-besters may need to be honest with themselves about the extent to which this type of emotional connection is important for them. While pursuing it can reduce resources for helping others, it may be a worthwhile investment in order for donors to stay emotionally connected to the areas they know help others the most. On the spectrum between do-bester and do-gooder, these people may be somewhere in the middle, but much closer to the do-bester side. Nevertheless, for them, it is still important to acknowledge and satisfy both sides. Understanding one's own motivations is a first step to becoming more effective.

Although do-besters don't necessarily have personal life experience or passion for a particular cause, a do-bester approach is neither impersonal nor impassionate. In my own observations, I've seen a number of people who start donating in a typical do-gooder style because they didn't know any other way, and as they gained more information about what helps others most, their giving evolved to have a more do-bester flair. I believe that for many do-gooder donors, becoming more experienced with philanthropy has a tendency to transition them closer to do-besters. That is, they will reduce donations to causes they believe have low impact and increase donations to causes they believe have high impact. This will happen with different speeds and magnitudes for different donors, depending on their level of research and critical thinking, and it will happen to some extent for nearly all people who think critically about their giving. This movement northeast on the Axis of Altruism is a natural progression, and I've seen how the donations tend to become more fulfilling as donors have more conviction in their impact.

I've also known a number of people with do-bester mentalities who don't donate at all; they don't believe they have enough information to know that their gifts will make a strong positive impact. In fact, I was not too different from them for several years. When I became more confident in my ability to identify the most effective ways to give, my giving increased more than tenfold. For people who share this trait, a philanthropic sector that better supports and informs do-besters will be more likely to drive both larger and more effective donations. There should be no doubt that there is a role for emotions in the giving process, and if harnessed well, it can dramatically increase the impact of the giving. For the remainder of this book, I'll try to lay out a process for the nuts and bolts of how donors can develop a practice of do-bester giving.

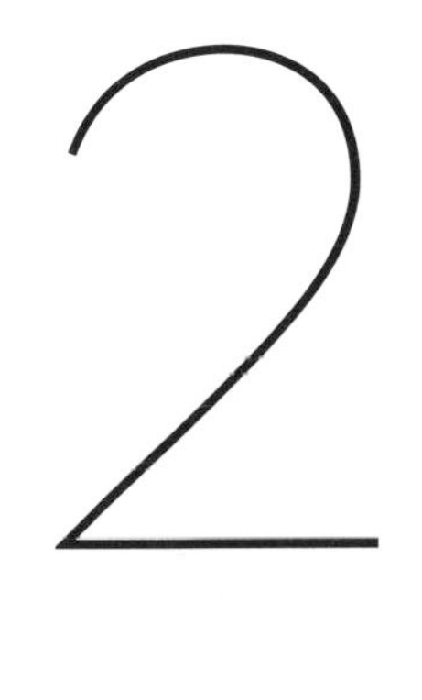

PRACTICAL STRATEGIES FOR EFFECTIVE GIVING

5

The Paucity of Helpful Information

Where facts are few, experts are many.
—Donald R. Gannon[1]

JPMorgan Chase and Facebook conducted a multimillion-dollar experiment in allocating philanthropic resources. They teamed up to let the army of Facebook users decide who would win charitable grants from Chase. Starting from a database of 500,000 nonprofit organizations, Facebook users voted for their favorites, narrowing the field to 100 finalists, and ultimately one grand prize winner. The $5 million giveaway, Chase Community Giving: You Decide What Matters, included a whopping $1 million for the grand prize winner.

"The grassroots nature of Facebook will allow us to hear directly which local charities matter most to our communities, hopefully creating an even bigger impact," said Jamie Dimon, chairman and CEO of JPMorgan Chase & Co.

Chase appears to believe that crowdsourcing of Facebook users is the best way to allocate philanthropic resources (unless this was just a $5 million publicity stunt). The grand prize winner in December 2011 was To Write Love on Her Arms (TWLOHA), a group that describes itself as "a non-profit movement dedicated to presenting hope and finding help for people struggling with depression, addiction, self-injury and suicide. TWLOHA exists to encourage, inform, inspire and also to invest directly into treatment and recovery."[2]

Chase Community Giving is not the only example of explicitly putting the power of giving decisions into the hands of the "average" person. Other examples from corporate philanthropy include the Pepsi Refresh Project, Kohl's Cares, and American Express's Members Project. Even beyond corporate giving, this type of grassroots decision making is part of a broader trend in the philanthropic sector of allowing average donors a tremendous amount of influence in where their money goes. There are other examples:

- DonorsChoose.org allows individuals to browse project requests from public school teachers and give to the ones that inspire them.
- Kiva, a microfinance charity, allows person-to-person microlending.
- GlobalGiving is an online marketplace that connects donors to the causes and countries they choose, and further allows them to select the specific projects they want to support, then get regular progress updates.
- Modest Needs allows donors to browse its online catalog of requests for help and select individual ones to fund.

For many donors, this type of giving is more rewarding because not only do they get to see precisely where their donation goes, but they also get to pick the people they help and how. This trend applies not only to the moderate-size donations the organizations given as examples cater to, but also to corporate, foundation, and major individual donors. These donors typically (though not always) pick specific projects to earmark their donations for rather than allowing the recipient organization to determine the best use for the donation.

But are most donors good at allocating philanthropic capital? Are there specific skills or experiences that make someone better at it? Is the trend toward empowering donors actually making philanthropy better at improving the world? Where can do-bester donors turn for help when they don't have all the skills and information needed to make the best decisions?

These are very important questions—questions that are not asked often enough. But before addressing them, a reminder is in order about who decides where to give: donors, donors, and donors. This is true for do-gooders as well as do-besters, regardless of whether they give to impactful causes or inconsequential ones, strong organizations or weak ones. It's the donor's money, so he can do almost anything he wants with it. That is natural in a free society and appropriate for philanthropy.

However, this doesn't mean that donors are actually good at choosing the best, most impactful causes and organizations. Facebook users aren't the group best able to direct the philanthropic checks that Chase signs. If there is any theoretical merit to the concept of allocating resources with a democratic process, the practical reality is that restricting the voting to only Facebook users isn't the least bit democratic. Domingos Antonic, his neighbors in Malanje, and his peers in extreme poverty are left out of this type of "democratic" process; they are too poor to have the computer needed to vote in such an election.

Most individual donors are actually quite bad at giving. And why should we expect them to be good at it? People have a limited set of life experiences, and few individuals have day-to-day life experiences that will allow them to acquire expertise in all of the fields necessary to give well. A hedge fund millionaire probably doesn't know much about poverty in the third world, an heir to the family fortune probably doesn't know much about the most pressing environmental concerns, and a real estate tycoon probably doesn't know much about promising medical research. And people with more typical occupations are unlikely to have greater expertise in these areas. There are experts in each of these charitable sectors, and they can be helpful. But where would someone acquire the skills to compare solutions for third world poverty to those for the environment and medical situations? Most donors who want to be impactful do-besters may want to seek help in selecting a sector. While there are many resources donors can turn to, most have major limitations in providing what do-besters need. For those who want to be do-bester donors without spending excessive amounts of time evaluating giving options, there are some resources available, but the donor must still put in a certain amount of thought to assess their skill in evaluating charitable options. After all, despite not being experts, donors are still in control because it's their money. There is no effortless path to being a do-bester. Let's explore this further by looking in more detail at the advantages and limitations of several resources donors look to for guidance.

The first place many donors turn for help is a charity rating agency. The largest of them—Charity Navigator, GuideStar, CharityWatch, and the Better Business Bureau—focus largely on finances, poring over the financial information of thousands of nonprofits to measure their financial efficiency.

The rating agencies typically analyze various metrics to understand the relative proportions of nonprofit budgets that are spent on programs versus administrative and fundraising costs.

Although few donors want their gifts spent on administrative overhead, even the rating agencies acknowledge that their analysis is insufficient. "There is a place for financial measures, but donors need a more complete picture of a charity to make a smart choice. We believe too many donors are paying too much attention to measures like overhead," noted Ken Berger, president and CEO of Charity Navigator.[3] This was a huge step forward for Charity Navigator, which has historically been one of the primary sources driving the focus on financial metrics.

Rating a charity solely by financial metrics is like rating a restaurant based solely on its health code scores. You only want to give to charities with decent financials just as you only want to patronize restaurants with acceptable health code scores, but what about the quality of the food and charitable programs? Acceptable health code scores and charity financial metrics may both be minimum standards for consideration, but neither is sufficient to determine whether the organization is actually good at what it does.

What's the alternative? Donors can focus on the effectiveness of the programs, not just what proportion of the money goes to them. It is far better to donate to an organization that spends eighty cents of every dollar raised on really effective programs than to one that spends ninety cents of every dollar raised on average programs. Charity Navigator—the largest of the rating agencies,[4] with over six million users annually[5]—has taken action to advance their rating methodology accordingly. Beginning in 2011, they've implemented "CN 2.0," changing their rating methodology from being solely based on financial metrics to incorporating the organization's accountability and transparency. They chose these two characteristics because they "believe that charities that are accountable and transparent are more likely to act with integrity and learn from their mistakes."[6] But they still do not yet incorporate results. They're working on that for CN 3.0.

But assessing effectiveness is easier said than done. Unlike profit-seeking corporations, which have an easy bottom line to measure their results, charities have more ambiguous social goals. While most charities can describe what they've done, it's difficult to measure the impact they have had. How many lives are expected to be saved by the research funded by the American

Cancer Society, and how much has quality of life been improved by the Metropolitan Museum of Art? Charity Navigator plans to rate effectiveness based on their reporting of five "results reporting elements":

1. **Alignment of mission, solicitations, and resources.** Does the charity do what it tells donors?
2. **Results, logic, and measurement.** Is there a plausible link between the charity's activities and its intended outcomes?
3. **Validators.** Does the charity have any third-party credentials, memberships, awards, or other indicators of accreditation?
4. **Constituent voice.** How well does the charity collect and report feedback from its beneficiaries?
5. **Published evaluation reports.** Are there published evaluation reports for the charity's programs?[7]

Though these updates would be a giant step forward, Charity Navigator doesn't expect to have them ready until 2016.[8] But even then, Charity Navigator explains the limitations on how this will be incorporated into its ratings: "At least for the first few years, charities will not be rated on their results, but on how they report those results. This puts the focus on the integrity of their measurement practices while avoiding penalizing organizations for what might be interpreted as poor results."[9] It appears that Charity Navigator's constituents should expect to wait until close to 2020 until their ratings actually reflect the quality of their results.

Though still a long way off, it is worthwhile to understand more about Charity Navigator's future methodology and consider how donors will eventually be able to use it. Deanne Pearn, a member of Charity Navigator's advisory panel on developing their future methodology, as well as the cofounder and chief development officer of First Place for Youth, succinctly sums up Charity Navigator's approach and illustrates how it might work: "To determine effectiveness, look at the organization's mission statement and see if its programs are able to fulfill that mission. For example, the mission of First Place for Youth is to support foster youth in their transition to successful adulthood. . . . Before making a gift, donors should ask . . . how they measure results and what 'grade' they would give a program."[10]

Not only does this characterize the future approach, it also clearly articulates another one of its biggest weaknesses: it doesn't evaluate the merits of the organization's mission—only the effectiveness toward meeting that mission. Supporting foster youth sounds like a mission that would do good, but is it really the most effective way to improve the world? How does it compare to improving education, the arts, hunger, or medical services? Donors must choose between these diverse areas. Does anyone at Charity Navigator try to compare them? How can you measure (and compare) such diverse areas?

Even Charity Navigator—possibly the most progressive of the four largest charity evaluators—refuses to make these judgments. By creating a system in which hundreds of extremely different charities get their top rating, Charity Navigator has watered down the value of its ratings and expressed little conviction about what really works best. The evaluations that Charity Navigator and other watchdog organizations provide are important, especially as a screen to filter out the very poorly managed organizations, but they are not a substitute for judging impact. Donors looking to fill this gap must supplement this information with more comprehensive analysis. Where else can they turn?

There are professional experts in the field of giving. For example, the Rockefeller Philanthropy Advisors (RPA) is one of the largest and most well-respected consulting organizations that helps donors develop and implement their philanthropic plans. The president of RPA, Melissa Berman, describes how many ordinary people seem to claim expertise in giving: "While your car mechanic would not (I hope) give you advice about your teeth, and your dentist would probably decline to look at your carburetor, both will likely happily tell you where to donate your money."[11] The consultants at her firm have professional expertise in philanthropy, and as an example of their work, RPA posted a case study on their website:

> In 2005, Sidney E. Frank started thinking seriously about his philanthropic ambitions. A highly successful entrepreneur who created Grey Goose vodka and marketed and distributed other premium liquor brands such as Jägermeister, Mr. Frank turned to Rockefeller Philanthropy Advisors to put together a plan for a foundation that would live well beyond him. After Mr. Frank died in 2006, RPA began to integrate his family into the foundation in order to continue his legacy. RPA helped to formalize all the operational and governance aspects of the foundation, including hiring an investment consulting firm and auditor and developing policies and

procedures so the foundation operated smoothly and efficiently. RPA also sat down with the trustees to identify and develop their preferred areas of giving.

BUILDING ON A LEGACY

The trustees had a strong interest in maintaining Mr. Frank's legacy but also wanted to explore new interests for the foundation. RPA assembled a team of advisors with deep expertise in each giving area under consideration. And in early 2008, the trustees and their RPA advisors developed the foundation's first docket of grants, with substantial amounts committed to the arts, education, medical research and climate change.

FINDING A CAUSE

In April 2008, after attending an RPA symposium on climate change, the trustees asked RPA to develop a docket specifically aimed at addressing environmental issues in relation to the creation of new coal power plants, which would be a major source of global warming emissions. RPA provided due diligence and analysis and made a series of recommendations, which were approved by the foundation's trustees. A series of grants to the Energy Foundation, the Rockefeller Family Fund and the Sierra Club helped to establish a campaign coordinator in relation to the coal issue.[12]

When donors like Mr. Frank hire RPA to assist with their giving, RPA might start by helping the donors think through a set of questions that RPA describes as their four-step "Philanthropic Roadmap":

1. What internal forces drive *you* to give?
2. What external issues tug at both *your* heart and *your* head?
3. How do *you* want the change to happen?
4. How do *you* want to get involved?[13]

Notice that all four of these steps are focused on "you," the donor. Why didn't RPA include steps about assessing the issues of greatest need (instead of those that emotionally tug on the donor), determining the methods that are most effective for making change happen (instead of how the donor wants it to happen), or deciding the best ways for donors to get involved (instead of how the donor wants to be involved)? Though RPA did assemble a team of advisers with deep expertise in each giving area under consideration, it appears that RPA did not suggest that experts help in the decision to focus on arts, education, medical research, and climate change instead of a range of other causes. That decision appears to have been made based on the personal preferences of the donor and board. I'm not suggesting that it would be better to have the opposite extreme—completely ignoring the donor's needs—but a better balance is needed.

An alternative philanthropic process might include questions like these:

1. What areas are in greatest need?
2. What interventions have the greatest opportunity to make improvements?
3. How do you (and experts) believe improvements happen?
4. What resources do you have that others can make the best use of?

You may wonder if the assertions I'm making here are based on a too literal interpretation of the RPA's description of its Philanthropic Roadmap. In practice, surely there would be *some* focus on the potential impact on recipients. Certainly this is a valid point, and it is not my intention to misrepresent the RPA's Philanthropic Roadmap. However, another quote from the RPA's president illuminates its perspective on its relationship with its clients and its role in the philanthropic process. When there was a public controversy over whether it was a poor allocation of philanthropic resources to focus on donkey sanctuaries, RPA president Melissa Berman weighed in:

> I'm not sure how donkey sanctuaries became the litmus test of our field, but I'm pretty clear on that issue: if a donor wants to protect donkeys, that's his/her right, and I'm in no position to declare that donkeys are less worthy of a sanctuary than any other species.[14]

Despite the RPA's expertise in operational and governance aspects of philanthropy, it does not believe it has a role in taking positions on certain key issues. This is consistent with the mainstream philanthropic practice of making this type of decision primarily based on the donor's personal experiences, with donors determining their direction based on their interests and passions. It is not that different from the mentality of the consultant who advised the donor to diabetes research regardless of whether there were other areas of greater potential impact, as described in chapter 4. It is too much to ask consulting firms like RPA to only help do-besters, but maybe they should at least adjust their roadmap to ask donors whether they have predefined a specific area to focus their giving or if they want to first determine the most effective areas. If consulting firms like RPA aren't willing to take a stronger view on the relative merits of supporting donkey sanctuaries, funding the arts, endowing scholarships, or vaccinating children, then they may not be able to help do-besters with some of their most important decisions.

When it comes to developing strategy, most philanthropy consultants, like RPA, will tell you that they are skilled at advising in this area. As evidence, they may point out that they have helped donors through strategy development for different types of giving, from the arts to education to the environment to international aid. That diversity, however, makes one question whether they are actually skilled at helping develop the highest levels of strategy for donors concerned about maximizing impact. One would expect someone skilled at strategy development to have higher conviction in their views about which sectors are most impactful. It can legitimately be argued that such conviction depends on the objectives of the donation, and even donors with do-bester objectives will not agree on a single "best" sector of philanthropy. However, if a consultant is equally happy to help donors implement programs in almost any philanthropic area, it seems more likely that the consultant's strategy-setting philosophy is to guide donors to their own personal do-gooder objectives rather than influencing them toward a do-bester approach.

It isn't fair to fault RPA or its competitors for this, because it is a direct function of their role as an adviser. Advisers help clients pursue their objectives, rather than impose objectives on them. This is what they get paid for, and they probably wouldn't be able to stay in business if they were not malleable enough to adopt their clients' objectives as their own. They don't judge their clients harshly. Most wouldn't point out to a client, "Hey, doesn't it seem a bit inappropriate to fund donkey sanctuaries when people are starving?" Or, "Excuse me, I know it's your money, but are you sure you'd rather build a new wing to the art museum than improve basic education for underprivileged children?" It's not their role to have those conversations.

By no means am I trying to diminish the importance of RPA's strengths. The governance, process, and operational areas they help with are vital to implementing philanthropy well, especially as the dollar amounts of gifts increase. These are a major way organizations like the RPA create value in the philanthropic sector.

Nevertheless, it is important for donors to take this lesson to heart: even well-intentioned philanthropic advisers with a tremendous amount of expertise in some aspects of philanthropy are unlikely to be full service providers for a do-bester.

In this context, it makes one of the RPA's projects even more fascinating. As they describe it,

> Many potential donors have trouble finding the on-ramp for issue-oriented philanthropy programmes. They are strangers in a strange land, and justifiably mistrustful of random encounters with advisers or recommendations when they lack a sense of the landscape as a whole. Research and interviews—formal and informal—have revealed over and over that donors feel they can't get access to basic information, whether about a topic or how to begin a family programme. The resources in our field are too narrow and too far flung. . . .
>
> At Rockefeller Philanthropy Advisors, we are thus particularly grateful to the Gates Foundation for a new three-year grant to help develop some of these donor resources, and to make them available to philanthropic advisers and others who work with private donors or potential donors.[15]

Maybe one of the reasons donors are so "mistrustful of random encounters with advisors or recommendations" is because much of the philanthropic establishment isn't debating some of the most important questions donors face. Thoughtful donors notice that almost everybody in the philanthropic sector has tried to avoid robustly addressing the relative validity of donating to donkey sanctuaries, the arts, education, or vaccinations. "Experts" have failed to differentiate between do-gooders and do-besters. This isn't an easy task, but many donors are looking for more. Consultants can help donors achieve their objectives once their geographic and programmatic areas are well defined, but often they are not able to help donors starting with a blank slate. As Berman noted, donors are looking for "a sense of the landscape as a whole," but she may not realize everything this entails.

Consultants aren't the only professional experts in philanthropy. Many large foundations hire dedicated staff to implement their giving. While they can provide expertise in a number of key areas, they also have limitations. Fundamental to those limitations are similar issues to those for consultants: the limited capacity for making value judgments about the relative philanthropic merits of different areas, whether it is the arts, education, health care, the environment, or donkey sanctuaries.

Foundation staff implement the philanthropic direction provided by others—typically the original donors. Their main responsibilities generally include writing requests for grant proposals, reviewing responses, and monitoring the results of grants. Staff members often become content area experts who can work with several different organizations in a particular area to pursue the foundation's goals. For example, a foundation that makes a significant number of grants in microfinance might have a few specialists in this area. They can develop intimate knowledge of the nonprofits working in the area, thus gaining the experience needed to be able to evaluate the strongest partners to support with grants. This is an extremely important role, but it also means that they are not responsible for or have expertise in assisting the foundation with deciding whether to focus on microfinance, donkey sanctuaries, or some other area.

If some of the best advisers in the philanthropic sector can't give donors comprehensive advice, then where can donors turn?

There are real advancements in resources for donors seeking to be do-besters. As an example, GiveWell may be the closest thing to a one-stop resource for do-bester philanthropists. It was started in 2006 by a pair of hedge fund analysts, Elie Hassenfeld and Holden Karnofsky, who wanted to be do-bester philanthropists themselves but quickly found that there was little information available to help with this goal. Karnofsky commented on GiveWell's genesis on his blog: "[Someone called] us the 'pissed off donor model,' which I hadn't thought of, but it's accurate: GiveWell grew straight out of our attempts to donate, and our realization that the resource we wanted and needed doesn't currently exist."[16]

Hassenfeld and Karnofsky's quest for measurable and reliable data on the best causes and organizations led them to give up their careers in the hedge fund industry and focus on helping create and distribute this information for other philanthropists. GiveWell is the result. They describe their organization in more detail:

> GiveWell is an independent, nonprofit charity evaluator. We find outstanding charities and publish the full details of our analysis to help donors decide where to give. Unlike existing evaluators, which focus

> solely on financials, assessing administrative or fundraising costs, we focus on how well programs actually work—i.e., their effects on the people they serve. GiveWell started as a group of donors . . . discussing how to accomplish as much good as possible. . . . Individual donors give over 100x as much as the Gates Foundation and over 6x as much as all foundations combined. We aim to direct as much as possible of this large pool to the best charities we can find, and create a global, public, open conversation about how to best help people.[17]

GiveWell is trying to turn do-gooders into do-besters, or at least provide them the resources to do it themselves. GiveWell does thorough analyses of individual charities and gives high ratings to the top performers. Its ratings and rationale are publicly available on its website. It incorporates value judgments on the relative merits of saving lives versus improving quality of life—this is not to imply that it ideologically favors one over the other, but just that it provides comparative ratings for organizations with both focuses. And it has a tremendous focus on measurement, so to the greatest extent possible, they do attempt to measure things like the cost to save a life (sometimes under $2,500[18]) and to provide various human services.

GiveWell differentiates itself from most other charity evaluation groups by describing the three categories these groups tend to fall into:

> 1. Groups that rate as many charities as possible. Donors come to them already having a particular charity in mind to give to, and search for that charity.
> 2. Groups that suggest charities for as many causes as possible. Donors come to them knowing what sort of cause they want to support (U.S. education, global health, etc.) but not which charity, and get a recommendation.
> 3. Groups that simply focus on finding outstanding charities. Donors come to them looking for outstanding giving opportunities (they are often issue-agnostic).
>
> We started GiveWell as issue-agnostic donors looking for the best giving opportunities we could find, and we have always primarily been interested in #3.[19]

The organizations GiveWell rates most highly tend to focus on proven low-cost health solutions for the world's poorest people. This is not an ideological preference of GiveWell's staff, but rather a conclusion of their research. It certainly incorporates philosophical judgments on areas such as the relative values of saving lives versus different ways to improve the quality of life. Hassenfeld and Karnofsky also included their own subjective judgments about analytical issues such as certain measurement techniques for evaluating the results of donating to various causes.

One of their unique characteristics is their extreme focus on transparency. They don't just tell you which organizations they rate highly, they tell you why, making their full analysis publicly available online. Further, they demand transparency from the organizations they review. The standard reports most charities send donors are not sufficient, and a large number of the organizations they review get poor ratings due to a lack of data provided to document their impact.

GiveWell is so forthcoming about their approach and reasoning, donors may find more things to disagree with than with less rigorous approaches. For example, some people believe that GiveWell's recommendations place too strong of a preference for organizations with track records over new ones. For their first several years of existence, GiveWell focused exclusively on proven organizations rather than ones with potentially new innovations, although GiveWell's research is now expanding to include a wider array of potential opportunities. There is no perfect way to compare the relative opportunities of scaling up today's best ideas versus looking for tomorrow's, and GiveWell's views may be different from those of others. Another criticism of their methods is the extreme focus on quantitative measurements of results, which risks favoring something that can be measured over something that is potentially more impactful, but also more difficult to measure. Both of these are valid concerns. In fact, most nonprofits aren't even able to provide GiveWell with enough information for GiveWell to assign a rating. It is certainly legitimate to wonder whether this points to a flaw in GiveWell's rating process or a failure of so many charities to demonstrate their success.

GiveWell is still a relatively new player in the charity evaluation world and their focus is somewhat limited. Despite this, I've personally donated to them because, simply put, they are the only organization I know of that takes such a strong do-bester approach to philanthropic strategy, does robust research, and makes well-defined recommendations based on that approach and research. Their research and thought processes are among the most well-informed and comprehensive resources available to do-besters.

While the completeness of their approach and transparency of the reasoning behind their views is appealing, GiveWell may be inadequate for some do-besters who have different philosophical views about judgments made as part of the quantitative research and the qualitative aspects of the analyses. Nevertheless, donors need to ask themselves whether the magnitude of any philosophical differences they have with GiveWell is greater than the advantages of using its research. GiveWell fills an important and largely vacant role in the philanthropic world. Ideally, there would be a crop of "competitors" to GiveWell, providing information to donors based on a similar do-bester philosophy, but with different people who would have different perspectives on the areas where subjective views are needed. In essence, this would create a true marketplace of ideas for those with do-bester philosophies to get the information they need to make decisions.

When Warren Buffett wanted to start giving away his money, he was wise enough to acknowledge that he didn't have the skills to do it alone. So he asked Bill and Melinda Gates to take the lead in giving away his fortune. In explaining his rationale for outsourcing his philanthropy to someone else, he said, "What can be more logical, in whatever you want done, than finding someone better equipped than you are to do it? Who wouldn't select Tiger Woods to take his place in a high-stakes golf game? That's how I feel about this decision about my money."[20]

Buffett was humble when he admitted his own weakness and declared that the Gates Foundation was more skilled than he was at philanthropy, thus outsourcing the majority of his philanthropy to it. However, Buffett had to retain the most important decision for himself: who to outsource his giving to. He could have chosen any number of other foundations, created his own foundation, or asked a different friend or family member to make his giving decisions. Though he wanted to outsource his giving decisions because he acknowledged that he wasn't exceptionally skilled at giving, Buffett still had to figure out who was the most skilled at giving.

What resources were at Buffett's disposal to help him determine who was the best steward for his giving—either by evaluating the Gates Foundation or any of the other potential options? While there are many resources available, most have significant limitations, as described in this chapter. His choice of the Gates Foundation, for better or for worse, will have a tremendous effect on the ultimate impact of the donation.

Some donors will want to totally outsource their giving as Buffett did and many GiveWell supporters do, while others may want to retain most of the decision making. Regardless, it's important to realize that even though there are many parties that are available to help with a donor's giving decisions, do-besters must make the most high-level strategic decisions. To a large extent, do-besters must do the critical thinking themselves.

6

Developing a Mission

OBJECTIVES AND CONSTRAINTS

> Fit no stereotypes. Don't chase the latest management fads. The situation dictates which approach best accomplishes the team's mission.
>
> —Colin Powell[1]

With so many potential avenues for giving, it's important for most donors to have an anchor to provide clarity of thinking and a consistent direction. Formal giving structures like foundations often do this with written mission statements, expressing a mile-high view of their core beliefs and how they intend to direct their giving. Many individual donors also develop some sort of guiding philosophy for their giving, like mission statements, but these are usually much less structured and formal. It's a good idea to have clarity of mission to help guide your decisions, making sure that all of your giving choices reflect your best thinking, regardless of whether you write down your mission statement or just have it in mind.

Mission statements can be as simple as "I want to help A by doing B because of C" or "I believe the best giving opportunities will have characteristics such as W and X and can be identified by looking at Y and Z." Those are variations on mission statements, even if the donor didn't explicitly write it down or call it a mission statement. The donor's mission is simply what he wants to do, how, and why. While there is no definitive "right" and "wrong" way to develop a mission, it is important to understand the three major elements: there are the broad objectives the donor is trying to achieve and the two types of constraints that help narrow down the methods for achieving the goals. Some constraints are designed to enhance the ability to achieve the objectives by providing specificity on the most important areas, and they would be changed if the donor believes a change would help better pursue the objectives. They support the pursuit of the donor's objectives, so I call them "supporting constraints." Other constraints do the opposite, limiting the donor's ability to achieve the objectives, and they may be called "impeding constraints." These often exist to meet the donor's emotional or personal needs, and these constraints are not necessarily changed, even in light of significant evidence that they impair the donor's ability to pursue the objectives.

As an example, let's illustrate the three major components of mission statements by looking in detail at the mission statement for the Robert Wood Johnson Foundation (RWJF)[2]:

> The Robert Wood Johnson Foundation seeks to improve the health and health care of all Americans. Our efforts focus on improving both the health of everyone in America and their health care—how it's delivered, how it's paid for, and how well it does for patients and their families.
>
> We are guided by a fundamental premise: we are stewards of private funds that must be used in the public's interest. Our greatest asset isn't our endowment; it's the way we help create leverage for change.
>
> We create leverage by building evidence and producing, synthesizing and distributing knowledge, new ideas and expertise. We harness the power of partnerships by bringing together key players, collaborating with colleagues, and securing the sustained commitment of other funders and advocates to improve the health and health care of all Americans.
>
> To ensure that our programs are effective, we developed a framework to organize our grantmaking practices and areas of focus.
>
> This framework recognizes that we do several different kinds of grantmaking and that improving the ways these grants work together can enhance the measurable progress we make toward our overall mission. The framework groups most of our grantmaking into four clusters we call portfolios—Human Capital, Vulnerable Populations, Pioneer and Targeted. Within the Targeted portfolio, we have chosen a group of critical issues to address—Childhood Obesity, Coverage, Public Health and Quality/Equality—by setting specific time-limited objectives, benchmarks, a plan of action, and a budget to accomplish the objective.[3]

We can dissect the RWJF's mission statement to see how it includes each of the three components.

1. Objectives

These are high-level goals that the donor will pursue, and they are typically extremely broad. The objective of the RWJF is in the first sentence of its mission statement: to improve health and health care. Other examples of objectives include the following:

- To reduce human poverty
- To promote global peace
- To protect the environment

Objectives state what the donors want to do and possibly why, but not where or how objectives will be pursued.

2. Supporting Constraints

These provide more specificity on the best ways to implement the donor's objectives—they often address the issues of where and how the donor will pursue the mission.

The RWJF's mission statement goes into significant detail about its areas of focus, such as childhood obesity, and how the foundation will create leverage, set goals, and measure progress.

One of the key features of a supporting constraint is that it could be eliminated, replaced, or changed if the donor finds a better way to achieve his objectives. For example, the RWJF might divert its focus away from childhood obesity if it perceived the issue to have become less of a problem, felt less able to effectively address it, or if a more compelling issue emerged. Childhood obesity is not part of their fundamental charter to improve health and health care for Americans, but rather how they implement their objective.

Here are a few other common types of supporting constraints:

- Program-based, such as focusing on vaccinations or education, when the donor thinks this is the best way to pursue certain objectives (e.g., saving lives or economic development).

- Geography, as the donor might believe that certain areas have the worst problems or the costs of improving conditions are lowest, often reasons donors implement poverty reduction objectives in the third world.
- Expertise, such as a donor with medical expertise being more skilled in evaluating the effectiveness of medical causes, and thus implementing in that area rather than an area in which the donor is not as knowledgeable.

To combine objectives and several different types of supporting constraints into a mission statement, a donor might want to reduce human suffering and death as much as possible, and choose a supporting constraint of funding tuberculosis vaccines for children in Asia and Africa. This doesn't necessarily mean the donor believes that the lives of West African children with tuberculosis are more important than those of children in Seattle with cancer (or tuberculosis), but just that these two alternatives have different opportunities for effectiveness.

Supporting constraints are extremely important, as they express the specific direction donors will take to achieve their objectives. If you approached giving as a pure do-bester, the only two components of a mission statement would be the objectives and the supporting constraints. But most donors have a third component.

3. Impeding Constraints

Impeding constraints are limitations placed on how the objectives will be pursued. They are like handcuffs donors place on themselves toward meeting their objectives.

The RWJF has a major impeding constraint in its mission statement, listed in its first sentence: its focus is exclusively on Americans. Given that America has significantly better health and health care than many other nations, and thus opportunities for improvement are more challenging, this is a fairly significant impeding constraint. It prevents the RWJF from addressing many of the most preventable health-related problems such as tuberculosis, malaria, and illnesses related to unsanitary water, as these are not prevalent issues in America. Interestingly, this may not have been as significant of a practical constraint when the foundation was started decades ago, because at that time it was more difficult to effectively implement global health care programs.

It could even be argued that another impeding constraint of the RWJF's mission is its focus on health care. In that line of reasoning, the objective, which is not explicitly listed in the mission statement, would be something broader, such as improving human welfare.

Common types of impeding constraints include many of the same categories as supporting constraints, but for different reasons:

- Geographic, such as only focusing on a certain country or locality. Geographic constraints, when chosen based on areas the donor has a personal connection to, rather than areas of greatest need or ability to help, become impeding constraints.
- Emotional proximity to the donor, such as focusing on schools the donor has attended or medical issues that have impacted the donor's family.
- Relations to the donor's particular area of interest, such as an athlete donating to sports-related causes or an arts patron supporting a favorite cultural institution.

Impeding constraints tend to be based on underlying do-gooder mentalities and limit impact far more than is typically recognized.

Sometimes supporting and impeding constraints look alike, but it is important to understand the difference in order to effectively pursue the donor's objectives. We can see the difference between the two based on how they relate to positions on the Axis of Altruism.

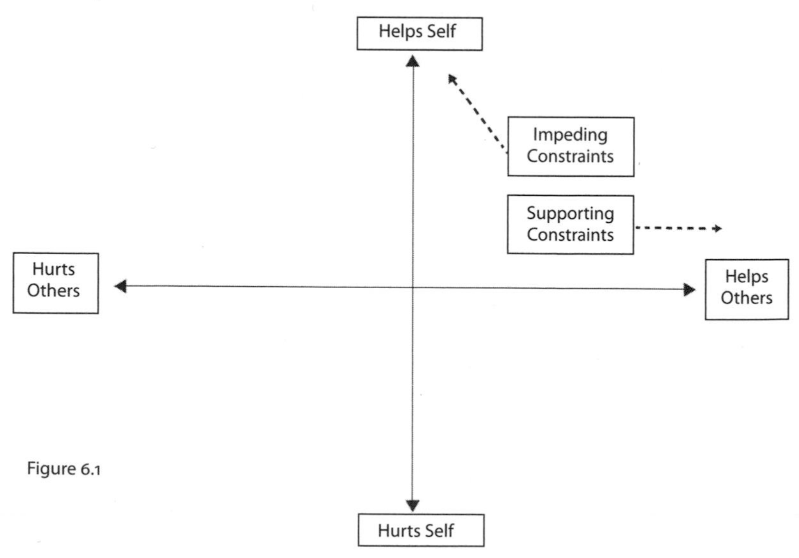

Figure 6.1

Impeding constraints are usually about the personal preferences of the donor, so they tend to be designed to provide emotional benefits to the donor at the expense of impact on others. Supporting constraints, alternatively, are usually intended to create a more focused giving program in order to make a greater impact. Let's look at a few examples.

Suppose a donor gives to local organizations. This constraint could be impeding or supporting.

Impeding: Maybe the donor wants to give locally, simply because he believes "charity begins at home." This cliché is commonly applied as an impeding constraint. The donor may want to "give back" to the community or he may want to see the impact of his donation. These reasons have purposes, but they arise from a do-gooder mentality and the donor should be aware of the impact this constraint has on the effectiveness of his gift. Can the hospital in your country (e.g., St. Jude) save more lives with your donation than any other hospital on the other side of the world (e.g., Malanje Provincial Hospital)? Are the schools in your area the most worthy of additional funds? Are the homeless shelters and food pantries near you the best ways to reduce hunger and poverty? For most donors, the answer to these questions is "no." The world is huge, and it would be a coincidence if the places best equipped to use your donation happen to be right by you. The reasons a donor might constrain gifts to local geographies are legitimate considerations if they are necessary for the donor to get sufficient emotional benefits to continue donating; however, donors shouldn't fool themselves into thinking that it is easy to focus on their favored region without also reducing the impact of their donations. Rather, donors should weigh the advantages and disadvantages of the constraint.

But maybe the same exact constraint—to focus giving on local organizations—could be a supporting constraint. A rationale for this might be if the donor chose to support local organizations because he didn't have the time or expertise to find better organizations in other geographies. This is often the case when the size of the gift is small relative to the amount of effort necessary to expand the geographic search—as with most "average"-size donations. This may have also been the case for major donors several decades ago (such as when the RWJF was formed).

However, for today's major donors, a constraint to focus locally is likely to diminish the donor's impact. The donor may consider spending more time and effort to broaden the search, possibly delegating some of these responsibilities to others, such as a full-time staff, or funding an organization with local presence that also works overseas. Of course, the additional cost of efforts to work globally would need to be justified by an expectation of improved effectiveness.

Earlier I noted that RWJF's focus on America was an impeding constraint, and that the decision to focus on health-related issues might be as well. But the real story could be more nuanced: both of these could be supporting.

At the time of its founding, the focus on America could have been because the challenges of implementing global programs were much greater than they are today, and the RWJF decided that it could be more effective with programs locally. Further, it was founded by someone with expertise in health care, who might have been in a much better position to effectively implement programs in health care than in any other field. Although the same analysis would probably produce different results for a typical large foundation starting up today, the RWJF is not a start-up. The staff has developed significant expertise in American health issues over the years and is extremely skilled at implementing programs in the area; continuing in their area of strength may be a logical supporting constraint.

Differentiating Impeding and Supporting Constraints

Does it matter whether a constraint is impeding or supporting? Absolutely, because it affects when and how the donor's decisions might change. In the RWJF's situation, if its geographic emphasis on America was a supporting constraint from decades ago when international giving was more difficult to implement, then it would shift to a global emphasis when conditions changed and the opportunities for international giving became more promising. Alternatively, if it was an impeding constraint, then it is not likely that their geographic giving patterns would change, regardless of the circumstances.

I don't know whether the RWJF's focus on health issues for Americans is really impeding or supporting. It has a strong reputation for a history of impactful programs. Could this be due to relatively few impeding constraints with smart supporting constraints, or could it be due to outstanding implementation in spite of significant impeding constraints? Only insiders in the RWJF have a strong basis to judge how they've made decisions about the constraints in their mission statement.

One of the most valid reasons for impeding constraints is related to donors' need for emotional benefits in order to maintain their generosity. Just as someone surely would be more willing to spend more on the well-being of himself and his family than on that of a stranger, he might also have a preference for someone in his neighborhood or country, or to someone who attends the same university he did or is suffering from a disease that has touched his life. In essence, this is prioritizing the well-being of one set of people over others because of a kinship donors have to them. Further, donors often want to see and emotionally relate to the impact of their giving, which can often be easier with impeding constraints. Such feelings—which are more pervasive in do-gooder approaches—are a part of human nature and not necessarily wrong, but donors must ask themselves questions about how far they are willing to take it. Would you rather save the life of a fellow American than two people in a foreign country? What about ten? Would you be more willing to save someone's life if you saw them or visited their community? Practical realities make these questions difficult to answer, but they are nevertheless important to consider.

More broadly, while a gift would have the same impact regardless of why it was selected, donors should explore their missions fully in order to improve their effectiveness for future gifts. Impeding constraints often drastically reduce how effective a gift is at meeting the donor's objectives, but they continue to be common. Donors who want their donations to go far should think twice before incorporating impeding constraints. Why would you diminish your own effectiveness? Are impeding constraints really necessary? How much impact are you willing to sacrifice for the priorities expressed in your impeding constraints? There may be good reasons to have self-imposed impeding constraints. If so, donors should be aware of those reasons and not be naïve about the fact that they reduce impact.

Impeding constraints survive and thrive in today's philanthropic sector. One of the culprits is an approach that goes by the buzzword "strategic philanthropy," which legitimizes impeding constraints without acknowledging their effect on impact. This approach links the donor's mission and implementation. Paul Brest and Hal Harvey say that "the basic imperative of strategic philanthropy is to deploy your responses to achieve your goals most effectively. . . . All this means [is] that accomplishing philanthropic goals requires having great clarity about what those goals are and specifying indicators of success before beginning a philanthropic project."[4] On the surface, this sounds logical and relatively benign, if not helpful. Why wouldn't anyone want to practice this? But its common implementation is where problems arise.

As an example of strategic philanthropy, Brest and Harvey describe the Thomas & Stacey Siebel Foundation's focus on methamphetamine abuse in Montana:

> Traditional law enforcement efforts to try to reduce the supply of the drug were not succeeding. Using print media, radio, and television, the Siebel Foundation's "Not Even Once" campaign was targeted at teens who had not yet used meth. The ads were scary, vivid, and blunt, portraying the negative physical, psychological, and social effects of meth use—teeth falling out, attempted suicide, physical violence—through personal testimonials. A preliminary report by Montana's attorney general indicates large declines in the use of meth in the workplace, meth-related crimes, and in arrests where the suspects tested positive for meth use.[5]

This initiative was "strategic" in that it had clarity in its goal and creatively considered how to deploy its responses to reduce meth use. It appears to have been successful in accomplishing that goal. However, Brest and Harvey make no mention of how the goal itself was determined. Was the focus on meth use in Montana a supporting constraint, or was it impeding? That is, would the donation have been better spent reducing meth usage in a different state, supporting education, or providing health care in the developing world?

One of the deepest flaws in "strategic philanthropy," as commonly practiced, is that strategic thinking doesn't usually start until after many impeding constraints have been set—only then is the strategy developed to best achieve the philanthropic objectives. While the approach of strategic philanthropy may be a very good way to achieve previously specified goals, the philanthropic world would be better served if the approach to strategic philanthropy were expanded to encourage mission statements to be developed with more strategic thinking in setting the objectives and constraints themselves.

Despite all the negative consequences of impeding constraints, it isn't realistic to expect donors not to impose them. Real people are not emotionless robots. Not only do people want their gifts to have a positive impact, they want to see and feel the effect. The relationship between helping others and feeling good about a donation is not as pure for most do-besters as described in chapter 4 ("The Role of Emotional Giving"). Donors want to personally connect with their giving, and they tend to feel most connected to their own life experiences. This is why impeding constraints are typically imposed. What should a donor do when his mind is telling him to avoid impeding constraints but his heart wants them?

Because it is not practical to ask donors to completely ignore the preferences and pet causes that tug on their hearts, an alternative for donors struggling with this would be a four-step process:

1. Acknowledge. Do you really want to give to your university because you loved your experience there? Do you feel passionately about supporting the medical cause that affected a family member? That's human, and there's nothing wrong with it. Start by becoming self-aware of how you feel and why. Ask yourself what level of impact reduction you are comfortable with and how strongly you believe the constraints you're considering impede objectives. If the impact is minimal, then maybe you find it acceptable. If the loss of impact is too significant, then someone with strong do-bester tendencies might be uncomfortable with the impeding constraint. This step will not be an exact science; it may be as simple as some critical thinking and a gut check.

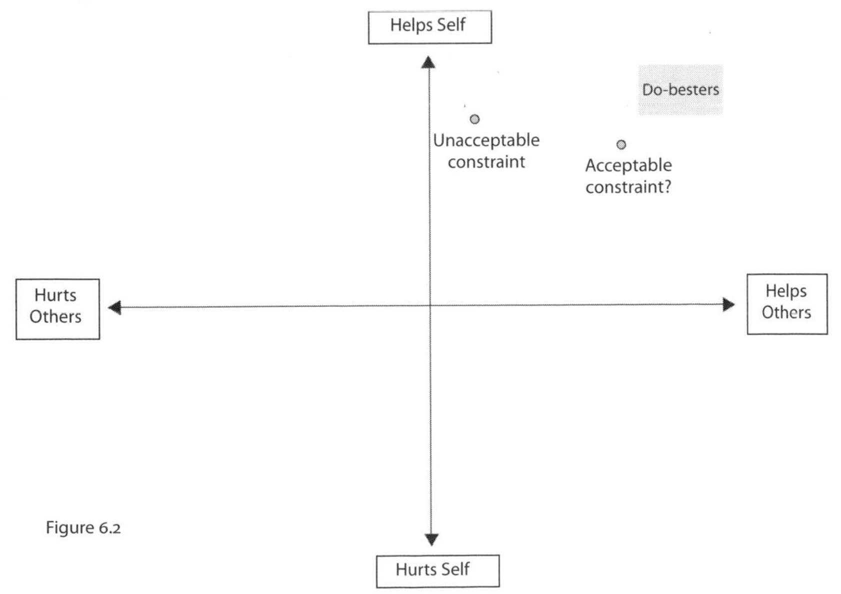

Figure 6.2

2. Loosen. Instead of just considering your university, expand your opportunity set to other educational causes. Your family may have been touched by a particular medical cause, but think about what other causes have affected other families. Loosen one impeding constraint at a time. Loosen them enough to push your comfort zones, but not so much as to lose your inspiration. This will bring you closer to a do-bester's level of impact. Consider the effects of each impeding constraint. How would the donation change without it? How would the impact change? What is the opportunity cost of the constraint? Don't just pick a direction and drive—consider other options. The ultimate choice is yours, so you should make that choice with with an eye on alternatives. And it's okay to test the limits of your comfort zone a bit as you're loosening impeding constraints. For many, loosening impeding constraints may be a natural reaction to the thought process about their effect on impact.

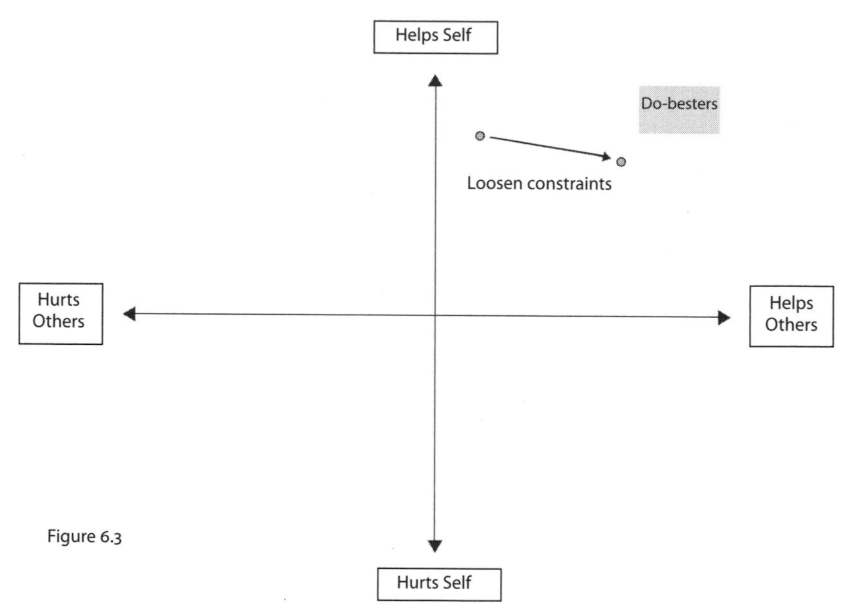

Figure 6.3

3. Connect. As you loosen constraints and give to causes that help more people, you're likely to start to feel a stronger emotional connection to the new areas. But you may want to take a step further to engagement, actively doing things to connect yourself emotionally with the causes you support. This might mean learning more about them, meeting the people involved, or even going to visit a program in a foreign country. Whatever it takes to give you that emotional warm glow when you know you've done something good, do it. This will give you greater emotional benefits.

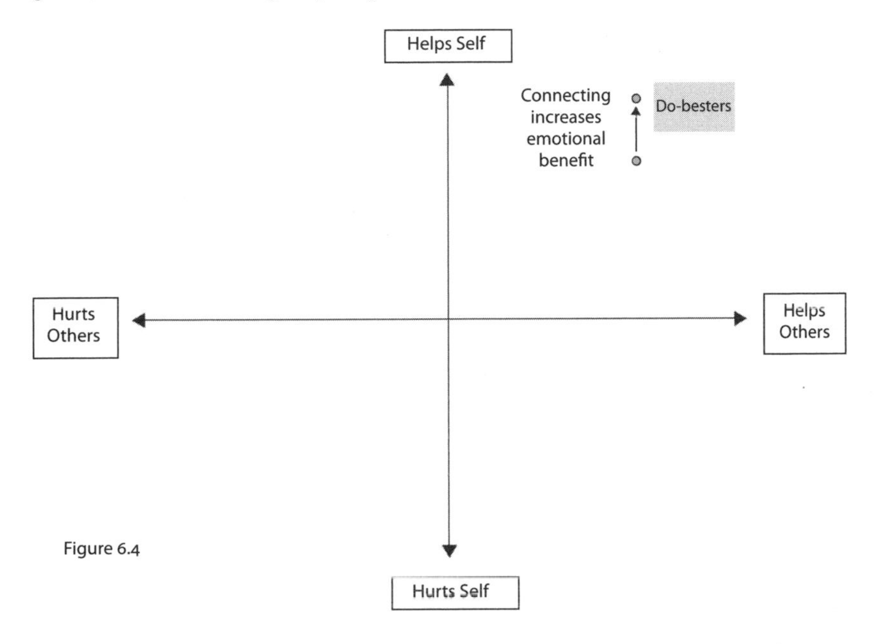

Figure 6.4

4. Repeat. Acknowledge the impeding constraints that remain, loosen them gradually, and make sure you still feel emotionally connected to your philanthropy. This will bring you closer and closer to do-bester-caliber results.

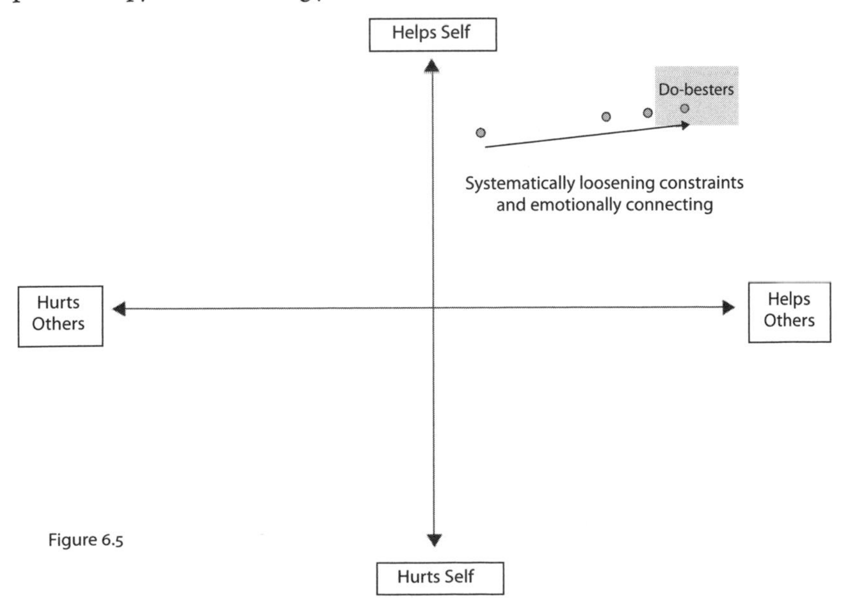

Figure 6.5

One important aspect of figure 6.5 is that the process of donors loosening constraints and connecting to their giving not only helps them move east on the Axis of Altruism, but also helps them move north. This improvement on both axes occurs for donors who care about the impact of their donations—they get more emotional satisfaction as they are providing greater help to others. It is truly a win-win situation for everyone.

This process is designed to align the donor's head and heart, maximizing the emotional benefits of giving with what is most impactful. This is the do-bester ideal. While there is some conflict between the emotional do-gooder and intellectual do-bester in all of us, donors shouldn't have to pick one to the complete exclusion of the other.

I believe these concepts can be brought together with a formula I call the Law of Mission Impact. It states:

$$\text{impact} = \frac{(\text{dollars}) \times (\text{quality of supporting constraints})}{\text{restrictiveness of impending constraints}}$$

Applying it to the example of the RWJF, the impact of its giving is primarily based on three factors:

1. Impact is proportionate to dollars donated. For example, holding everything else equal, the more that RWJF gives, the greater its impact will be.[6]
2. Impact increases with the quality of the supporting constraints. This relates to how skilled RWJF is at effectively identifying causes, determining how to address those causes, and choosing grantees to implement its vision. In fact, its mission statement is very explicit about how much RWJF focuses on the quality of implementing its supporting constraints: "Our greatest asset isn't our endowment; it's the way we help create leverage for change."
3. Impact is reduced by the restrictiveness of the impeding constraints. RWJF's constraint to focus in America may have been a smart supporting constraint when the foundation was started decades ago, but today it may be a more restrictive impeding constraint for a foundation in health care.

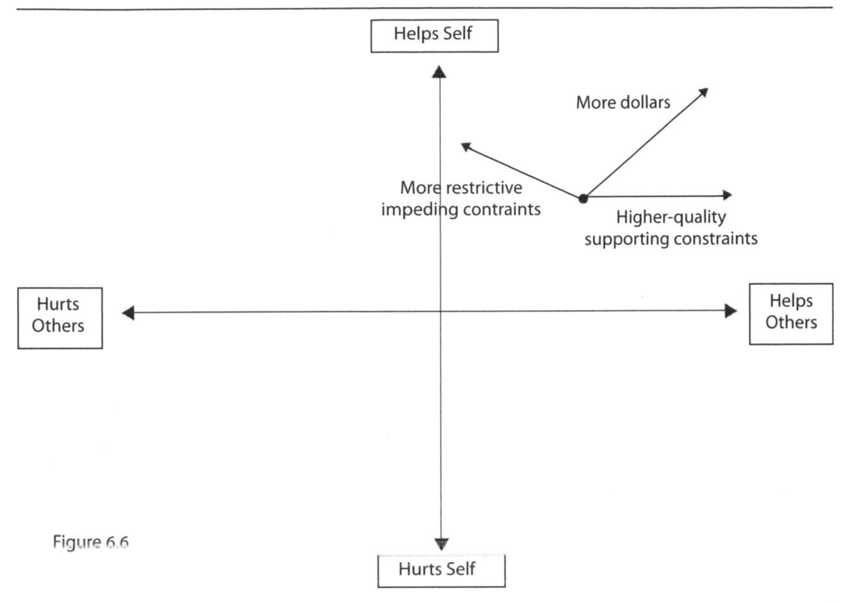

Figure 6.6

There are two big points that can be gleaned from reviewing the Law of Mission Impact. First, while more dollars increase impact, the constraints can be more important influencers of impact. The biggest gift isn't necessarily the best one.

Second, and probably less recognized, is that restrictive impeding constraints significantly reduce impact. Many donors impose them to reflect their own personal passions and desires. This is not necessarily wrong—giving is often personal and expressive, and might not occur without these constraints—but donors concerned about impact should consider their effect. Whether they are geographic, as with RWJF's focus on America, or programmatic, impeding constraints reduce impact.

While the Law of Mission Impact is not as exact in practice as shown in its mathematical form, it holds true that giving $100,000 with a significantly constrained mission may not do as much good as giving $10,000 to one of the most impactful areas.

Figure 6.6 was presented with the assumption that the impeding constraints increase the emotional benefits to the donor. This is because such constraints are usually designed explicitly for that purpose. While that may be true in many situations, we showed earlier how loosening impeding constraints and reconnecting to the cause can give many donors greater long-term emotional benefits from their giving. In these situations, our example will look more like figure 6.7.

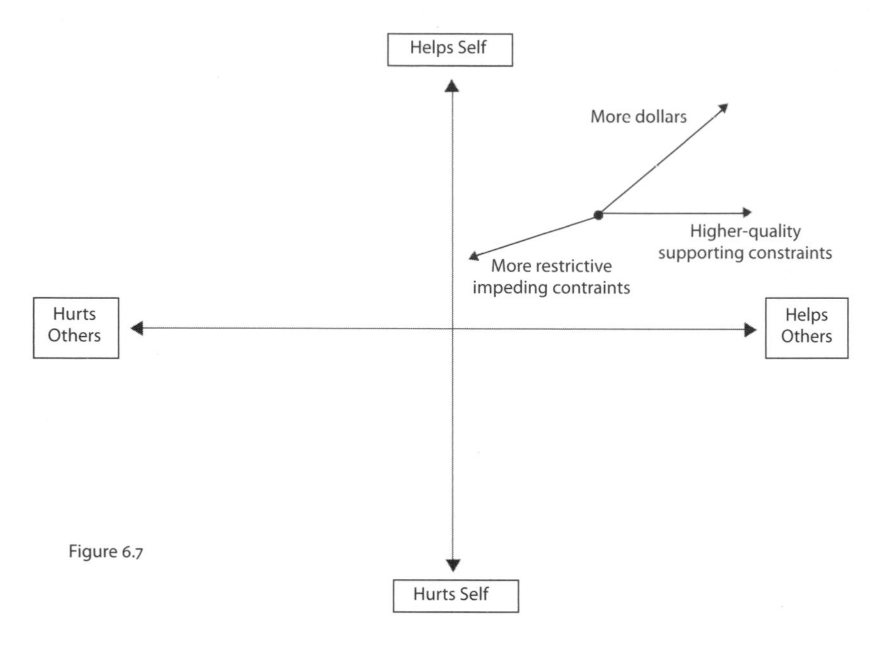

Figure 6.7

The Law of Mission Impact gives you some guidance on how to structure your own mission. How restrictive are your impeding constraints? Constraining your health care focus to Japan—ranked 1st in life expectancy at eighty-three years—is much more restrictive than constraining it to Swaziland, ranked 191st at forty-seven years.[7] Constraining your donation to a school you attended is much more restrictive than constraining it to any educational institution. Constraining your focus to the disease that affected your family is much more restrictive than considering any disease that affects families. Loosening up restrictive impeding constraints can have a tremendous effect on the impact of the donation.

Every donor has a mission statement, whether formally written or not, and the way they construct it will direct the most important decisions influencing the ultimate effect of their giving.

7

The Most Important Decisions

The premise of this foundation is one life on this
planet is no more valuable than the next.
—Melinda Gates[1]

Adopting the philosophy of the do-bester is a key step for donors to increase their impact. It is, however, where the challenges begin. With about 1.1 million nonprofit organizations in America,[2] many of which have several programs, it's important to have some method for filtering them out. Do-besters need to understand what criteria should be most important. While it's impossible to write a definitive instruction manual for do-besters, there are some general guidelines to offer. Do-besters should focus on the most important decisions.

Once the amount of a donation is set, the three most important decisions affecting the impact of a donation are these:

1. **Geography:** Local, national, or international.
2. **Cause:** Examples include education, health care, environment, religion, art, etc.
3. **Implementation:** The methods for making change happen as well as the organizations to work with.

This chapter won't articulate exactly how to make these decisions, because there isn't a single process that every do-bester can adopt. But it will help

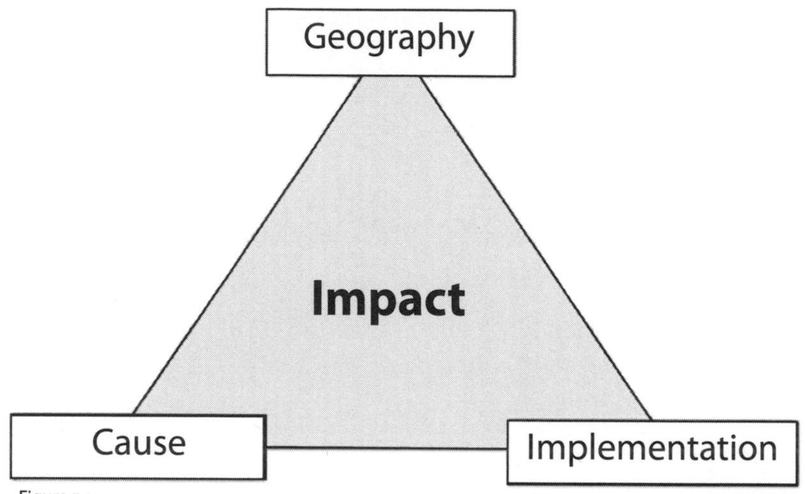

Figure 7.1

clarify what the most important decisions are, so donors can focus their thinking on these areas.

Conversely, there are processes for making these decisions that are inconsistent with the do-bester philosophy. Many donors set impeding constraints on one or more of these factors: focusing locally because "charity begins at home," selecting a cause that has touched their lives, or implementing with an organization they know personally. These approaches are donor-driven, not focused on needs or opportunities. Impeding constraints in the most important areas tend to significantly limit the donor's impact. As a result, the do-bester approach addresses all three of these with an eye for impact.

Geography

Suppose you're considering ways to improve health care and debating whether to support American causes versus those in the developing world. What would your donation do in each geography, how much would each cost, and what would be the results?

What you would do in each geography?

In America, you might donate to a local hospital or clinic. They might use your donation to provide subsidized medical supplies for the poor, care for people with certain illnesses, or support research initiatives for improving treatment. As an example, the Ann & Robert H. Lurie Children's Hospital (formerly Children's Memorial Hospital) in Chicago recently sent a solicitation letter for an opportunity just like this:

> Imagine the birth of your child, a moment you'll remember forever. Now imagine that your son was born with Down Syndrome, and needed emergency surgery *just to live*. Where would you turn? It happened to Jim and Sandra Brown, and their infant son Chris. . . . Your gift of just $75 or more ensures that we can be here for families like Chris's, and helps pay for needed items like advanced sensory equipment to comfort a child in pain. . . . As soon as Chris arrived, a team of Children's Memorial specialists performed the emergency surgery that saved his life. Chris spent his first year of life at Children's Memorial, and he endured three open-heart surgeries *before his third birthday*. Chris and his parents became like family to the hospital staff. Today, Chris is in the 10th grade, and he's won several medals at the Special Olympics. "He surpassed what I ever thought he'd be able to do," says his mom, "[a]nd he's happy!"[3]

Certainly this is a very inspiring story about success at the Children's Hospital, and it is the type of thing that motivates its donors to help.

For the developing world, there is a very different type of story being told to donors. There are rarely references to advanced sensory equipment or year-long stays in hospitals. Instead, donors would probably support initiatives such as immunizations, providing clean water, deworming, and providing anti-malaria mosquito nets. For example, UNICEF's website describes some of the health-related work they do:

> [S]ince its first tuberculosis campaign in 1947, UNICEF has been a leader in global immunization. Today we provide vaccine to 40 percent of the world's children and help save two million lives a year. But thousands of children still die needlessly every day from diseases like measles, polio, or tuberculosis. UNICEF is committed to vaccinating every single child against preventable childhood diseases.
>
> When war or natural disaster strikes, we do whatever it takes to get children immunized. We help broker ceasefires so that we can enter a war-torn region and vaccinate its children. After a disaster, we go door-to-door in the remotest areas to distribute lifesaving vaccines.[4]

Clearly this type of life-saving help is different from what happens stateside.

How much would it cost?

When it comes to someone's health and well-being, this may feel like a terrible question. But unless a donor can fully fund every health care need for every person in the world—which is impossible for even the wealthiest of billionaires—it is a question that thoughtful donors must ask. Donors who consider what it truly means to care for others must dig deep to understand where their donation will have the greatest impact. Returning to our example, the solicitation from the Ann & Robert H. Lurie Children's Hospital practically boasted about how expensive it was for them to save lives; the patient they described spent the entire first year of his life in the hospital. The solicitation letter went into more detail on how much things cost (see table 7.1).

TABLE 7.1

At this level . . .	*You make this possible . . .*
$10,000+	A neuroendoscope, which enhances surgical precision for children undergoing complex surgeries
$5,000–$9,999	One Vecta Cart, a specially designed interactive device to help distract and relax children during difficult medical procedures, such as spinal taps
$2,500–$4,999	An exercise bike for children with limited physical abilities
$1,000–$2,499	A one year supply of musical instruments and materials for music therapy in all areas of the hospital
$500–$999	A scholarship to send one diabetic child to summer camp for one week
$250–$499	Housing one family for one week at Kohl's House while their child recovers from transplant surgery
$100–$249	Sensory equipment to help children in pain
$1–$99	Special dolls that absorb a parent's scent to place in neonatal intensive care beds with babies

In contrast, UNICEF can stretch your money to save many lives in the developing world (see their description of costs in table 7.2).

TABLE 7.2. *What Your Money Can Buy*

$6	can provide a hundred auto-disable syringes to immunize a hundred children with safe equipment.
$60	can provide enough vaccine to immunize four hundred children against polio.
$200	can provide a large cold box for the transportation of vaccines to remote locations.
$4,000	can provide a Solar Refrigerator, used for the storage of vaccines in areas with non-existent or unreliable electrical energy.

While the true costs for both organizations are unlikely to be as exact as reported, they give a general indication of differences of working in different geographics. Comparing the two, it is a clear reminder that paying American salaries for doctors, nurses, and researchers in addition to advanced technology would be far more expensive than any of the labor or products necessary to assist in the developing world. Further, many of the causes of illness and mortality in the developing world are much cheaper to address—they're problems that wealthier countries have already fixed.

What would be the results?

There is a fundamentally different value proposition to helping the poorest people in the poorest countries as compared to helping the poorest people in the richest countries. Because illness and mortality rates in the developing world are so much higher and the preventable ways to improve them are so much cheaper, there would almost certainly be a more powerful impact for donations that focus on the developing world.

For donors who truly believe that the value of every human life is equal, independent of nationality, there is a compelling case that any health-related philanthropy should be directed at the developing world. This means things like clean water, deworming, protection from malaria, and child immunizations—which most people in the developed world take for granted. Common areas of focus like cancer and heart disease would receive a smaller piece of the global philanthropic pie than they currently do—that's not to imply that these are not important issues or that the people who suffer from them are less important. Rather, in a world of scarce resources, priorities must be set and these issues would be a lower priority than they currently are. While the example provided here is for health issues, the concept can be extended to many other areas.

When I've spoken with people from international charities, they often say that the biggest obstacle to getting more donors is that many donors prefer to help people "here" rather than "there." The real issue for donors is more complex. The question of geography is not just a question of where to help people, but also about how much help can be given.

Cause

In 1983, Susan G. Komen died of breast cancer. She was young—in her mid-thirties. Her younger sister, Nancy Goodman Brinker, promised to do everything she could to end breast cancer forever. That promise eventually became the Susan G. Komen for the Cure organization, which has contributed more than $1 billion to fight cancer.

One of its biggest fundraising events is the Susan G. Komen 3-Day. Participants use a three-day, sixty-mile walk as an opportunity to raise money for the organization and its programs. Although participants come from all walks of life, it should come as no surprise that there are more women than men participating—breast cancer is about a hundred times more prevalent in women than men. And there is also a disproportionate number of cancer survivors and close family members of victims and survivors participating.

Donors and activists, like Nancy Brinker and 3-Day participants, typically gravitate toward causes they've felt personally. They give to medical causes that have affected their families, universities they attended, programs they've benefited from, and artistic organizations they've enjoyed. This is only natural, as donors are inspired by experiences they've had. And it also means that the people getting involved are truly passionate about whatever cause they are supporting, making them more dedicated than an average person, and thus more likely to be impactful. Further, there is something inherently pluralistic about this: the causes that have affected the most people will tend to get the most support, at least to the extent that the people they affect have the financial means to become donors.

Despite these advantages, there are also unfortunate side effects of this method of selecting causes. First, programs that personally touch the wealthy tend to be funded better than those that affect the poor. According to the World Health Organization, forms of cancer occupy four of the top ten causes of death in high-income countries, one of the top ten causes in middle-income countries, and aren't among the top ten causes of death in low-income countries.[5] Cancer causes a larger proportion of deaths among those with higher incomes, so if donors give to the causes that touch them, cancer is likely to get a disproportionate share of the philanthropic pie.

There are several items on the top-ten list for low-income countries that don't even make the list for high-income countries: tuberculosis, neonatal infections, malaria, and prematurity and low birth weight. Despite extensive focus on these areas by UNICEF, the Gates Foundation, and some other high-profile organizations, they remain far underserved relative to the top causes of death in wealthy countries. Not only does cancer rank lower as a health problem in the developing world, but it is also more costly to prevent, treat, and cure than many of the diseases ahead of it. Certainly there is some overlap between the decisions on programs' geography, but the issue for donors to address should be clear.

That's not to imply that more funding in the battle against cancer is bad, but that there may be higher priorities when that funding takes away from other causes. Does it? Sometimes, but not always.

Most philanthropy experts consider it a best practice for donors to focus on a small number of causes. An unfocused giver is much more likely to engage in "peanut butter philanthropy," spread thin across diverse areas—so thin that the donor would be unlikely to have the expertise to know where to give. In his book *The Foundation: A Great American Secret; How Private Wealth Is Changing the World,* Joel Fleishman expresses this view:

> Other, more tangible benefits flow from [foundation] founder constraints. As I've already noted, the hardest task foundation trustees face is choosing specific program areas on which to focus. When a foundation creator has already made that choice, the trustees' job is greatly simplified. They can concentrate on how best to implement the founder's choice, a task of lesser complexity and subjectivity. Ironically, then, the more constrained the trustees, the better their performance is likely to be. . . . And the staff members who are ultimately selected will have a better chance of mastering their field of operations when strategic limits reduce the universe of social problems with which they are expected to deal.[6]

Constraining the causes to focus on is important for many of these reasons.

It may be the hardest task for foundation trustees, as Fleishman noted, but it may also be among the most influential on the foundation's ultimate impact. Thus it is important to question the rationale for the constraints foundation founders put on their trustees—are they impeding or supporting constraints? If they were chosen with an impeding mentality, then the foundation trustees and staff will have an easier time being very effective in a less impactful area—perhaps a dubious way to "succeed."

Will the world be better off if charitable contributions are directed toward education or health care? The environment, the arts, or disaster relief? The options are so diverse that it is difficult to create a structure for comparison.

As a result, although cause is one of the most important decisions, it is usually made with a shift in focus away from the program and toward the donor. Donors look at their hobbies, experiences, and lives and try to improve something that they have encountered along the way. Health-related causes have a disproportionate number of donors that have personal or family experiences with the illness or problem they focus on. Organizations with arts-related missions tend to be supported by those with a taste for that type of art. These reasons for selecting a focus are donor-driven, not need-driven.

There are definite advantages to this trend. Donors tend to be more passionate about the areas of their personal experience, which can make them more effective. For example, they often give more, raise more awareness among others, or fundraise more effectively as their personal interest shines through. They may also be more motivated and knowledgeable about the cause, which means that they can better implement their goals.

As donation sizes get larger, the advantages of focusing on causes outside the donor's area of interest become greater. With larger donations, charitable giving should be less of a hobby/extracurricular activity and more to have an impact on the world. There are also stronger reasons for the donor to spend time and resources to learn which causes are most effective, rather than simply giving to causes they already know.

Implementation

Of the three most important decision areas for donors, implementation is the area that the mainstream philanthropic community often focuses on when addressing effective philanthropy. As a result, it is the area that needs the least reinventing. That is not to imply that the average donor does it well, but that the current "best practice" among professionals in the philanthropy sector (e.g., large foundations and consultants) addresses this area well.

Implementation involves selecting organizations to work with and choosing projects. It includes decisions about whether to innovate or invest in proven solutions, how much emphasis to put on scalability and sustainability, and the best means to deliver services.

So what are other ways for donors to evaluate the relative merits of the diverse array of approaches to implementation? The answer is as much philosophical as it is empirical. Many people believe that the core of it relates to the donor's "theory of change." The term "theory of change" has a linguistically impractical sound, but it's actually a very practical and important concept that every philanthropist uses—whether they know it or not. While there are several ways to define it, I will use the following definition: Theory of change is a belief about the processes and methods by which change happens.

A theory of change concerns how to implement a desired result. To consider a specific example, let's look at donors who focus on education. The specific educational organizations and programs that a donor supports would depend on his theory of change. To give further insights:

- If he believes that governmental policy is the strongest driver of change, he might support programs that lobby the government to change education policy.
- If his theory of change is that governmental funding of education programs would do the most to achieve his desired change, then he might support programs that lobby the government for more money.
- If he thinks his desired change can best be achieved by local programs, he might support small programs that help individual students or schools at a local level.
- If he believes that modern teaching methods are flawed, he might fund research on alternative methods.
- If he thinks that elite leaders are extremely influential, he might focus on education for the gifted rather than the typical student.
- If he thinks that the most important years are the early ones, he might focus his efforts on preschools or elementary schools rather than universities.

The list could go on and on, and there could be other lists for other issues. There are not necessarily clear "right" or "wrong" answers, they are simply beliefs about how the desired social change can best be achieved. While many people determine their theories of change based merely on ideologies and gut instincts, there are better ways. Instead, they can be determined largely based on research and testing. There are numerous studies on nearly every area that philanthropy touches, which give insight into what works and what doesn't. There is still a certain amount of subjectivity in how to interpret them, allowing room for different opinions. Nevertheless, it is this research that should drive a large part of how donors determine and refine their theories of change. Ultimately, these beliefs should dictate how philanthropists make implementation choices.

Of course, theories of change don't have to be absolute. For example, one could believe that increased governmental funding is the best way to improve education in some countries, but in other countries the government is so corrupt that implementing the same theory of change would not be effective.

Often two organizations will have very similar high-level objectives, but extremely different programs. One of the reasons for this is that they may have different theories of change. A do-bester should know not only what he is trying to achieve, but also how he thinks it can be implemented most effectively—a key for mainstream donors to turn into do-besters.

Without a theory of change, a philanthropist may have difficulty determining how to implement his donation. But with a theory of change, donors still have more work to do to choose organizations and projects. (Chapters 10 and 11 dive deeper into those areas, so this chapter won't cover them in more detail.)

This chapter has discussed the three most important decisions donors make, and they are all interrelated. Donors focusing on the developing world will be choosing from different causes and organizations than those focusing on wealthier countries. Similarly, donors focusing on certain causes will have a limited menu of organizations to work with and implementation mechanisms, and their geographical emphasis may be narrowed down by the nature of the causes.

It can be tricky for donors to navigate these three types of decisions to determine where to ultimately give money. Some donors may prefer a top-down approach, choosing the cause and/or geography first, then selecting implementation methods. Others may favor a bottom-up approach, selecting the best organizations and implementations first, letting that dictate the geographies and causes. Presumably, donors with that approach would need a method for narrowing down the 1.1 million nonprofit organizations in the United States.

Processes aside, the three most important decisions donors make are intertwined. Do-besters should recognize that all of them are key to the ultimate impact, and making any of them based on purely emotional criteria would not be consistent with their goal of maximizing impact.

It is useful to understand how these three decisions are often viewed in mainstream philanthropy to avoid common pitfalls. The prior chapter introduced the concept of strategic philanthropy, which is deeply embedded in today's dominant paradigm of effective philanthropy. It is worth reviewing how this paradigm, in practice, is applied to each of the three most important decisions outlined in this chapter.

The approach of strategic philanthropy generally starts by defining a specific problem the donor wants to solve, determining the specific strategy to solve it, then giving to organizations and projects to implement that solution. For example, a donor might want to reduce homelessness in Chicago, and might then develop his strategy of supporting a combination of education, job training, housing, and other areas. Then the donor would select the actual organizations and programs to fund.

It seems logical on the surface to define the problem first, determine the solution, then implement. However, strategic philanthropy, as commonly practiced, doesn't use any strategic analysis to determine the problem or answer the first two important questions (geography and cause). For example, philanthropists are donating millions of dollars to research diseases that are rare and have few short term prospects for a cure, while 19,000 children die every day of preventable causes.[7] It is ironic that strategic philanthropy tends to use little analytical strategy in deciding which problem to address, though this method of selecting problems is a major reason donors fail to maximize the impact of their giving.

Strategic philanthropy, as commonly practiced, emphasizes a do-bester approach to finding the right implementation, but suggests a less analytical, do-gooder approach for selecting the geography and cause—these are simply constrained when defining the problem to solve. While such a process may be appropriate for many donors, it is not suitable for do-besters. It is unfortunate that many professionals in the philanthropy industry hold this type of "strategic" philanthropy as the gold standard in giving, and this is much of the reason why philanthropy needs reinventing.

Do-bester philanthropy must consider impact when evaluating all three of the most important decisions: geography, cause, and implementation. Further, do-bester donors need to evaluate these three issues in tandem to maximize impact. Though this chapter has discussed the importance of decisions about geography, cause, and implementation, it probably still isn't immediately obvious how donors should make those decisions. That's natural—these are hard questions. Hopefully the issues discussed will help advance your thinking, as these decisions, whether made through supporting or impeding constraints, will be the most important influences on the ultimate impact of the gift.

8

Measuring Performance

The most elegant evaluation is only meaningful
if its findings are used to inform decisions and
strengthen our work to improve people's lives.
—Fay Twersky, Jodi Nelson, and Amy Ratcliffe[1]

What's so special about VillageReach? What did it do to become GiveWell's number-one recommended charity?

VillageReach is a medical charity that improves the transportation and logistical systems that provide vital medical supplies to rural, hard-to-reach areas in extremely poor African countries. For example, they operate refrigerated trucks that deliver vaccines to medical facilities, so the vaccines are more likely to be in stock and unspoiled. Though the work is not very exciting, it does not take much imagination to believe that it has the potential to save lives.

But this doesn't answer the question about what makes VillageReach so special. There are many other charities doing other things that are important.

One example is Build Africa's "Build a School" program. They build classrooms, staff rooms, toilet blocks, water supplies, and teachers' accommodations, as well as providing desks, books, and teacher training. They also train and support school management committees and work with parents to ensure that the children receive the best education possible now and in the future.[2] As with VillageReach, it is very easy to see how this type of program could do a lot of good, using education to help the next generation escape extreme poverty.

Another example is the American Association for Cancer Research (AACR). Its mission is to prevent and cure cancer through research, education, communication, and collaboration.[3] This is quite a lofty mission, but the impact of complete success would be huge—quite possibly larger than what VillageReach and Build Africa are seeking to accomplish.

These three organizations have very different approaches toward improving the world:

- VillageReach widens a bottleneck to giving life-saving medical care.
- Build Africa supports education to have a ripple effect on the lives of those it works with.
- The AACR is swinging for the fences with research to conquer cancer.

Whether a do-bester prefers one of these organizations over the others largely depends on his or her beliefs regarding which organization has the best theory of change and is most capable of implementing it well.

We still haven't answered the question about what's so special about VillageReach. Does it have a better theory of change than the other organizations? Is it more skilled at implementing its projects? If either or both of these are true, how would GiveWell know? Or does the staff at GiveWell simply have subjective, personal philosophies that are aligned with those of VillageReach?

The answer is surprisingly concrete: there is more compelling analytical research that measures and demonstrates the effectiveness of VillageReach. GiveWell evaluated that research and concluded that they "believe its activities have had and will have significant impact, under $1000 [of money donated] per infant death averted."[4] GiveWell believed in VillageReach because of data-driven analysis. The other organizations GiveWell reviewed don't have results that are as measurably compelling.

That is a big caveat, though: donors may believe that the results for other organizations may be more impactful, but not as measurable. This belief is valid, but it doesn't require that abstract philosophy replace analytical thinking.

Suppose a do-bester wants to evaluate a philosophical belief or intellectual hunch that donations to Build Africa may be particularly impactful. That do-bester can still flesh out his theory of change in more quantitative detail. How far could his donation go to buy desks and books, build classrooms, and train teachers? What would be the incremental improvement in school attendance, learning, or graduation? How much would this translate into long-term economic development or life enhancement?

Following the logic model of these questions may give insight into the assumptions necessary to favor Build Africa, but it won't be precise. Comparing an organization with known, measurable impacts, like VillageReach, to one whose impacts are less measurable, like Build Africa, is challenging.[5] Do-besters might give to an organization with an unproven level of success over one with a proven track record, but only if the uncertain approach has the *potential for and likelihood of* making a greater impact. That is, projects whose benefits are unproven should naturally have a higher hurdle to justify funding.

That's where the AACR might come in. If its research actually produces a cure for cancer, then that would be big—really big. But the odds of that happening are slim. It is more likely that their research has an incremental impact on improving prevention and treatment. While many incremental improvements over time might sum to a giant leap forward—which has been the case from the past several decades of cancer research—it raises the question of what proven organizations like VillageReach could have done with the equivalent amount of money. Even if the AACR were to develop a breakthrough cancer treatment, cancer treatments typically cost thousands of dollars, so that intervention probably would cost more than the amount VillageReach can use to save a life right now.

A common measure for evaluating nonprofits is the percentage of contributions spent on program services, rather than fundraising or administrative overhead. This is further promoted by several of the major charity rating agencies, as discussed in chapter 5, and many donors find this metric very appealing. Unfortunately, this type metric is fraught with problems. Aside from all the inconsistencies in how it is calculated (and the manipulative accounting methods behind the common claim that "100 percent goes to charity"), the biggest issue is that it does not address the quality of the program services.

Many charities are more advanced than relying purely on this metric. One level of advancement is reporting their *outputs*. In a fundraising brochure, Africare will tell you what "your money" can buy:

- $10 pays for "cereal for 40 orphans and vulnerable children"

- $80 pays for "10 shovels for rehabilitating 1 kilometer of an impassable farm-to-market road, improving access to market for 3 communities"
- $1,000 can help "combat maternal morbidity by providing 'Mama Kits' to a targeted 6,690 women who deliver at Africare supervised clinics"[6]

Despite the frequency of this type of reporting of outputs, it doesn't take much to realize that it is far from complete. Does the $10 just pay for the cereal, or does it actually include the cost of acquiring, transporting, and preparing it? Is the $80 donation actually the only financial cost needed to rehabilitate the road? Does the $1,000 donation include the cost of training the 6,690 women to use the Mama Kits, and are all the kits actually used? Probably not. This type of measurement rarely includes the full cost of implementing programs.

Other organizations, such as Build Africa, use a broader method for reporting outputs. Their 2009 Annual Review lists their achievements for the year:

- We supported 25,600 pupils in 2009, up from 19,586 in 2008 (a 30 percent increase);
- 54 classrooms were constructed and 27 classrooms were renovated;
- 95 toilets were built, providing sanitation facilities for 12,468 pupils;
- Desks were provided for nearly 5,000 pupils;
- 49 School Management Committees have been trained to identify the needs of their school and develop a three year School Development Plan;
- 173 teachers received training in English, Maths and Science.[7]

Combining this information with the program's budget, £1,268,000 (about $2 million), we can get a sense for what Build Africa does with its money. This measures the program's *output*, but it doesn't measure its *outcomes* or *impacts*.

To report outcomes, they should measure how much their program improves educational outcomes. This would address questions like how much does their support increase attendance, graduation rates, literacy, and test scores.

Measuring outcomes is a step further in the right direction. However, it is not sufficient—understanding impact is necessary for robust measurement. Build Africa's theory of change is based on their assertion that "education is the key to a better life."[8] Measuring impact would test this view specifically, helping to understand how much better education makes life. This is much more difficult. It would likely require a long time to measure the impact of education on life outcomes such as income. Alternatively, donors can try to understand the impact of education by relying on data from other organizations to measure the long-term impact of education on life, and combine that with the outcomes from Build Africa's programs.

Either way can be valid, as each is trying to reduce the leap of faith required to believe that the organization is successful. Perhaps most people believe Build Africa's theory of change that education is a key to a better life. But what isn't as obvious is how much the desks, teacher training, and other services provided by Build Africa result in better lives. Of the 25,600 pupils they supported in 2009, are an incremental 10,000 of them likely to escape extreme poverty due to Build Africa's programs? Or is the number closer to 100? Both are better than nothing, but each paints a different picture when comparing Build Africa to VillageReach.

Build Africa and VillageReach have very different theories of change, but it's important to realize that theories of change are not purely theoretical. Most can, and should, be empirically evaluated. This is not to imply that these measurements can be done with extreme accuracy—that is rarely possible. But an inability to measure impact perfectly is not an excuse for not making an attempt to measure it at all.

It is unfortunate that nonprofit measurement often has too narrow of a focus, preferring outputs and outcomes over impacts. Do-bester donors need to focus on measuring impacts, not outputs or outcomes.

A common concern with measuring nonprofit performance is that it is a costly exercise focused on the rearview mirror. To be clear, I believe that the most important purpose of measurement is to improve expected future performance. And measurement is a beneficial activity only when the expected improvement of future performance exceeds the cost of the evaluation.

In contrast, Innovation Network did a survey of nonprofits and found that performance evaluations were ranked as the second-lowest organizational priority of ten areas. Further, the highest-priority audience for nonprofit program evaluations was donors.[9] It appears as if many nonprofits view evaluating performance as relatively unimportant for running their organizations, but may acquiesce if it will bring in more donors. Donors should be turned off by nonprofits that evaluate performance only to please them and impressed by organizations that evaluate performance to understand what is working and what isn't, and then make adjustments to improve their approach. If the evaluation methods provide sufficient information for the nonprofit to understand the impacts of its programs, usually that should be sufficient for donors. Whereas the nonprofits need to think critically about the results to figure out how they can use the information on past performance to improve future performance, donors need to think critically to translate the past performance of the programs into judgments about expected future performance. Donors should ask questions like these:

- Is the evaluation reliable? Does it present a strong enough case that the nonprofit made positive impacts? Organizations that see measurement as a tool for fundraising, rather than analysis, often slant their analysis so it is biased to inflate perceived performance.
- What would be the marginal impact of an additional donation? Can the program be replicated in the future for the same cost? Would costs increase or decrease? It could be cheaper because of economies of scale, or it could be more expensive because of differences in environments or key personnel. As an example, at the time this is being written, GiveWell is expressing concerns that if VillageReach continues fundraising at its current pace, it may reach its organizational capacity and not be able to deploy future donations with the same efficacy as current ones. So GiveWell replaced VillageReach as its number-one recommendation—not because GiveWell has lost confidence in VillageReach's programs, but because they may be adequately funded for their programs and have less room to use additional funding.[10]
- What would be the impact if the program was replicated in the future? There may have been cultural or location-specific factors that suggest that the impact would be different if the program were run at a different time, place, or under different circumstances. So the impact of future programs may be very different from past programs.

Donors who ask these critical questions are much more likely to effectively use measurements of past performance to identify the nonprofits most likely to generate future performance.

Though measurement can be used to improve the effectiveness of philanthropy, there are some causes and nonprofits whose impact cannot be measured well.

Take, for example, the International Physicians for the Prevention of Nuclear War (IPPNW). The IPPNW was founded in 1980 by physicians from the United States and the former Soviet Union who shared a common commitment to the prevention of nuclear war.[11] Upon awarding it the Nobel Peace Prize in 1985, the Nobel Committee stated: "It is the committee's opinion that this organization has performed a considerable service to mankind by spreading authoritative information and by creating an awareness of the catastrophic consequences of atomic warfare."[12]

It is impossible to measure whether the IPPNW's efforts have actually prevented a nuclear war in the decades since it has been founded. And it is equally impossible to measure whether future donations to the IPPNW will prevent a future nuclear war. Nevertheless, by any standard, preventing nuclear war would be pretty impactful.

There are plenty of other organizations whose impacts cannot be measured. It would be naïve for a do-bester to dismiss the IPPNW simply because its impact cannot be measured, but nonprofits whose impacts are uncertain should correspondingly have a higher hurdle to justify funding.

Organizations whose innovations are breaking new ground are a notable group whose impacts are difficult to measure. VillageReach may have been one of them in 2000 when it was a startup, before its results had been proven. Would a focus on measurement prevent a do-bester from funding the "next VillageReach"? Would innovation come to a halt if there were a wholesale adoption of funding only those with proven results?

These are good questions. As you read this, there are probably dozens, if not hundreds, of startup projects that could be the next big innovation—one of the GiveWell's future top-rated charities. But only a very small fraction of those innovations will materialize, and we don't yet know which of them will make the cut. So to fund the innovation that will be among GiveWell's future top-rated charities, a donor probably would have to fund a lot of failures. While this isn't necessarily prohibitive, it does mean that the innovation should have the potential to be much more impactful than the best solution currently available.

This isn't anti-innovation. It simply means that the cost of R&D must be justified by the potential for better solutions. This notion is obvious in the for-profit sector, but it appears to be continually violated in the nonprofit world. This is especially true among foundations, many of which primarily focus on projects that are innovative, unique, and potentially groundbreaking, and rarely emphasize scaling up existing, proven solutions. In reality, many of the potential innovations—even if successful at the highest expectations of the funders—would not be as impactful as some existing, proven solutions that have yet to be brought to scale. This is partially due to a lack of robust, comparable measurement systems for evaluating alternative uses of grants.

Measuring the effect of a donation can be a tricky endeavor. Take the $20 million gift that Robert and Myra Kraft made to Partners HealthCare. The following excerpt from a press release describes one of the central elements of the program:

> In an effort to immediately increase the number of qualified providers delivering care in community settings, the program will include a loan repayment incentive of $50,000 for physicians who commit to a minimum of two years of service in a community-based program. Additionally, a loan repayment incentive of $30,000 will be made available for nurse practitioners, nurse midwives, psychiatric nurse practitioners, and other master's-prepared nurses who make the same commitment. This effort is expected to yield an additional 100 care providers, creating capacity for about 200,000 patients.[13]

It isn't clear, however, whether the donors considered all of the incremental effects of the program.

- Were the one hundred professionals who will enter the program over the next five years likely to work in community care even without the program?
- Will the additional professionals this program entices to enter community care take jobs that could crowd other professionals out of this area?
- Of the fraction of the hundred professionals in the program who wouldn't otherwise be in community health care, what would be the impact on the patients they would have served if they hadn't entered into community care?

There are ripple effects to giving, and while it is impossible to measure all of them, donors should at least think about them. Most important might be directionality. The prior example had ripple effects that are likely to diminish the positive impacts of the donation. But with insecticide-treated (mosquito) nets (ITNs), the ripple effects may enhance the impacts of the donation. ITNs are one of the most cost-effective ways to combat malaria, which is one of the biggest killers in many parts of Africa, Asia, and South America. GiveWell reviewed the data on ITNs and estimated that when ITN distributions are effective, under $2,500 prevents a death from malaria *and* prevents 320 less severe malaria episodes, with the caveat that the impact would depend heavily on the effectiveness of the specific implementation program.[14]

While this alone might be enough to cause a do-bester to consider donations to organizations that support ITN distributions, there's substantial evidence that malaria can also be economically debilitating to some of the poorest people in the world.

> Freedom from Hunger's research documents that families living in rural poverty in Burkina Faso and Benin spend one-third of their income dealing with malaria. Money that could be spent on food, growing a business, providing shelter or sending children to school instead goes to coping with this one terrible illness.[15]

Not only does malaria kill, it also causes economic damages such as expensive medical bills and lost wages. The exact measurements from Freedom from Hunger's study may not apply to other geographical areas, but the general conclusions likely do: preventing malaria has a ripple effect that goes beyond saving lives.

While measuring second-order ripple effects accurately is often more challenging than measuring the primary impacts of a donation—which isn't an easy task itself—it is important to try to get a general understanding of the total impact of a donation.

Despite its effectiveness, some donors may not find ITN distribution to be an appealing philanthropic approach because it is simply a stop-gap measure to help a single family for a short period of time. These donors often have ideological preferences for causes that address problems at their roots, rather than just provide short-term "Band-aid" fixes that don't provide sustainable solutions to the underlying issues. When faced with the choice of providing a stop-gap fix or developing a sustainable solution, they inherently gravitate to the latter. Reversing the root cause of problems is

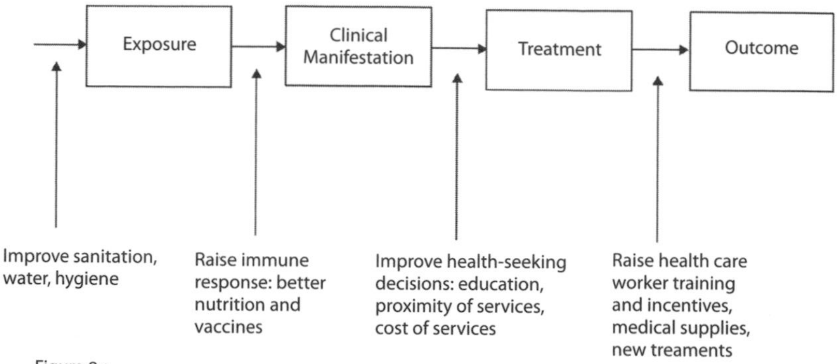

Figure 8.1

Source: Boone and Johnson, "Breaking Out of the Pocket," p. 68

the best kind of philanthropic prevention. The concepts of Band-aids and sustainable solutions don't just apply to medical situations, as there are analogs in other philanthropic areas: helping alms to poor people versus providing economic empowerment to help them avoid or dig out of poverty permanently, providing educational support for individual kids versus making lasting improvements to the entire education system, and cleaning up polluted areas rather that transitioning to a society that pollutes less. While the concepts of Band-aids and deeper solutions are fundamental, philanthropic interventions can be done in more than those two ways.

Peter Boone and Simon Johnson developed the framework for looking at the four major categories of intervention points for reducing early childhood mortality.[16] Let's apply their model to the problem of dirty drinking water in the developing world (see figure 8.1). As background, children are most susceptible to illness from dirty water, and they often develop diarrhea so severe that the dehydration it causes can be lethal. Figure 8.1 shows the four different points at which an intervention can be made to prevent a child from dying. The first is to reduce exposure to dirty drinking water, which is the only true way to get at the root of the problem. A philanthropist focused on reducing exposure to the problem might develop more clean water systems. The second potential area of intervention is after a child has been exposed to dirty water, but before manifestation of illness; philanthropists focused on this area might try to improve childhood nutrition so they have stronger immune systems. The third potential area is after clinical manifestation of the illness, but before treatment; philanthropists focusing on this area might be educating parents on how to respond to diarrhea. And the final point of intervention is at treatment, and philanthropists might invest in finding and administering better treatments for the illness.

Which of these areas should philanthropists focus on? Not only does a measurement-based approach provide no ideological guidance on this question, it rejects the validity of an ideological response to the question itself. Instead, a measurement-based approach asks about what we are good at. Preventing exposure may be "better" than Band-aid fixes that treat the illness, but if we are a hundred times better at applying Band-aids to sick people, then that should influence the philanthropist's decisions. A philanthropist focused on root causes and prevention might have the very expensive task of building and maintaining water and sanitation systems in hard-to-reach, rural areas. Alternatively, donors focusing on educating parents might simply provide (or even sell) 15-cent packets of oral rehydration salts—like a powdered form of the drink Pedialyte that is sold in the United States for children suffering from diarrhea—that can dramatically reduce the severity of dehydration. Or these donors might support an educational campaign, correcting a misconception of about 30 percent of mothers in India who wrongly believe that fluids should be withheld from children with diarrhea, a practice that has a significant impact on mortality.[17] A measurement-based approach would not have an ideological preference between the "Band-aid" fix and more lasting solutions addressing root causes. Rather, it would try to figure out which one we are better at, and in effect, which would have a greater impact.

Sustainable solutions to the root of problems are better than short-term Band-aids, but sometimes—certainly not always—Band-aids are more practical. This doesn't mean that cheap, short-term methods should be preferable, but simply that do-bester donors should be open and critical. Ideological preferences to solve the root causes of problems can get in the way of rigorous, measurable methods for figuring out what would have the greatest impact.

After so much discussion about the importance of high-quality measurement of the impact of donations, it's worth saying a few words about how to do it.

There are many different methods for measuring impact. Some, such as estimating the social return on investment (SROI) quantify results in financial terms. Others, such as disability-adjusted life years (DALY) saved, quantify results in terms of health improvements. In addition to these common methods, there are many other ways to do it. Every method has its own strengths and weaknesses.

This book is not intended to be a technical dissertation on how to make these measurements. Typically donors have a much easier task than measuring impact—evaluating the quality of the measurements that others have done. Different organizations will measure their results differently, often for appropriate reasons based on the nature of the organization and project. The most important thing for donors to do is make sure that the methods used are robust and appropriate for the situation at hand.

For do-bester donors, it is usually important to seek organizations with known, high-performance, measured results that are likely to persist in the future. The primary exceptions are (1) when an organization is innovating in an area that has a potential for impact that is significantly greater than anything expected by proven options, by a large enough margin to justify the risk, or (2) when an organization's activities have been proven impactful by other organizations pursuing similar activities.

Unfortunately, with so many challenges to accurately measuring impact, donors have no choice but to get comfortable making decisions based on imperfect information. It may be tempting to throw the concept of measurement out the window, and many people do this.

Some people further criticize measurement by saying that different causes need to be measured by different yardsticks, so donors have an "apples to oranges" comparison. That, too, is a fair point. It may be a judgment call whether a donor prefers to save lives or lift people from poverty. Maybe the donor must choose between saving one life versus lifting ten from poverty. Or maybe the question is whether to save ten lives versus lift one from poverty. Without measurement, however, donors won't even know which of these questions they face.

9

Examples of Do-Besters

It is well to respect the leader. Learn from him. Observe him. Study him. But don't worship him. Believe you can surpass. Believe you can go beyond.

—David Schwartz[1]

The Copenhagen Consensus claims to have found the holy grail of solutions to some of philanthropy's greatest issues. In short, they've attempted to determine a do-bester's approach (and answer) to one of the three most important decisions: choosing causes to support. Here's how they describe their project:

> If we had more money to spend to help the world's poorest people, where could we spend it most effectively? Using a common framework of cost-benefit analysis, a team of leading economists, including five Nobel Prize winners, assesses the attractiveness of a wide range of policy options for combating ten of the world's biggest problems.[2]

Philosophers can debate the relative merits of the many ways to improve the world, such as saving lives, reducing illness, or combating poverty. But donors have a more challenging problem. It is not sufficient for a donor to simply have a view on the relative merits of, say, saving one life versus lifting ten out of poverty. Donors must also have knowledge about the effectiveness (i.e., costs and benefits) of immunizing children, improving education, increasing economic opportunities, preventing malaria, etc.

Each of these will have different impacts on saving lives, reducing illness, combating poverty, and other areas that improve the quality of life. It is extremely subjective and challenging for donors to develop views on these issues, and it requires a level of expertise that few individuals have.

But some people have tried to address these issues head on. Every four years, Copenhagen Consensus gets a team of world-renowned economists to analyze the benefits of many different causes and prioritize them. They try to determine what causes do-besters should give to.

It would be naïve to suggest that the Copenhagen Consensus has presented an objective, be-all, end-all solution for do-besters that closes the book on prioritizing causes. What makes it useful is that this is one of a surprisingly small number of rigorous, public attempts to prioritize causes in a framework resembling that of a do-bester.

This chapter will examine the Copenhagen Consensus as well as several other rigorous attempts to address resource prioritization from a do-bester perspective. Each of them is trying to find this holy grail of philanthropy. And each has strengths and weaknesses. There are common threads throughout them and there are differences. Although most people won't completely agree with the methodology, analysis, or results of any of these methods, seeing how they approach the issues and what causes they favor may be helpful for others trying to refine their own views.

The methodology used in the Copenhagen Consensus is fairly simple. It brought together experts to analyze and evaluate the answer to the following question: "What are the best ways of advancing global welfare, and particularly the welfare of developing countries, illustrated by supposing that an additional $75 billion of resources were at their disposal over a four-year initial period?"[3]

Thirty opportunities were selected from ten different categories to improve global welfare. For each category, a specialist in the area wrote a paper to analyze the opportunities within the framework of cost-benefit analysis. Two critiques of each paper were also prepared to increase the rigor of the analysis.

Then a panel of leading economists—experts in prioritizing resource allocation—reviewed those analyses and ranked the thirty opportunities. The views of the panel members were aggregated to determine the group's views. So what were the top-ranked opportunities?[4]

TABLE 9.1

Rank	*Opportunity*	*Category*
1	Bundled interventions to reduce undernutrition in pre-schoolers	Hunger & Education
2	Subsidy for malaria combination treatment	Infectious Disease
3	Expanded childhood immunization coverage	Infectious Disease
4	Deworming of schoolchildren	Infectious Disease
5	Expanding tuberculosis treatment	Infectious Disease
6	R&D to increase yield enhancements	Hunger & Biodiversity & Climate Change
7	Investing in effective early warning systems	Natural Disasters
8	Strengthening surgical capacity	Infectious Disease
9	Hepatitis B immunization	Chronic Disease
10	Acute heart attack low-cost drugs	Chronic Disease

Key to this analysis is that the measuring sticks were standardized, so proposals aimed at improving very different areas such as health and economic empowerment could be compared on an "apples to apples" basis. This was centered around the DALY metric. DALYs essentially measure the number of years of life lost, then adjusts for morbidity by including years lost due to disability. As an example, preventing someone from going blind is assumed to be 40 percent as valuable as saving the life of a healthy person with the same life expectancy. Adjustment factors like this were developed for many different types of conditions.

Further, price tags were put on DALYs and discount rates were set to normalize the value of current versus future benefits. The analysis was done with multiple price tags for DALYs and discount rates, so readers could evaluate the sensitivity to those assumptions. In addition to summarizing the technical analysis and conclusions of their research, the Copenhagen Consensus Center publishes a *Guide to Giving*[5] to translate these findings into tangible advice to donors.[6]

Although the Copenhagen Consensus provides a lot of useful information, donors still need to know whose name to write on the top line of the donation check. The *Guide to Giving* acknowledges this issue and provides the names of some "inspiring organizations that are actively working in the area that we describe." However, it stops short of making recommendations, noting the following:

> The Copenhagen Consensus Center does not intend to endorse any particular organization. We have not closely vetted the work that they do. We do think, however, that it is sensible to point to reputable organizations working in the areas where small donations could make a big difference. . . . [W]e recommend that you conduct your own research before deciding where to make a donation.[7]

This appears to imply that the Copenhagen Consensus Center prefers a very top-down giving process: the most important thing is to select the best cause to support, but the specific organization is less important. Any "reputable organization working in that area" will do.

The Copenhagen Consensus is not—and does not claim to be—the last word in giving priorities for do-besters. It doesn't take much to find flaws in their use of DALYs as a standard metric for welfare and their translation of DALYs into dollars. Some are critical of their use of economists as the professionals tasked with evaluating the opportunities, and others have disagreed with the specific set of economists chosen. Many have expressed concerns that the cost-benefit analysis methodology used is biased against some opportunities, like environmental ones. Further, it could be argued that the Copenhagen Consensus understates the performance differential between the best organizations implementing these programs and the typical ones. This is certainly not an exhaustive list of all the potential reasons to discount the conclusions of the Copenhagen Consensus.

But these critiques miss the point. The Copenhagen Consensus has tried to do what most others have refused: to prioritize charitable resources. Further, it has used a transparent process so the public understands how their conclusions were reached. The very transparency that allows us to poke so many holes in the process can help donors see where their beliefs are different, and how that might affect their giving. It is informative to understand not only what the Copenhagen Consensus did, but also what causes it recommended.

Fortunately, the Copenhagen Consensus is not the only rigorous, public effort to help donors prioritize philanthropic resources.

GiveWell, as described in earlier chapters, has a different process for determining the best way to prioritize philanthropic resources. While it is also heavily focused on measurement, there are several major differences between its processes and those of the Copenhagen Consensus.

First, GiveWell looks directly at organizations, not just causes. While GiveWell generally believes that the most impactful organizations are likely to be global health and nutrition charities, they don't always prioritize causes significantly more granularly than that. This suggests that GiveWell may believe the quality of the organization implementing them is too important to prioritize causes too independent of the charities themselves. In this way, they are able to simultaneously address both the cause and the effectiveness of the charities they evaluate.

Another difference is that GiveWell does not attempt to standardize measures for different causes on the same measuring stick. So they don't have to measure DALYs and put a dollar value to them. This allows each organization to measure its impact in the manner most appropriate to what it does and also allows GiveWell to use the measurements that each organization has readily available, rather than requiring organizations to create a set of metrics customized just for GiveWell. Their approach leaves more room for subjective judgments, which may be appropriate for the task.

Of course, GiveWell also has different people passing judgment on what organizations to recommend.

Let's look at the three charities GiveWell rated highest in early 2013 (listed in table 9.2).[8]

TABLE 9.2

Charity	*Rank*	*Description*
Against Malaria Foundation (AMF)	1	Provides insecticide-treated nets (for protection against malaria) in bulk to nonprofits which then distribute them in Africa
GiveDirectly	2	Distributes cash to extremely poor individuals in Kenya
Schistosomiasis Control Initiative (SCI)	3	Treats children for parasitic worm infections in sub-Saharan Africa

GiveWell has a strong preference for organizations working in the developing world. Their favorite charities, including other organizations they rated highly, span a variety of different causes, as their emphasis on the quality of the organization shares significant influence with the cause itself. GiveWell also tends to focus on relatively small charities that concentrate on a small number of solutions. Larger organizations tend to have more diverse program areas, which can include a significant number of programs that GiveWell would not prioritize.

There is some overlap with the conclusions of the Copenhagen Consensus, but the results are far from identical.

- GiveWell's first-ranked charity, Against Malaria Foundation, focuses on the same issue as the second-ranked cause of the Copenhagen Consensus, malaria, though GiveWell's recommendation focuses a different intervention (bed nets versus combination treatment).
- GiveWell's second-ranked charity, GiveDirectly, is not among the causes rated highly by the Copenhagen Consensus.
- GiveWell's third-ranked charity, Schistosomiasis Control Initiative, would be categorized with the fourth-ranked cause of the Copenhagen Consensus, deworming of schoolchildren.
- GiveWell's prior first-ranked charity, VillageReach, would be categorized with the third-ranked cause of the Copenhagen Consensus, expanded childhood immunization coverage.
- GiveWell's prior second-ranked charity, Stop TB, would be categorized with the fifth-ranked cause of the Copenhagen Consensus, expanding tuberculosis treatment.

It is interesting that GiveWell's top-rated charities are not clustered within the causes most favored by the Copenhagen Consensus. One explanation is that GiveWell may have had difficulty finding organizations in the areas most highly recommended by the Copenhagen Consensus that they could confidently recommend. Alternatively, maybe this reflects a belief in the importance of an organization with high-quality programs relative to a cause with a high opportunity for impact.

GiveWell's list of recommended charities may change by the time you're reading this book. Although they are a great case study in do-besters, they are not the only ones.

The Mulago Foundation doesn't accept grant proposals—they proactively find organizations to support. Their goal is to maximize social impact, and they look for

- A priority problem
- A scalable solution
- An organization that can deliver[9]

They also have a strong emphasis on measurement. In their own words,

> We measure impact because it's the only way to know whether our money is doing any good. In fact, we don't invest in organizations that don't measure impact—they're flying blind and we would be too. Those organizations that do measure impact perform better and evolve faster, and discussions around measuring impact almost always lead to new ideas about effectiveness and efficiency.[10]

The roughly two-dozen grantees listed on their homepage span a wide array of sectors, though they almost always focus on the developing world. One common trend among their grantees is the scalability of their solutions. For example,

- Aquaya has developed a "business in a box" kit to help individual, profit-seeking entrepreneurs start clean-water kiosks to reduce the instances of sickness from dirty water. The for-profit nature of the businesses gives them the potential to be maintained (and expanded) without ongoing donor funds.[11]
- Population Media Center creates entertaining TV and radio programs packed with themes that educate the audience on topics like female circumcision (Sudan), safe sex (Nigeria), child labor (Burkina Faso), and poaching of gorillas (Rwanda). They are able to train writers and use existing broadcasting channels. Popular programs may pay for their own continuation and expansion through advertising revenue.[12]
- Bridge International Academies is developing a franchise of high-quality, ultra-low-cost schools for the poor. These schools are for-profit, so the franchises could be maintained and expanded with market forces.[13]

These are three very different organizations in diverse areas. What they all have in common is the potential to scale broadly. Aquaya doesn't simply build wells or give away clean water; rather, it develops a distribution channel for selling clean water that can ultimately fund itself through the profits of the individual entrepreneurs. Population Media Center doesn't pay for all the broadcasting—they pay to train writers, and the broadcasting is intended to pay for itself through advertising. And Bridge International Academies isn't intended as a school system requiring a constant flow of subsidization from donors; it is intended to be able to be replicated without donor funds.

It remains to be seen the extent to which these organizations will succeed. But each has a vision of impact that is potentially very large-scale and financially sustainable, an implementation structure that is clearly attractive to the Mulago Foundation.

EBay's first president, Jeff Skoll, created the Skoll Foundation with the following mission statement: "The Skoll Foundation drives large scale change by investing in, connecting and celebrating social entrepreneurs and the innovators who help them solve the world's most pressing problems."[14]

Like the Mulago Foundation, the Skoll Foundation appears to have few ideological preferences for specific geographies or issues, other than its perception of what the world's most pressing problems are. A disproportionate number of their grantees tend to work in the developing world on a few very broad issues such as economic and social equity, environmental sustainability, and health. This implies the view that the most pressing problems are in the developing world.

Another similarity to the Mulago Foundation is that both are very focused on funding those with the ability to scale solutions to create a massive impact. However, Skoll focuses almost exclusively on investing in people, the so-called social entrepreneurs.

Who are the social entrepreneurs? "Society's change agents: creators of innovations that disrupt the status quo and transform our world for the better."[15] The Skoll Foundation's theory of change is that the best opportunities for it to make impacts lie in supporting individuals with the best ideas and the ability to implement those ideas. How does the Skoll Foundation identify the best of the best social entrepreneurs? They call their approach the "4-I framework":

- **Issue:** The world's most pressing problems
- **Innovation:** A solution with the potential for large-scale expansion

- **Inflection point:** An environment in which the timing is ripe for the change sought
- **Impact potential:** Issue, innovation, and inflection point combine to create an opportunity for outsized impact[16]

Grants for the Skoll Awards, the foundation's flagship program, are not generally given to early-stage programs. Recipients must have already developed, tested, and proven their approach, with a track record of at least three years. The foundation's president, Sally Osberg, explains that "there were a few organizations focused on early stage social entrepreneurs, but no one who was investing in social entrepreneurs at the mezzanine stage, where the entrepreneurs' models had been sufficiently proven and poised to scale their impact significantly."[17] In a sense, the Skoll Foundation doesn't create new innovations from scratch: they refine and expand innovations that social entrepreneurs have already proven to work. Skoll's grants help these successful social entrepreneurs scale up their programs for even broader impact. In describing the foundation's strategy, Skoll often repeats a quote from one of his role models, John Gardner, "betting on good people doing good things."[18]

Each of the illustrations presented in this chapter thus far describes the views of a private organization with expertise in philanthropy. Want to know what the United Nations thinks are the areas with the greatest opportunity for impact? The Millennium Development Goals (MDGs) are eight development goals (and measurable targets) set by the UN in 2000 to reach by 2015.[19] Further, they have largely been embraced by the development community. Freedom from Hunger's Chris Dunford describes them as

> more than a laundry list of unrealistic recommendations to governments, like the typical U.N. conference outputs. They are SMART objectives: specific, measurable, attainable, relevant and time-bound. . . . When you think about all the problems in the world that we hear about in the media, this is a surprisingly short list. That is the genius and the courage of the MDGs. They focus on the few changes most likely to make a world of difference.[20]

What is especially important about the MDGs is that they represent both the areas where the problems are greatest and where the progress is most attainable. Although these goals were not designed exclusively for private donors—some are best achieved through governmental actions—they are a great place to start for donors looking for the areas of greatest potential impact.

Goal 1: Eradicate extreme poverty and hunger
- Halve, between 1990 and 2015, the proportion of people whose income is less than $1 a day
- Achieve full and productive employment and decent work for all, including women and young people
- Halve, between 1990 and 2015, the proportion of people who suffer from hunger

Goal 2: Achieve universal primary education
- Ensure that, by 2015, children everywhere, boys and girls alike, will be able to complete a full course of primary schooling

Goal 3: Promote gender equality and empower women
- Eliminate gender disparity in primary and secondary education, preferably by 2005, and in all levels of education no later than 2015

Goal 4: Reduce child mortality
- Reduce by two-thirds, between 1990 and 2015, the under-five mortality rate

Goal 5: Improve maternal health
- Reduce by three-quarters the maternal mortality ratio
- Achieve universal access to reproductive health

Goal 6: Combat HIV/AIDS, malaria, and other diseases
- Have halted by 2015 and begun to reverse the spread of HIV/AIDS
- Achieve, by 2010, universal access to treatment for HIV/AIDS for all those who need it
- Have halted by 2015 and begun to reverse the incidence of malaria and other major diseases

Goal 7: Ensure environmental sustainability
- Integrate the principles of sustainable development into country policies and programmes and reverse the loss of environmental resources
- Reduce biodiversity loss, achieving, by 2010, a significant reduction in the rate of loss

- Halve, by 2015, the proportion of the population without sustainable access to safe drinking water and basic sanitation
- By 2020, to have achieved a significant improvement in the lives of at least 100 million slum dwellers

Goal 8: Develop a global partnership for development

- Address the special needs of least developed countries, landlocked countries and small island developing states
- Develop further an open, rule-based, predictable, non-discriminatory trading and financial system
- Deal comprehensively with developing countries' debt
- In cooperation with pharmaceutical companies, provide access to affordable essential drugs in developing countries
- In cooperation with the private sector, make available benefits of new technologies, especially information and communications[21]

These are very broad goals. They don't articulate the best ways to reduce child mortality: vaccinating more children, preventing and treating malaria, providing better access to clean water, etc. But they do give guidance on the areas of greatest opportunities.

As the original 2015 deadline approaches, some of these goals are closer to being met than others. Nevertheless, the list remains a good focal checklist of opportunities for governments and philanthropists. Focusing on one or more of these areas is likely to be a reasonable approach for do-besters.

We've seen several examples of approaches from do-besters, from the Copenhagen Consensus and GiveWell to the Mulago and Skoll Foundations and the Millennium Development Goals. There are many similarities as well as differences among all of the different attempts—and this should not be surprising.

Being a do-bester is not about choosing the top-rated charities from an objective list. It's about evaluating options and making judgments. Donors never know the ultimate impacts before deciding where to give, and each donor will have a unique perspective on what is most likely to work.

The commonalities are there. Most do-besters tend to be focused on helping the poor people in the world's poorest countries, as the governments of wealthier countries have already addressed the problems that have the most cost-effective solutions. Do-besters also measure results, not as a score-keeping mechanism, but as a way to improve performance by understanding what is working and what isn't.

There do, however, appear to be mixed views on the relative importance of selecting the best organizations and projects to focus on. This may be due to the tremendous challenge of identifying the best organizations, which is why we'll focus on that next.

10

Choosing a Charity

> When we consider contributing, we really need to know two things: First, is there good reason to think this idea will work to solve this problem in this setting? Second, will this particular organization implement this idea effectively and efficiently?
>
> —Dean Karlan and Jacob Appel[1]

One of the most revealing discussions I had while writing this book was with the executive director of an international development organization; let's call him Sam. He originally suggested we meet so he could tell me about his organization and ask for a donation, and I told him that I was writing this book and I'd be interested in discussing his thoughts on effective philanthropy. The two topics overlapped, as I would need to understand why his organization was more worthy of my giving than other organizations.

Sam had certainly heard others ask a thousand times before why donors should give to his organization. His response to me was probably similar to how he responded to others: he told me what they do and asked if I was interested in supporting them. Unfortunately, this didn't answer the question. He gave me little information to evaluate whether what they do is more worthy than what other organizations do or whether they are good at it. I probed further, but he couldn't—or at least didn't—directly answer the question.

This would hardly be tolerable in the for-profit sector; most companies are continuously trying to differentiate themselves from their competitors. But it is the norm in the charitable sector. Donors must compare multiple organizations and select from them. In his refusal and inability to compare his organization to others, Sam failed to make his case.

I told Sam that although I had no reason to believe his organization wasn't very good, he didn't seem to have compelling evidence to persuade me that it was. I explained further that his organization was not the only one I knew of with this issue. I then asked him not just how donors should evaluate his organization, but how donors should evaluate *any* organization. Sam noted (and I agreed) that it would not be good to focus on purely financial metrics like the percentage of revenue dedicated to overhead. Other than that, he seemed stumped.

Sam is far from the only person I talked with about this issue. Nevertheless, I still have not been able to find an answer that is satisfying. I don't think I am trying to do something unreasonable. I'm not seeking an objective standard to rank every nonprofit with absolute confidence—that will never be possible. But having some reasonable principles, standards, or methods for evaluating the quality of a charity doesn't seem like too much to expect.

Donors need a way to sift through the nonsense and evaluate organizations. To address this, I've come up with a set of eight principles do-besters can use. This list augments, rather than replaces, the top-down decision factors described earlier. If you believe that a charity follows these principles, then it is a pretty good bet that it would be a good steward of your donation.

Principle 1: The organization should share your do-bester values.

Though this may seem obvious, it should not be taken for granted. If you have do-bester goals, then it is preferable to look for organizations that have do-bester values.

There may be some charities with programs that appear very impactful and could be appealing to a do-bester, though their leadership actually has a value system that has more in common with do-gooders. This can be a notable concern about organizations that do many different types of projects. For example, many large international development charities have programs for disaster relief, clean water, HIV/AIDS, malaria, education, economic development, and other areas. It is easy for them to assert that their constituents have needs in all of these areas, but that is a naïve view because it doesn't acknowledge resource prioritization. Do-besters need to be comfortable with how priorities are set when allocating resources among the areas.

The problem with giving to these types of organizations—even if the donation is earmarked for the most impactful programs—is that donors will never be able to know or influence all the decisions made within the organization. If they don't appear to have do-bester values in areas such as resource prioritization, then the decisions they make behind the scenes may be different from what a do-bester might prefer.

This is very different than in the for-profit sector. Consumers don't have to have the same values as the companies that receive the money they spend—the consumer's goal is to get useful products and services, and the company's goal is to earn money. Each party has a different goal, and they are making an exchange that benefits both. But in the charitable sector, donors are entrusting their money to nonprofits in expectation of helping third parties. Both should have the same goal of helping others, so it is best to have shared values about *how* to help others.

Unfortunately, it is easier to find out what a charity does than the reasons it chooses to do those things. Determining whether an organization shares your do-bester philosophy can require a lot of judgment. By understanding an organization's ideological DNA, donors can be more confident that the decisions made would incorporate the desired reasoning. Donors should talk with senior staff (usually not the fundraising specialists) to find out how the organization makes decisions about priorities. Find out how they allocate unrestricted gifts and how they decide which programs are worth pursuing and expanding. Ask deep, open-ended questions that require thoughtful responses and see the direction they take to answer your questions. The people you talk with will usually be professionals in their areas with many years of experience, so they should be able to respond to hard questions. If they are initially unable to answer these questions in a way that demonstrates conviction in their values, you may be talking with the wrong person (e.g., fundraising staff) or they may simply not be accustomed to donors asking such questions. Continue probing, and if they still cannot provide a sufficient response to your questions, then that may be all the response you need.

Principle 2: The staff should be top-notch.

Donors should have immense confidence in the staff of nonprofits entrusted with their money. Not only should they have the same values as the donor, but they should also be good at managing people, projects, and money in order to ultimately be successful at executing their programs. They should be educated and experienced in their area.

How can a donor assess whether the staff is strong? This is not fundamentally different from interviewing someone for a job: ask a lot of probing questions and hope that you do a good job evaluating their answers. And as with interviewing candidates for a job, interviewers who make the wrong choice will eventually find out, but only after investing a lot of time and money. Challenge them with the most difficult questions. Check references by asking other informed people in the sector what they think. Unfortunately, donors tend to avoid asking really tough questions. I've wondered if this may be because people see it as socially unacceptable to critically question people who have dedicated their lives to helping others. Maybe, but donors who are dedicating their wealth to help others have an obligation to ask questions to make sure they're funding top-notch teams.

Principle 3: The organizations should focus on cost-effective solutions to big problems.

Pick the lowest-hanging fruit first. The majority—if not all—of a charity's programs should focus on the biggest problems with the most cost-effective solutions. Despite the apparent obviousness of this statement, many donors and charities simply don't do it. St. Jude will spare no cost to save the lives of the small number of people it admits, while many others are dying of much more easily solvable problems. This is not to suggest that St. Jude is doing bad things—it is saving lives—but that donors have other options that may be able to help more people. In a world with limited resources, do-besters should require that charities focus on cost-effective solutions to big problems.

One potential exception is for charities that receive earmarked grants from donors or foundations. In these cases, the organizations may not have discretion to use the funds in ways that they see best. A common example is when donors earmark significant amounts of money for aid for a specific disaster like the tsunami in Asia, earthquake in Haiti, or hurricane in New Orleans. The organization might believe that there are better uses of the money elsewhere—there is significant evidence that "everyday" developmental aid is more efficient at doing good than disaster relief because of the high costs and planning challenges associated with disaster relief operations—but donors constrain the charities they support with earmarked donations. Similarly, many foundations give grants for specific projects that may be different from what an organization might do with unrestricted funds (otherwise, the purpose of the grants wouldn't need to be specified).

While donors may not want to focus their evaluations of charities primarily by the activities they do with restricted gifts, do-besters may find it inherently problematic when unrestricted funds make up only a small portion of the organization's budget. This should be an especially large concern when the restricted gifts require the charities to deviate far from their missions. These signs suggest that the organization's activities could be driven by the objectives on an uncoordinated set of donors with agendas different from the charity's mission. Even if the charity's mission sounds like that of a do-bester, their activities may be for other purposes.

While caution is warranted when restricted gifts become too dominant, donors should typically put more emphasis on what the organization does with funds over which it has discretion. And those should be used to focus on cost-effective solutions to big problems.

Principle 4: Give appropriate credit to organizations that emphasize scalable and sustainable solutions.

"If you give a man a fish, you feed him for a day. If you teach a man to fish, you feed him for a lifetime." This cliché advocates for long-term, sustainable solutions. Although some organizations like soup kitchens provide short-term help, others that focus on areas like economic development and education emphasize solutions that will have enduring, longer-term effects, even without continual donor funds. All else being equal, sustainability is certainly a desirable characteristic that increases impact. However, it can be much more challenging and costly to teach one man to fish than to feed a hundred people. Balancing sustainability with costliness and effectiveness is a key consideration.

Scalable solutions are those that can be efficiently expanded to reach more people, multiplying the impact. Expanding our example further, a scalable solution might be one that can be replicated to teach many people how to fish, with the potential for a very broad reach. Scalability is only important if funding is (or will be) available to bring a program to scale. Having the initial seed funding for a successful, scalable program doesn't imply that it will be expanded—it is unfortunate that building an effective, scalable solution is far from a guarantee that funds will come—so donors need to consider how the program will ultimately expand.

Freedom from Hunger is an example of an organization that emphasizes sustainability and scalability, as described on its website:

> Freedom from Hunger's self-help programs invest in women and their determination to feed their children, safeguard their health and send them to school. Our combination of microfinance, practical education and access to health care, helps women earn and save more money, buy more and better food, and pay for health care. We share our proven programs by training and collaborating with local partners who expand our reach and ensure that services are delivered effectively and sustainably.[2]

In other words, Freedom from Hunger provides technical support to help microfinance institutions not only develop their core microfinance services, but also provide education and services for both health care and business. This is sustainable because the solution can live on without perpetual funds from Freedom from Hunger's donors, and it is scalable because Freedom from Hunger partners with over a hundred microfinance organizations to expand the reach of their programs far beyond what they could do directly.

GiveWell reviewed Freedom from Hunger and rated them as "notable." This rating is much higher than that of most organizations, but falls short of the top ratings given. GiveWell describes its rationale as follows:

> Freedom from Hunger does not currently qualify for our highest ratings because:
>
> - The rigorous evaluations of Freedom from Hunger's programs found some effects on participants' knowledge, but found limited or no effects on business revenues and limited effects on health behaviors.
> - Freedom from Hunger relies on other organizations to implement its programs. It is concerned with the question of whether partners implement its programs well, but, due to the nature of its model (in which more people are reached by not running programs itself), it has limited ability to ensure that programs are consistently implemented well.[3]

Freedom from Hunger's then president, Chris Dunford, suggested that he believes that GiveWell may not have adequately considered the advantages of Freedom from Hunger's model to emphasize sustainability and scalability:

> "[H]elping the less fortunate" is a multi-dimensional task, and I do not believe GiveWell has yet captured this complexity in its assessments of organizational effectiveness. . . .
>
> GiveWell's system overweights the one dimension of impact and seems to ignore two other key dimensions—scale and sustainability. The Cadillac programs in international development typically are small in scale of outreach to intended beneficiaries, because they are expensive. There is a trade-off between the high cost of proving and constantly assuring impact (though I believe this is crucial and therefore applaud GiveWell's attention to this dimension) and the ability of organizations to reduce their costs per person served in order to reach large numbers of people in need. Moreover, this trade-off is even more pronounced if the organization is trying to sustain its outreach over years or decades without endless dependence on philanthropic subsidy. I would argue that Freedom from Hunger does not qualify for better than "notable" rating by GiveWell, because we are trying to support a variety of local organizations to pursue a multi-dimensional balance between assurance of impact, scale of outreach and sustainability of operations over long periods of time. Being "notable" in each of these dimensions would be high praise indeed.[4]

Freedom from Hunger is agreeing that their programs may not have as deep of a positive effect as some organizations with "Cadillac" programs, but they believe their model makes up for this through the sustainability and scale of its outreach. Providing a moderate amount of sustainable help to a large number of people may be better than providing a lot of nonsustainable help to a moderate number of people.

Sustainability and scalability are multipliers for impact. It is a very subjective issue to balance their advantages with their costs, and the analysis will vary with each specific program and organization. Donors should consider this carefully in their assessments.

Principle 5: Programs should not be built around donors.

DonorsChoose.org proudly describes its model as "citizen philanthropy." Donors can browse an online menu of school supplies and projects submitted by teachers across the country and choose which ones to fund.

DonorsChoose.org will deliver the materials. Afterward, donors will get photos of the project, a thank-you letter from the teacher, and a cost report showing how each dollar was spent. Those who give over $100 will also get thank-you letters from the students.[5]

This model was explicitly built around donors. Any public school teacher is allowed to request funds for discrete projects and sets of materials, and donors, who have minimal skill in identifying the best projects, are encouraged to fund whatever inspires them. Further, the structure of DonorsChoose mandates that it can only support a large number of relatively small initiatives, rarely extending beyond a single classroom. And finally, there are multiple layers of administrative burdens for relatively small grants: requiring teachers (who already have plenty to do) to spend time writing up their request, having DonorsChoose verify it and deliver materials, and requiring teachers and students to write thank-you notes. Presumably, the teachers wouldn't apply for the grants if the money wasn't worth the hassle, but in many cases it might only be worth slightly more. While the DonorsChoose system is very democratic and is attractive to many donors, it is unlikely to be the most effective use of donor funds.

There are plenty of other examples of donor-centric nonprofits. They are often extremely good at engaging donors and motivating them to maintain support. For example, Kiva, a microfinance organization, allows donors to choose who they lend to. Habitat for Humanity engages donors through volunteering to build homes. And most colleges and universities solicit from their alumni for the types of things they benefited from. These examples tend not to fare particularly well on the Axis of Altruism, as shown in figure 10.1.

Despite this, we should not necessarily chastise organizations that build their programs around engaging donors. After all, it can work well—many donors give more when they are inspired, and often don't seem to realize (or mind) that the program has built-in inefficiencies to meet their emotional needs. These programs are better than nothing, which is what many people might donate without them. They have a role in the philanthropic world, though not usually for do-besters.

One possible exception is that a do-bester may fund the infrastructure of such an organization if he believes it will ultimately result in significantly larger donations from do-gooders that would not otherwise happen. But as a general rule, do-besters should focus on organizations that build their programs around social needs, not donor emotions.

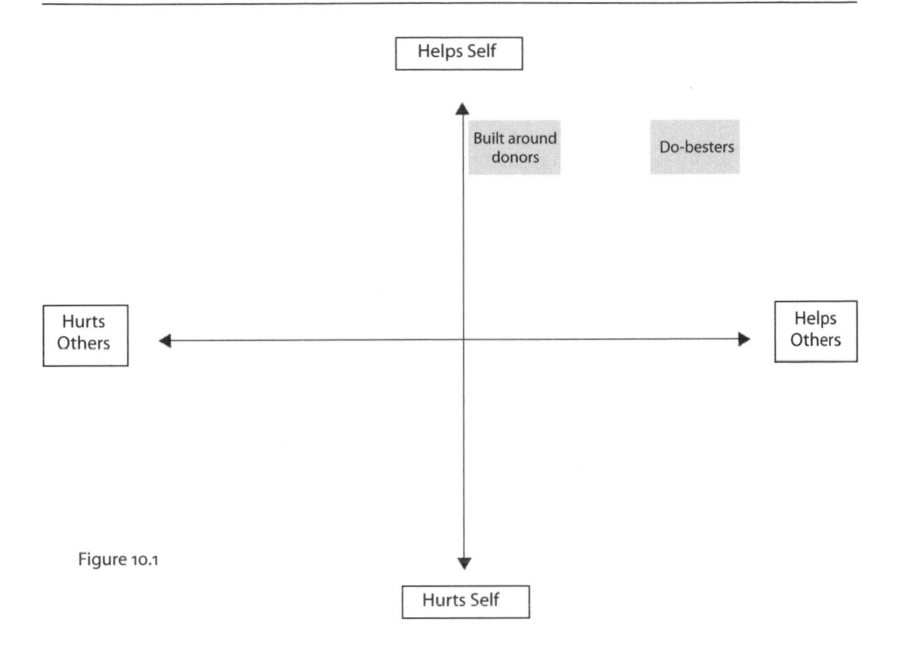

Figure 10.1

Principle 6: The organizations should have evidence on how well their programs work.

Feedback loops in the for-profit sector are par for the course. If a company develops a product that isn't in demand, it will find out quickly when nobody buys it. If it builds a product that doesn't work well, its customers will usually let it know. And if a company makes mistakes like these long enough, it is more likely to go out of business.

But the same thing isn't typically true for donors and charities. Donors often give to charities for decades based on little more than stories about individuals helped, or in the case of volunteers, seeing it with their own eyes. This may be a legitimate way to assess if there is impact for a single organization, but it is not sufficient for comparing multiple organizations. Favoring the visible over the impactful is a recipe for do-gooder philanthropy. It is a major factor causing biases toward geographies and causes close to donors. Do-besters should demand evidence of the impact of their giving—not simply to measure their impact, but as a tool to maximize it.

Similarly, charities often run programs for decades without knowing how well they work. Lack of knowledge can make it difficult to improve or reprioritize their programs.

Although this means that in most cases organizations should measure their results, it's not always possible to do so. For example, new programs haven't had the opportunity to measure performance—so they should have a plan to develop evidence of impact. Also, replications of programs that have already been measured—like distributing insecticide-treated mosquito nets to prevent malaria—may have less of a need to undertake costly efforts to measure impact than programs that have never been implemented before.

As an increasing number of donors are demanding measurement, some organizations are begrudgingly doing it solely to appease donors. This usually manifests itself in poor-quality measurements that inflate perceived impact; such misinformation can actually be harmful to organizations. Charities that engage in disingenuous measurement don't have shared values (principle 1) with those who believe measurement should be used to improve performance.

There isn't a one-size-fits-all approach to evidence, but that doesn't mean that donors should be less demanding of charities to understand how well their programs work.

Principle 7: Take it as a good sign when a charity receives funding from sophisticated donors who share your values.

Though every donor must do a certain amount of independent research, it can be made easier by finding a few philanthropic role models and following their lead. Many people do this by giving to organizations their friends and family recommend, although this is only effective for do-besters if those people share your do-bester philosophy and have done significant research into their recommendations. In most cases, recommendations from friends and family won't be sufficient for do-besters. But the opinions of well-staffed institutional donors might.

Warren Buffett applied this principle when choosing to give to the Gates Foundation. GiveWell donors, including my wife and me, apply it when giving to charities recommended by GiveWell. Of course, this method only works to the extent that you can find like-minded do-besters who have done significant research into finding suitable charitable organizations. One way to apply it is to find several such "role model" donors and look at their choices as your menu of options.

This principle does have unintended downsides. It creates a structural bias toward large organizations, which have many funders and programs. Also, it creates a bias against innovation, as donors relying on this principle would never be the first to fund an organization. And of course, the method is only as good as the role models a donor chooses—many are not good, and even the good ones make mistakes. So it may make sense to use role models as a starting point, continually challenging their rationale and conclusions to make sure you believe in their choices. Despite these limitations, this principle can provide very useful information and narrow down the field of candidates.

Principle 8: Donors should fund organizations only if they would be comfortable supporting all of the organization's projects and overhead.

Donors generally have the option of earmarking gifts for specific projects or giving unrestricted gifts. Nevertheless, it is a good rule of thumb for donors to only fund organizations when they'd feel comfortable supporting all of that organization's projects and overhead. If this is not the case, it is a likely sign that the organization fails to meet several of the other principles.

One exception is when an organization receives a significant amount of earmarked contributions from other donors. In this case, the organization may have programs its leadership would not independently prioritize. Although this can be less desirable than if the organization is able to pursue the projects it believes would be most effective, many strong charities take earmarked donations because they can fund a significant amount of good work.

While consideration should be given to such cases when it is difficult for donors to truly understand an organization's priorities, being comfortable supporting all (or most) of an organization's projects and overhead is a key principle donors can apply.

Many people wonder why overhead is included in this. Some form of "overhead" is necessary for nearly all organizations to function. In many cases, expenses that some people classify as overhead are important for a well-functioning organization. For example, competitive salaries for leadership may be necessary to maintain a talented staff, and that staff may need to attend conferences to become better educated about their work. Modern computer systems can make work more efficient, and monitoring and evaluating programs can ultimately improve an organization's work. Much of what donors call "overhead" is actually laying the infrastructure for a strong organization. While there are reasonable limits to the appropriate level of overhead—few people would want to donate to an organization that spends 90 percent of its revenue on overhead—squeezing pennies out of overhead doesn't necessarily make an organization better at its mission, and may have the opposite effect.

This eight-principle checklist can be daunting for many donors, as it would be difficult to research all of these areas, let alone find organizations that pass all eight tests with flying colors.

Do-besters can seek best-fit organizations based on the eight principles, but some will carry more weight than others. Many donors will usually focus on a few of these, like principle 7 ("Take it as a good sign when a charity receives funding from sophisticated donors who share your values"). This could be implemented simply by narrowing down the list of possible charities to only those currently funded by a few specific donors you believe in. There isn't a single "best" organization, and do-besters expecting to find the perfect fit may end up doing nothing.

Choosing a charity is not an easy task, and there's no perfect formula for doing it. I'm reminded of a quote one of my friends and former colleague used to say often. Although it was not intended to apply to philanthropy, it is appropriate as a concluding caveat to this entire chapter: "Don't delay action seeking perfection."

11

Project Selection

(OR DECIDING NOT TO SELECT PROJECTS)

> By delivering giving opportunities that will allow donors to pursue projects of interest, at attractive levels of engagement, and with profiles that suit the donors' desires, nonprofits are led to sublimate their real needs and their own preferences for structuring philanthropic relationships.
>
> —Peter Frumkin[1]

On July 21, 2011, billionaire philanthropist and New York City mayor Michael Bloomberg spoke under the backdrop of a coal-fired power plant in Alexandria, Virginia. "If we are going to get serious about reducing our carbon footprint in the United States, we have to get serious about coal."[2]

That same day, Bloomberg coauthored an opinion piece describing problems caused by coal plants: "Each year, the soot emanating from coal-fired power plants kills an estimated 13,000 Americans prematurely, and is responsible for an astonishing $100 billion in health costs."[3]

He further detailed those problems:

> In the U.S., coal is the leading cause of greenhouse-gas emissions, and coal's pollution contributes to four out of the five leading causes of mortality—heart disease, cancer, stroke, and respiratory illness. Coal emits almost half of all U.S. mercury pollution, which causes developmental problems in babies and young children, as well as being a major contributor to asthma attacks.[4]

In another piece published that day, Bloomberg is quoted as saying, "We don't know the names of the kids who are killed by coal, but it happens."[5]

Bloomberg's speech and the media campaign around it announced his $50 million donation to the Sierra Club's Beyond Coal Campaign, which is seeking to retire one-third of America's coal plants by 2020. This was far from Bloomberg's first entrée into philanthropy. He's donated over $1.6 billion to a wide variety of causes, and has been one of the ten most generous philanthropists in America in every year from 2004 to 2011,[6] including giving to nearly 1,200 different nonprofit groups in 2011.[7]

Bloomberg specified the direction of his gift, rather than letting the charity decide. In this case, his donation appears to have been earmarked for the Beyond Coal Campaign, only one of the Sierra Club's many activities. Such earmarks, often called "restricted gifts," are very common in the charitable sector. Not only do many foundations and large individual donors restrict their gifts, but many smaller donors also restrict gifts, such as those designating gifts to the Red Cross for relief efforts to a particular natural disaster. So not only must donors ask themselves which charities to support, but also whether they should earmark their support for specific projects—and if so, which ones. How should donors think about these decisions?

Bloomberg didn't intend to give the Sierra Club leadership leeway to allocate his donation to their other activities. He didn't appear to want to make such a sizable donation to fund their campaigns to protect and improve water quality or create "resilient habitats" for plants, animals, and people. Bloomberg's announcements do not indicate a significant desire to fund the many outdoor trips organized by the Sierra Club, or many of its other diverse environmental activities.

Bloomberg has a reputation for giving many of his largest gifts to organizations that focus on public health, education, the arts, and the environment. This included giving hundreds of millions to Johns Hopkins University to support its (renamed) Bloomberg School of Public Health, and contributing significant amounts to curb smoking and fight malaria. Despite his $50 million contribution to the Sierra Club, there are reasons to wonder how much Bloomberg supports its overall activities.

A careful review of his speech, Sierra Club's press release, and other interviews suggests that Bloomberg views coal-fired plants as a problem as much because of their implications for public health as for the environment in general. He might be making this donation by looking, in part, through the same lens as he did when he donated to fight malaria and tobacco use.

Bloomberg may have dual objectives—both environmental and health—but he gave to an organization primarily focused on the environmental aspects.

Based on the fact the Bloomberg restricted his gift to a single program of the Sierra Club, is it possible that he gave $50 million to an organization that has fairly different priorities than he does?

Imagine choosing between two organizations for your donation.

One is very good at implementing programs, and shares your goals and values. If you gave to them, they would spend the money exactly as you'd like them to. You don't need to earmark or restrict the donation for a specific purpose because you have confidence that they'd do exactly what you'd want. You fully believe in them.

The other is equally good at implementing programs, but their goals and values are different from yours. Maybe they aren't do-besters, or their philosophy places different values on sustainability and scalability than you do. Or maybe they just have many different programs, some of which you believe in more strongly than others. Although each of these programs is best-in-class for its particular goals, the organization uses different criteria than you do for deciding how to allocate funds among its programs. Nevertheless, you could give to them and earmark your donation for the specific program(s) you have the most conviction in. This would restrict the charity's freedom, but they would still accept the donation because, like most nonprofits, they don't have so much money flowing in that they have the freedom to reject earmarked gifts that are close to their core areas.

It might seem like a trick question to ask which organization you would rather give to. But it's not. Despite the apparent "obvious" choice to make an unrestricted gift to the first organization, over 80 percent of donations by foundations are restricted.[8] Foundations are supposed to be the smartest, most strategic, and experienced—and least emotional—philanthropists.

We've already wondered whether Bloomberg's gift to the Sierra Club might have been restricted because of different priorities between the two. Is that the case for 80 percent of foundation grants? If so, why and what are the implications?

Chapter 5, "The Paucity of Helpful Information," detailed numerous parties that could help donors choose where to give. One resource was notably omitted: the charities themselves. In fact, they might be among the most helpful resources. Of course, they typically have a bias: ask most charities where you should give, and they will put on their fundraising hats, smile, and open their *own* hands. That bias impedes their objectivity in comparing the relative merits of different organizations, but they can certainly be helpful in determining how to allocate resources given to *them*.

All donors should ask themselves whether to impose some type of restriction on their gifts or make unrestricted gifts that give the nonprofit free reign to spend it as they see fit. Restricted giving is a form of micromanaging the recipient organization. It is rooted in a view that the donor has concerns with how the organization might allocate the money without such restrictions. Unrestricted funds allow organizations to allocate the money where they believe it is best used—and they should know their priorities better than outsiders. As a result, a strong case can be made that unrestricted giving should be the default choice in the absence of special circumstances. More specifically, unrestricted giving is the most appropriate form of giving when two conditions are met:

1. The recipient organization's objectives and theories of change are consistent with (or a subset of) the donor's focus.
2. The recipient organization is at least as skilled as the donor at managing its own budget and allocating its resources.

When both of these conditions are met, the donor can have confidence that an unrestricted donation would be used more effectively than one with restrictions. With about 1.1 million nonprofit organizations in America,[9] it would initially appear that most donors should have good odds of finding organizations that meet both criteria. So when donors don't, they should think hard about why. Why is the donor's world view so unique that none of the existing charities share it (condition 1)? Is the restriction related to an impeding constraint in the donor's mission? Does the donor really know that much more than the charities with boots on the ground (condition 2)? Consistently favoring restricted gifts requires a large amount of confidence—maybe even arrogance—on the part of the donor. This is not to imply that there are no valid reasons for do-besters to make restricted gifts, but rather that it is important to understand the reasons in order to best structure a gift.

If an organization doesn't meet condition 2, then donors shouldn't give it anything (unless the donation is intended to help them strengthen capabilities). Alternatively, what if an organization meets condition 2 but not

1? In this situation, the organization is highly skilled, but its priorities are different from the donor's. This may be an appropriate situation for restricted giving, but it is important to investigate further because it is a counterintuitive situation when an organization is very skilled at something that is not its priority. Let's return to Bloomberg and the Sierra Club. There is overlap between the environmental and public health effects of coal-fire power plants. While Bloomberg's priorities may be a balance between improving the environment and public health—as evidenced by his explanation for this gift—he determined that an environmental organization, the Sierra Club, was most skilled to assist with his goal of retiring coal-fire plants. Because both the environmental and public-health benefits come from the exact same result—retiring coal-fire power plants—there is sufficient overlap for both Bloomberg and the Sierra Club.

There could even be situations when the organizations most able to succeed at your objectives have missions that are very different from yours. As an example, suppose there is extremely promising research for an AIDS vaccine being done at a university, and you believe it could save millions of lives. Making an unrestricted gift to the university probably wouldn't significantly impact the research for the AIDS vaccine, as the university's mission is based on education and research in broad areas. Instead, you may want to give to the university but restrict the donation for this specific research project. The misalignment of priorities between the donor and the university would not be a problem if there was alignment between the donor and the researcher. In essence, the restricted gift to the university could be informally thought of as an unrestricted gift to the researcher.

On the other hand, what if the researcher would have wanted to do a totally different type of research, but agreed to do the project on the AIDS vaccine anyway because that is what he could get funding for? The misalignment of priorities here is more problematic. It may be a sign that the researcher has less confidence in the project than the donor. The donor may want to reconsider.

This type of situation is not uncommon: nonprofits often take restricted donations because getting something is better than nothing. We see this when donors earmark their gifts to be used for the latest natural disasters, though there is substantial evidence that the best forms of everyday developmental aid are more effective than disaster relief. It also occurs frequently when foundations ask for grant proposals that are very specific, causing applicants to construct programs to fit the donor-driven strategy, though they may believe that there are better prospects for impact with their existing programs (where they spend their unrestricted donations) or some other potential new projects.

Donors need to be hyperaware of the practical implications of restricted versus unrestricted giving, and unrestricted giving should be the preferred form in most cases.

UNICEF recently issued an eighty-page report to make the case for unrestricted gifts—"Regular Resources," as they call them.

> Regular Resources are particularly valuable because they are provided by donors who not only believe in UNICEF's mandate but who have also chosen to trust that the organization will allocate their funds where they are needed most. . . . Regular Resources are not driven by any individual donor priorities or agendas. . . . Because such funds are not tied to any country or sectoral programme, they can be used to support those areas that will have the greatest impact on the largest number of children.[10]

The report describes a budget process in which regular resources are used to wrap around the restricted donations UNICEF receives, effectively filling the gaps between the projects with the greatest impacts and those designated to receive restricted gifts. UNICEF spends regular resources very differently than its other funds. Not only do regular resources go toward the areas of greatest impact, but they also help UNICEF maintain a long-term focus and continuity of programs, which they assert is vital for both efficiency and effectiveness. The report further describes the challenges UNICEF faces because only 26 percent of its income is regular resources—a proportion that has been declining for at least a decade. That is, UNICEF's leaders only have full control over 26 percent of their budget, which makes it much more challenging to implement their mission.

Despite UNICEF's clear preference for unrestricted giving, web-based donors to the U.S. Fund for UNICEF are greeted by a website offering the opportunity to give to the General Fund (unrestricted) or to give by program. There are eight choices of core programs:

- Education
- Emergency relief

- Immunization
- Malaria
- HIV/AIDS
- Nutrition
- Protection
- Water and sanitation[11]

Alternatively, donors can choose from over a dozen different countries.[12] It is striking how the organization must balance its own preference for regular resources with the preferences of many donors to direct the resources. Often organizations solicit donors for the types of gifts they think they can get rather than the types they need most.

Because of the budgeting process for regular resources, those who give restricted gifts may not be influencing UNICEF's actions as much as they think. Although donations restricted for a specific program or country are certainly routed as the donor requested, UNICEF sets their budgets for unrestricted funds with an eye for the levels of restricted giving they will get for each area. By allocating regular resources to the areas of greatest need, UNICEF must consider the resources already directed at various areas in their assessment of what are the areas of greatest need. That is, large amounts of restricted giving to one of their core areas gives them the flexibility to not allocate as much of their unrestricted funds there. In this type of situation, "restricted" giving probably won't affect the aggregate budget allocations as much as donors might naïvely expect.

Certainly there is not a direct, dollar-for-dollar reallocation whenever donors make restricted gifts. But it is reasonable to believe that donors earmarking their gifts for Mozambique are probably not impacting the amount of resources UNICEF spends there as directly as they expect. Budgets are fluid and restricted gifts can affect priorities for other resources.

For a restriction on a gift to truly have an impact (positive or negative), it must either be for a purpose that the organization wouldn't have dedicated resources to or for an amount greater than what the organization would have allocated. Bloomberg's $50 million gift was almost definitely large enough to do this, as it would allow the Sierra Club to double the staff working on this project. Nevertheless, many "restricted" gifts are not as influential to the charity's overall budgets as donors may perceive. While this may be a good thing for nonprofits seeking to meet their own objectives, it can present challenges for giving when the donor's goals are not in full alignment with the recipient's.

Is this type of budgeting process a technicality for nonprofits to avoid genuinely responding to donor intent? Possibly. I suspect that most charities would balk at any statement that acknowledges that they do not highly prioritize donors' wishes, but there is often an inherent tension between fulfilling donors' wishes and accomplishing the charity's mission. From the perspective of accomplishing UNICEF's mission of helping children, it would be negligent if UNICEF didn't consider the amounts and designations of restricted gifts in setting its budgets for unrestricted funds. Donors who want to maximize the impact of their gifts would expect UNICEF to have nothing less than a smart, strategic approach to determining where and how they deploy their resources. And that is exactly what their *Report on Regular Resources* describes. Donors who are more concerned with having an organization that blindly abides by donors' intent may need to partner with an organization that places a higher priority on fulfilling donor wishes than helping the people it is intended to serve.

Giving without restrictions means that your donations will be distributed to the areas of greatest need, as defined by the charity's goals and priorities. Donors should ask charities they are considering what they would do with incremental unrestricted donations. Many charities will direct them to their favorite programs that are not sufficiently funded, possibly scaling up a proven program or undertaking a promising new program that doesn't fit neatly into any of the grant guidelines for foundations.

But many charities would use additional unrestricted funds in ways that may appear on the surface as less inspiring. Those operating on shoestring budgets might put it in reserves to give them the financial cushion of a stronger balance sheet, allowing them to make decisions with a longer-term focus. This can make all of their programs better run. Other organizations might use unrestricted giving to monitor and measure the results of their programs, which can help them improve quality. There might even be some organizations that use incremental donations to give staff raises, which can improve morale and prevent costly employee turnover. Though these may not seem as inspiring, that doesn't make them less important. Of course, donors must trust an organization in order to make unrestricted gifts. But without trust, donors probably shouldn't be giving any gifts at all.

Most charities are unlikely to tell potential donors that their gifts would go to "overhead," even though it might be the honest truth. Ironically, this might be because givers of restricted donations often don't fund enough basic overhead costs to keep the organization's doors open and lights on. A less verbally offensive way of describing "overhead" is "infrastructure and capacity building," and there's nothing inherently wrong with it if it is needed to improve all aspects of the organization's programs. In fact, it might be a very good thing.

Donor restrictions have detrimental effects on the charitable sector as a whole. The programs being funded are not necessarily the ones preferred by the nonprofits with boots on the ground, but rather those preferred by the funders. Even more radically, in many cases megadonors or foundations design the programs themselves. The nonprofits receiving the grants and implementing the programs may only partially believe in these programs, and they certainly feel less ownership. These types of restricted donations inherently limit the nonprofit's abilities to use its expertise in solving social programs. Further, for nonprofits that receive primarily restricted gifts, it is challenging to maintain coherent strategies. They may be implementing ten different programs funded by ten different anchor donors, each of whom has their own world view and is contracting the nonprofit to implement programs based on that world view. How is the nonprofit supposed to have its own world view? How it is supposed to function effectively as a contractor for others without the freedom and flexibility to make its own decisions?

With all the advantages of unrestricted giving, why are over 80 percent of donations by foundations—considered among the most sophisticated donors—restricted? I've spoken with many people about this, and there appear to be several drivers of the phenomenon:

- The primary reason may be misalignment of objectives between the donor and recipient. There are certain situations when this is normal and warrants a restricted donation, as in the situation described earlier with an AIDS vaccine researcher at a university. However, donors who truly can't find organizations aligned with their objectives may want to question why this is the case—they might have excessively narrow objectives or impeding constraints that reduce impact.
- Some donors have do-bester philosophies that are different from those

of the existing organizations. This is more likely to be the case in emerging areas with potential for innovation. For example, it is possible that someone might believe that a cutting-edge technology might have the potential to provide a cheap and effective vaccine for malaria, but the technology is so new that even those researching in the area don't fully appreciate its potential. This is a perfect situation for a restricted gift, but when donors have difficulty finding others to agree with them, it could be a sign that they should examine their views carefully.

- Some foundations develop combinations of multiple restricted grants to different organizations, believing there is synergy among the grants that makes the value of the combination of grants greater than the sum of the pieces. So restricted giving may have been needed to get the individual organizations to pursue these projects, but the combined impact would be greater than if all of the grants were unrestricted. This could be an ideal situation for restricted giving, though it is rare and often requires a complex theory of change.
- For many donors, it is very important to be able to measure the results of "their" donation with more specificity than simply attributing partial credit for all of the projects of an organization. Sometimes this measurement can be very quantitative, and other times it can simply be the knowledge that a specific project (and its results) would not have happened without that donor. Those who give unrestricted donations have more difficulty getting such feedback. Ironically, unrestricted donors might even deserve more than a proportionate share of credit for the results of the organizations they support because their gifts went to the areas of greatest need. It is important for donors to realize that measurement is not important in and of itself; it is only important to the extent that it ultimately helps improve performance. So the potential performance benefits of better measurement would need to be carefully weighed against the detriment of structuring the gift around the desire for more precise measurement.
- Receiving credit for or ownership of a specific gift is enticing for many donors. The opportunity to have a building named after them or receiving public recognition can be influential. Ego, while a natural part of the human psyche, must be put aside to be a do-bester.
- Probably one of the least acknowledged reasons for restricted giving is because it is more fun. It's natural for donors and foundation staff

to enjoy being a deeper part of the process of helping others, rather than simply cutting a check. It allows them to select projects that are new and innovative, and it is more intellectually stimulating and emotionally engaging to be on the frontiers of new developments rather than simply participating in someone else's innovation—even though participating in someone else's solution might be much more effective at helping others.

- Last, among foundation staff and professional advisers for grant-making, there is a cultural assumed bias toward restricted giving. Recommending that donors make unrestricted gifts reduces the perceived value of their expertise, as it puts more decision-making power in the hands of the charities themselves. Unrestricting giving is often viewed as not being "strategic" because it implicitly adopts the objectives of the charity, rather than imposing the donor's own separate objectives. This view contributes to the norm of restricted giving.

Such a significant proportion of restricted giving hurts the entire charitable sector. The selection of programs being funded is disproportionately driven by those with the checkbooks rather than those who are close to the programs themselves. By tying up budgets of nonprofits, restricted donations inherently handcuff them from using their expertise in solving social programs. Further, not having control over large portions of the budget makes managing a charity challenging. Though the rationale for restricted giving often relates to making sure the money is used effectively, in reality this practice often has the opposite result.

There is no universal answer to the question about restricted versus unrestricted giving. Many major donors underuse unrestricted donations, which should be the default preference in most situations. There are a variety of reasons for this, and thoughtful donors with a do-bester approach should examine them carefully when deciding how to give.

Although the title of this chapter refers to "project selection," it may appear to have very little on selecting individual projects, other than not to do it in most situations. The unrestricted donor's version of project selection is to find out the answer to a simple question: *What would a charity do with incremental unrestricted donations and why?*

Then the donor would give to the organization(s) that are able to make the best use of the donation.

12

Volunteering and Other Ways of Donating Yourself

And some kind of help
is the kind of help
That helping's all about

And some kind of help
is the kind of help
We all can do without

—Shel Silverstein[1]

Bridget Clark Whitney gushes when she talks about Amway Global, and she's not referring to their cosmetics and cleaning supplies. Whitney is the executive director of Kids' Food Basket, a nonprofit that fights hunger in Grand Rapids, Michigan.

Kids' Food Basket makes "sack suppers" for about 3,800 children in food-insecure households, supplementing the meals they get from free school breakfasts and lunches to make sure they are getting all the nutrition they need. It isn't just about hunger, but also to make sure kids get enough nourishment to be able to focus on their education at school.

The Kids' Food Basket had a "good" problem. They were growing so fast they were bursting at the seams. There was a tremendous amount of food being donated and they had over 150 volunteers daily to pack the suppers. They had plenty of volunteers and donations, but they were running out of space. There wasn't enough room to store all of the donations and the volunteers were inefficient because they were tripping over each other and the stockpiles of inventory. Yet there was still major unmet demand for their services, which shouldn't be surprising since Grand Rapids had an 8.9 percent spike in poverty from 2000 to 2008, the largest among U.S. cities.[2] Kids' Food Basket was having major growing pains from its roots as a small organization.

An epiphany happened when they met the logistics experts in Amway Global's Operational Excellence team. Whitney describes how Amway helped:

> They offered to come in and volunteer their time to help us become more efficient. And so they actually did a series of projects working with us to improve some of our efficiencies. And they found just in our building tons more space. In fact, we were able to increase our production just in that building in one fiscal year 57%—a huge amount. They taught us how to use our inventory . . . to better deal with all of the food coming in. . . . How to better fragment out volunteer times, so we could have more people come in and have more people able to take the opportunity to volunteer.[3]

Amway's Operational Excellence team volunteered their time and unique skills, which the Kids' Food Basket desperately needed. The team was able to help the Kids' Food Basket grow 30 percent in a single fiscal year. Whitney raved about Amway: "Because of Amway's efforts, hundreds more children in Kent County won't eat lunch as their last meal of the day."[4]

Many people prefer giving time instead of money, or at least in conjunction with giving money. Volunteering can create a greater emotional connection, as the donor doesn't just know the impact, but also sees it, touches it, and directly creates it.

It is also common for volunteers to want to help in ways unique to their abilities. If the Operational Excellence team at Amway hadn't helped the Kids' Food Basket improve its efficiencies, who else would have? There are few—if any—other people in Grand Rapids with comparable expertise. Presumably, the Kids' Food Basket's need would have remained unmet. It simply would not have been able to expand its services as broadly or as quickly.

It is very likely that Amway's donation of time and expertise was more valuable to the Kids' Food Basket than an equivalent amount of cash—it may have been the most impactful thing Amway Global could have done to help the Kids' Food Basket. But even if this is the case, it may not have been the best outlet for Amway's philanthropy.

Unfortunately, many people volunteer by first deciding what they want to do, rather than thinking about how to make the greatest impact. This often means that volunteers are doing what they find most emotionally rewarding instead of what helps others most. Or, in many cases, it means helping an organization that is not especially impactful because its programs have desirable volunteer opportunities. Either way, impact is reduced.

This is not to imply that volunteering is always impact reducing; for some people, it is the most impactful thing they can do. But donors are most likely to make this happen when they consider the venue and method for volunteering just as carefully, and with as much rigor, as their cash donations.

Like Amway, Google also shares its expertise, pursuing philanthropy in a way that only it can. It pledged 1 percent of its equity, 1 percent of profits, and a significant amount of employee time to its philanthropic arm, Google.org, nicknamed DotOrg. Its uniqueness lies not in the amount that it pledged, but the way in which DotOrg operates. In Google's IPO letter, cofounder Larry Page explains, "We hope someday this institution may eclipse Google itself in terms of overall world impact by ambitiously applying innovation and significant resources to the largest of the world's problems."[5]

DotOrg was not set up as a nonprofit, which would have subjected it to the host of regulatory restrictions that are associated with the tax-exempt status of a nonprofit. Instead, it was set up as a part of the business. "Google .org can play on the entire keyboard," Google.org's first executive director, Dr. Larry Brilliant, said in an interview with the *New York Times* shortly after accepting the position. "It can start companies, build industries, pay consultants, lobby, give money to individuals and make a profit."[6]

Like Amway, DotOrg has further tried to refine its giving to be centered around what it does best. While the Operational Excellence team at Amway helped improve logistics and process efficiencies, DotOrg has focused its programs in areas it has the talent and resources to address better than anyone: computer engineering solutions. With the optimistic and ambitious flare that is characteristic of Google, DotOrg is intent on addressing many of the world's biggest problems.

Google Flu Trends is one of its most innovative projects, which it often features as an example of the kind of work it does. Using real-time analysis of trends for flu-related Internet search requests, Google engineers believe they can identify flu outbreaks a week or two earlier than the fastest alternative.

This is important because detecting outbreaks faster can lead to shorter response times and a better ability to curb the spread of illness.

Although not everyone who searches the Internet for flu-related topics has the flu, a meaningful uptick of searches tends to be correlated with increases in flu incidents. Google can do its analysis of search requests daily, which gives its forecasting technology a significant speed advantage over more traditional methods used by the Centers for Disease Control and Prevention, such as reports of physician visits. Is there anyone better equipped than Google to come up with this type of solution?

The Google.org website describes its mission: "Google.org uses Google's strengths in information and technology to build products and advocate for policies that address global challenges. We focus our efforts on activities that are uniquely suited to Google's engineering teams, global infrastructure and user-driven approach, taking advantage of our ability to innovate and scale."[7]

Google Flu Trends clearly supports this mission. But to counter Dr. Brilliant's analogy that "Google.org can play on the entire keyboard," it won't play every instrument in the band: DotOrg only focuses on engineering solutions that utilize Google's most unique and valuable skills.

A former DotOrg executive put it this way: "We concentrated on complicated engineering problems rather than large development challenges. That meant we were creating solutions that were looking for problems rather than the other way around."[8] Maybe early detection of flu trends is not one of the world's biggest problems, even though it has a clever computer engineering solution.

The reason most nonprofits working on global health and poverty don't hire a lot of computer engineers is because computer engineering is not usually the most important skill set for the problems at hand. And the fact that DotOrg will only work on problems with engineering solutions is why its impact is constrained.

While Amway Global's gifts of time and expertise may have been more valuable to the Kids' Food Basket than an equivalent amount of money, Google.org's gifts of time and expertise may not be. They might be coming up with extremely creative engineering solutions to problems that could be more effectively addressed with other means. That is not to imply that DotOrg's initiatives are not making the world a better place, but they may not be doing as much good as possible if they did not have the strict requirement of being focused on computer engineering.

Both Amway and Google use their specialized skill sets as part of their efforts, but they are choosing the problems they focus on very differently. Google is trying to emphasize the world's biggest problems, and Amway is choosing to work with those who need their skill set. Each approach has its own set of downsides. Google is constraining itself to computer engineering methods (usually involving data aggregation) to develop solutions. Amway doesn't necessarily focus on the world's biggest problems, but just those that can benefit from their skills. Google is tying its right hand behind its back, and Amway is tying its left hand. While both of these one-armed volunteers can do good things, neither appears to be thinking in an unconstrained way about what are the most impactful things they could do.

A lot of people prefer volunteering—donating their time and expertise—either instead of or in addition to giving money. Volunteering is much more personal. It is often emotionally more rewarding, especially when there is direct interaction with the people helped, and donors can literally see the impact with their own eyes. Further, many wealthy people don't find writing a check particularly rewarding because they have too much money for it to feel like a sacrifice. Those who view their time as their most scarce and personally valuable asset may find volunteering more rewarding precisely because it is a greater sacrifice.

But these reasons for volunteering are fraught with pitfalls for donors who want to maximize impact. Self-sacrifice and unique contributions are not a precondition for helping others. They are donor-driven, in that they relate to donors being able to see and feel the gift, its costs, and its results, instead of maximizing the positive impact on others.

A do-bester wouldn't want to volunteer for the sake of donating time and self, but rather because it is the method for giving that is most helpful to others. One of the fundamental problems with volunteering is that to have hands-on involvement in many of the most impactful areas requires large time commitments as well as specialized knowledge in unique fields—things the average person simply doesn't have. As a simple example, let's revisit a few of the top-ranked causes recommended by the Copenhagen Consensus in chapter 9:

- Bundled interventions to reduce undernutrition in pre-schoolers
- Subsidy for malaria combination treatment
- Expanded childhood immunization coverage[9]

Volunteers won't be able to address these types of issues by spending a couple of hours a week at the Kids' Food Basket, local library, hospital, or elementary school. Though some global charities offer "volunteer vacations," it is not the most efficient use of a donor's charitable budget to spend thousands of dollars to travel across the world to do unskilled labor in areas where there are plenty of people looking for jobs. There simply aren't many volunteer opportunities for the most impactful areas without living overseas for extended periods of time and/or having deep expertise in niche technical areas.

Warren Buffett, when pledging to give away over 99 percent of his wealth, contrasted his gifts with those of others:

> Measured by dollars, this commitment is large. In a comparative sense, though, many individuals give more to others every day. Millions of people who regularly contribute to churches, schools, and other organizations thereby relinquish the use of funds that would otherwise benefit their own families. The dollars these people drop into a collection plate or give to United Way mean forgone movies, dinners out, or other personal pleasures. In contrast, my family and I will give up nothing we need or want by fulfilling this 99% pledge. Moreover, this pledge does not leave me contributing the most precious asset, which is time.... Gifts of this kind often prove far more valuable than money.[10]

Though his statements demonstrate a remarkable amount of humility, Buffett was wrong in implying that his gifts are less valuable because he didn't feel that he was giving up something important to him. Just because Buffett considers his most precious asset to be his time doesn't mean it is the asset others need most. When Buffett goes on to note that "[a] struggling child, befriended and nurtured by a caring mentor, receives a gift whose value far exceeds what can be bestowed by a check," he fails to acknowledge that he can write checks large enough to fund entire organizations with full-time employees serving as caring mentors—people who otherwise would have to take different jobs. Had he decided to spend his time mentoring individual children, rather than making money with his financial wizardry, his philanthropy would be much smaller and do less good.

Of course, that doesn't mean that volunteering should be excluded from the do-bester's toolkit. Many of the organizations that work on these issues need help from lawyers to set up the structures to operate legally, web designers to develop an online presence necessary for fundraising, and leaders in a variety of areas to sit on their boards and provide the top rung of governance and direction. Volunteers who fill these roles well are valuable. Nevertheless, this suggests that the opportunities for do-besters to volunteer are very limited. Intuitively, it seems that there must be something more that do-besters can do with their time. The key for do-besters is to look more broadly than traditional volunteer opportunities, considering more creative ways to think about how to give "yourself" to help others. Do-besters must look at the full range of what they can do for charities through the lens of their impacts on others.

In pursuing a graduate degree in philosophy at Oxford University, Will Crouch is trying to change how people think about the best ways to spend their time to help others. Crouch is not just thinking about volunteering; he founded the group 80,000 Hours, which encourages people to think differently about how their career choices impact the amount of good they can do.

How differently? Crouch thinks that it may be morally superior to pursue a lucrative career as a high-earning investment banker than as a charity aid worker—that is, if the banker is a "professional philanthropist": going into the career with the intention of earning a lot of money to give away. "The direct benefit a single aid worker can produce is limited, whereas the philanthropic banker's donations might indirectly help 10 times as many people," Crouch explained in a BBC interview.[11] Crouch presents three main reasons for this:

- The banker might be able to make enough money to pay the salaries of multiple aid workers.
- By not becoming an aid worker, that would open a position for someone else to be an aid worker. Whereas by becoming a banker, he would be taking the position from someone who probably would not be as philanthropic.
- The banker can give to the most impactful areas, but the aid worker may be more limited in career opportunities. Further, though the most impactful areas of aid may change over the course of one's career, it may not be as easy to change career specialties within the aid sector as it would be for the banker to change where he donates.[12]

Along these lines, Buffett's decision to spend his career making billions running Berkshire Hathaway, then giving 99 percent away, may have been the best way for him to spend his time.

Crouch goes so far as to say that it might still be ethical even if that lucrative job requires working for an immoral corporation. He describes a situation of working for an arms company supplying an unjust war. If you didn't take the job, someone else would; they would be more ruthless than you and wouldn't help others with donations. As an example, Crouch points out Oskar Schindler, made famous by the movie *Schindler's List*, who ran a munitions factory supplying the Nazi army in order to buy off the lives of 1,200 Jews. Crouch argues that had Schindler not run the factory, someone else would have made the munitions instead—probably of higher quality, helping the Nazis more—and the 1,200 Jews would have died.[13]

Of course, some people might not have the ability to be successful in investment banking or any other high-paying job. But Crouch notes that making a lot of money and giving it away is not the only way to have a high-impact career.

> In fact, it's plausible that one can do even more good by taking a career that enables one to influence others than one can through professional philanthropy. Trivially, if one can influence 10 others to become professional philanthropists (perhaps through one's role as a teacher or lecturer) then one would do 10 times as much good as those professional philanthropists themselves.[14]

Though volunteering is often thought of as doing "hands on" aid work, that may not be the best way for many people to use their time to help others. A skilled banker might help others most by working overtime and donating a cut of his bonus to the best charities. A clever computer programmer at Google or a member of Amway's Operational Excellence team might spend their time improving their employer's core business and donating their earnings. And those who are talented at persuasion and have a network of potential donors might do far more good by inspiring others to give to the best causes.

When a massive tsunami hit East Asia on December 26, 2004, many Americans wanted to donate to the relief efforts, but didn't know how to choose a charity. Former president Bill Clinton teamed up with his ex–political rival, President George H. W. Bush, to form the Bush-Clinton Tsunami Relief Fund. Many donors believed that if Clinton and Bush could agree that this organization would make good use of their money, it must be true. They rejoined forces again in 2005 to help fundraise for relief efforts for Hurricane Katrina. Clinton did a similar tag-team with the younger President Bush to fundraise for relief efforts helping victims of the Haitian earthquake of 2010. All together, the joint efforts raised tens of millions of dollars, if not more.

Though these types of activities aren't traditional volunteering tasks that the average person could pursue, the former presidents were donating their time, reputations, and specialized skills. They were donating themselves, which is a form of volunteering. And this wasn't Clinton's first entrée in volunteering after finishing his two presidential terms. He started the Clinton Foundation in 2001, spending much of his post-presidential time on philanthropic efforts.

Roughly a decade later, the 2011 financials for the Clinton Foundation included over $300 million in contributions and grants. Further, the foundation brings together over 1,200 leaders in the nonprofit and philanthropy sector for the annual Clinton Global Initiative (CGI), a major conference designed to "turn ideas into action."[15] CGI members are expected to make a "commitment to action"—new, specific, and measurable initiatives—and they must later report progress on it.

Most charities love celebrities volunteering as spokespeople to help them reach broader audiences and get those audiences to reach deeper into their pockets when making donations. When well-known people put their names on causes, it creates a culture of giving that has positive ripple effects throughout society.

Though there are plenty of different views on Bill Clinton's performance as president, few can deny that he still has a strong backing of followers. One of his best skills is to motivate and mobilize others. His ability to do this may dwarf the impact of anything he could do by simply writing personal checks. Volunteering his time, reputation, and skills may be the most impactful thing Clinton can do now to improve the world.

I don't know if Clinton is a do-bester, but I suspect that his actions—publicly volunteering his time and reputation for the efforts he thinks are most important—are consistent with a do-bester approach.

A lot of donors want to do more than just write checks. Aside from the emotional warmth that volunteering brings, it seems intuitive that there must be something more we can do than just give money. And that intuition is right. Although few people can replicate what Clinton and Bush did, most have some combination of time, skills, reputation, and network that can add value to their charitable interests. Like traditional volunteering, giving any of these things is a form of giving yourself.

For some, the path is clear. Those with the unique skills needed by the most impactful organizations—whether those skills are medical, leadership, agricultural, engineering, or anything else—may know exactly how they can use those skills to best help the world.

Without such unique skills, the path may not be immediately obvious, but it certainly exists. Increasing and improving philanthropy isn't reserved for ex-presidents, movie stars, and foundation chiefs. Everyone has a social network, and one of the most important things "ordinary" donors can spend their time doing is to persuade others to give and (possibly more important) give better. Signaling to other potential donors might be the most basic form of improving the infrastructure of philanthropy, and it is a type of volunteering.

In fact, this was my premise in writing this book. Although my professional background didn't lend itself to traditional volunteering for the most impactful causes, I realized I might be able to do more by being evangelical about the do-bester perspective, helping others be more effective donors. Maybe this book will positively influence the direction of much more money than I could actually donate.

Bill Gates and Warren Buffett are also volunteering their time and reputations to change the culture of philanthropy. They joined forces to start the Giving Pledge, asking America's billionaires to publicly pledge to donate the majority of their wealth during their lifetimes or after their death. It is ironic that the world's two most generous donors are spending much of their "volunteer" time and effort encouraging others to donate. Nevertheless, as billionaires themselves who are giving large amounts, they may be able to persuade other billionaires more effectively than anyone else. It is a very valid strategy for increasing their impact—despite the size of their financial gifts, their impact could be multiplied if they started a movement that influenced many other billionaires to give.

Although the Giving Pledge and this book are both designed to improve the philanthropic sector's infrastructure, Gates and Buffett are approaching this from a different angle that I am. They are encouraging people to donate more, while I'm encouraging people to donate better (or at least, in a way that I think is better). There is a correlation between giving more and giving better: people who give more tend to make more effort trying to give better, and people who believe they are giving effectively tend to be willing to give more.

Each approach can be perceived with its own set of pros and cons. Some may perceive it as better to suggest how much people should give away, without passing judgment on how they do it. Others may find it more palatable to suggest a specific framework for how to give better, without explicitly asking for more money. Gates and Buffett are certainly not encouraging people to donate worse, just as I am not encouraging people to donate less. It's just that we are focused on different aspects of improving philanthropy.

Readers may have different views on the best ways they can improve the infrastructure of the philanthropic sector. You may believe you can increase the amounts people give. For example, if you know people who are willing to give but don't because they can't identify organizations that will make good use of their money, it may be as simple as providing them with information. Or you may know people who are very generous, but are not giving to the most impactful areas. While some may not be open to changing their practices, others might be willing to consider alternatives.

It would be impractical for readers to spend their time going door to door, giving their neighbors lectures on giving more or better—that is unlikely to be persuasive. Being evangelical about giving more or adopting the do-bester perspective usually requires more subtle actions to help others be more effective donors. It may be as gentle as letting people know your philosophy and approach to giving—research shows that people are more likely to give if they know their peers are doing it. It may involve becoming informed about the charitable sector so people know they can come to you as a resource when they want information. Or it could be recommending that other people read this book, GiveWell's blog, or whatever other things you believe may be helpful for other potential donors. Each individual would need to figure out what they are comfortable doing and would most likely succeed.

This may not be "volunteering" in the sense people most often think about it. It isn't a project like what Amway's Operational Excellence team is doing with the Kids' Food Basket or Google.org is doing with Google Flu Trends. But for many do-besters, improving the infrastructure of the philanthropic sector may be the most influential way they can volunteer their time to improve the world.

13

Leveraging Your Donation

Give me the place to stand, and I shall move the earth.
—Archimedes

A few years ago, *Slate* magazine published an article sharing responses from several people to the following question: "If you had a million dollars to give, who would get it?"[1] One of the contributors was Lincoln Caplan, then a partner at SeaChange Capital Partners. His chosen recipient would have been the Effective Practice Incentive Fund created by New Leaders for New Schools. The fund would support training school leaders—primarily principals and some teachers—and provide performance-based compensation and incentives. Caplan's reasoning was that he believed in the "teach the teacher" model, as better teachers would eventually cause a broad ripple effect to impact a large number of students. Teaching principals could have an even greater ripple if each principal is able to cascade the new skills broadly over many teachers to affect an even larger number of students. In fact, Caplan said that New Leaders expected to be training one-fourth of the new principals needed in cities across the country within six years of when that article was written.[2]

But that wasn't the only thing that made Caplan so enthusiastic about New Leaders. He explained that New Leaders had already raised $4.5 million of the $13.3 million in private funds it was seeking for this program, which would be matched five-to-one with grants from the U.S. Department of Education and other public funds. The hypothetical $1 million that Caplan would donate would result in an additional $5 million of government money to the organization, expanding its impact much further.

Caplan's case for New Leaders was fundamentally about leverage. He believed that it would make good use of the two main types of philanthropic leverage:

1. **Operational leverage:** Cascading benefits such that each dollar of funding generates an outsized impact. For New Leaders, the model of teaching the teacher (and principal) allows each participant in the program to improve the education of hundreds, if not thousands, of students. This has the potential to have a much more expansive impact than, say, tutoring students one at a time.
2. **Financial leverage:** Using other people's money so the dollars-at-work are greater than those donated. In this case, the five-to-one matching grants from the government are the financial leverage.

Both forms of leverage can be great tools for donors to increase their impact, but they are not as simple as it may appear on the surface. Donors should think critically about charities that claim to use leverage to make sure the impact multiplier is truly legitimate.

In the case of New Leaders, it would only receive the five-to-one matching public funds for the first $13.3 million in private funds it raised, which makes the marginal impact of a hypothetical $1 million donation from Caplan less clear. If he had made a donation, would it increase the total amount granted by the government or would it have crowded out other potential donors who would have resisted donating once New Leaders maxed out its opportunities for the five-to-one matching funds? If so, Caplan's donation might not have had any impact on the total amount raised by the fund, as other would-be donors may not have given once the $13.3 million target was reached. Alternatively, maybe the other donors would continue to donate, but their funds would not be matched—then Caplan's hypothetical donation would have only increased the marginal funding for New Leaders by the $1 million he donated, even though technically "his" gift was matched five-to-one. Or maybe the donors who would have been crowded out of the matching fund would give their $1 million to a totally different charity—likely the case for foundations that have mandatory spending policies—in which case the marginal impact of Caplan's donation would, ironically, be tied to where the other donors chose to give. While it is not typically known which of these alternatives would materialize, it's important to realize that the marginal impact of a hypothetical donation from Caplan would be highly related to the behavior of other donors, specifically whether they would cover the full opportunity for matching. At the time Caplan wrote the piece, it was not known whether this was the case.

Further, the government's matching funds would need to be raised somehow. Those funds could come from three broad sources:

1. Higher taxes
2. Reduced spending on other government programs
3. Government deficits (which would need to be paid for in the future by either higher taxes or reduced spending on other government programs)[3]

None of these are free for society, so the positive impact that matching government grants are expected to have on education would be mitigated by a negative ripple effect that is difficult to understand and quantify. While government spending on education is often considered a good thing, it is not the case that all additional spending on all programs related to education is good—otherwise governments would have likely already shifted expenditures accordingly. Governments are supposed to do their best to balance competing needs for the appropriate amounts (and types) of taxes and spending, including for public education. Presumably, the government officials who agreed to provide matching grants believe it is a worthwhile expenditure, but it is worth asking why the government wouldn't fund New Leaders program or something similar without matching private funds. Is the program not expected to be valuable enough without significant private funds to share the cost?

Certainly the government's track record of allocating funds is far from perfect, and I don't want to overstate the strength or reliability of the signal the government gave by refusing to cover the full cost of the program. But it is something donors should evaluate when considering the true leverage of this type of arrangement. Leverage is an important tool for donors, but its nuances must be understood well to use it effectively.

The government isn't the only source of financial leverage. Many donors issue matching gift challenges for other donors to respond to. A typical example is the $100,000 challenge issued by David Levi, Kathleen Hamm, and David and Kelsey Lamond, who challenged alumni of the Duke University Law School.[4] They offered a dollar-for-dollar match of contributions to the school's Annual Fund. Many potential donors may have been encouraged by the two-to-one leverage of "their" contribution, while the issuers of the matching challenge may have been similarly encouraged by the fact that "their" contribution was leveraged by its linkage with the other donors. Each donor believed they were getting financial leverage from the money of the other.

As with the case of New Leaders, the beneficial leverage of matching gifts is only real if a certain set of circumstances occurs. One way for the leverage to have real benefits is if the matching challenge actually increases the total amounts donated. It cannot simply put a "matching" label on donations that would have occurred anyway. The issuers of this matching challenge had a clever way of addressing this: the matching challenge only applied to those alumni who did not make a gift the prior year. Under the theory that alumni who didn't donate last year are less likely to donate this year, the matching gift challenge might bring in new donors. In the very least, it wouldn't be maxed out by a few of the Annual Fund's perennial major donors.

But even if the matching fund challenge doesn't encourage additional philanthropy, it could entice donors to reallocate gifts they would have given to other nonprofits. This could happen for individual donors with fixed giving budgets or for foundations. In that case, the leverage is only real if that reallocation is toward better nonprofits. Presumably, the issuers of the matching challenge believe that Duke's Law School is one of the best organizations to donate to—that's why they initiated the challenge there rather than with a different organization. But the responders may not have the same view, as they would have preferred to donate elsewhere absent a match. As with a gift to New Leaders, the actual impact of the match leverage is not as simple as doubling the gift's dollar amount.

Social commentator and pundit Matt Miller has advice for billionaires who want to make the greatest positive impact on the country:

> [T]he impact of direct philanthropy pales next to the impact of shaping more effective and efficient uses of the vastly larger public resources

> available to government. For this reason, farsighted philanthropists all come to realize that advocacy—i.e., efforts to shape how public resources are utilized—offers the best possible bang for the charitable buck. So if the choice for a high-net-worth patriot is to devote himself or herself to a foundation, or to run for president or invest in related efforts, there's no question that the presidential campaign is the path to greater impact.[5]

Miller is arguing for advocacy as a source of financial leverage, as it has the potential to tap the full financial resources of the government. He goes on to assert that the billionaire doesn't even have to win the election. Running a strong campaign will change the substance of the issues being debated, and the other candidates would be forced to adjust their own focuses. Miller pointed to Ross Perot's presidential run in 1992 that made the federal budget deficit and national debt key issues all politicians needed to address. The campaign itself could be sufficiently influential to have an impact.

Miller is discontent with the level of extremism influencing U.S. national politics, and believes that the country could benefit from a wealthy patriot in the "far center" financing a campaign outside the two major parties. Although this view closely relates to Miller's appreciation—or lack thereof—for the candidates running for office then, it has an element of truth that may transcend his personal views of the political environment. The cost of a presidential campaign, though expensive, pales in comparison with the federal government expenditures it would seek to influence—$3–4 trillion annually[6]—not to mention the other areas that the presidency influences such as military strategy and judicial appointments. While it would take an extremely wealthy individual to self-finance an entire presidential campaign, a similar concept could be applied to smaller-scale lobbying of governmental entities to reallocate their resources. This could certainly be considered a form of leverage that do-bester donors might want to employ. And many donors, foundations, and nonprofits do seek to influence governmental actions.

But Miller appears to overstate the consensus about the merits of his view when he states that "farsighted philanthropists *all* come to realize that advocacy . . . offers the best possible bang for the charitable buck"[7] (Or maybe he is accusing a lot of philanthropists of being shortsighted.) While advocacy for governmental policy has the opportunity to influence more money, that influence is far weaker than the control donors have when spending their own money. Ross Perot spent millions on his presidential campaign, but the national debt has increased almost continuously since then. Would it have gotten larger, faster, without his campaign? It's hard to say. Would the money he spent on the campaign have been more influential if he had funded a think tank to research the impacts of government debt or ways to reduce the debt? That is also hard to say. What we can confidently say is that advocacy is a potential leverage tool in the do-bester's toolkit.

Though many nonprofits working on health issues in the developing world give away important health care products like insecticide-treated bed nets (to prevent mosquito bites that transmit malaria), oral rehydration salts (to prevent dehydration from diarrhea after drinking dirty water), and deworming pills (to treat intestinal parasites), Living Goods' founder Chuck Slaughter had a different idea: he wants to sell those products. He's developing a network of door-to-door microfranchise saleswomen, effectively becoming the Avon of "pro-poor products."[8] Living Goods also seeks to emulate Avon's size and scope, by hopefully having thousands of community health promoters—its version of the "Avon lady" saleswomen—serving millions of customers. But Slaughter isn't looking to make a fast buck on the backs of the global poor; he's looking to use operational leverage to succeed where the traditional nonprofits have struggled.

Living Goods is built on the assumption that the traditional methods of giving away health care products are unsustainable. While providing these products to the poor for free will help, such a system will always be reliant on perpetually underfunded charities. Living Goods is trying to develop an efficient, scalable, and sustainable distribution system to get these important products to the world's poorest people, starting in Uganda. It is using operational leverage by developing a system in which donor funds are only needed for the start-up years, and the program will be self-funding thereafter.

Living Goods is relying on many of the same techniques that other franchise businesses have used successfully. Its products are branded. Its community health promoters are local women, well trained in how to use the products they sell—for example, knowing when to administer Artemisinin-based combination therapies (ACTs)—the second-ranked cause in the Copenhagen Consensus—as treatment against malaria and when danger signs warrant a referral to a hospital or clinic. It also combines high-impact, slow-moving products like insecticide-treated bed nets with high-velocity products like toothpaste and soap. This helps the community health promoters maintain ongoing relationships with their customers and contributes to their own income. Also, as a business with a social purpose, it provides profit incentives for selling the most essential health supplies and requires community health promoters to stock them at all times.

Of course, Living Goods' idea relies on the assumption that there will be consumer demand for their products at the prices charged. Because of inefficiencies in the retail distribution system in the developing world, especially in rural areas, Living Goods is typically able to price its products 10 to 40 percent below retail. And for many products, the savings customers get by having products brought to them more than make up for the transportation costs associated with the alternative: going to a clinic to get the product for free. In some cases, Living Goods' community health providers describe their products as "cheaper than free."[9]

Living Goods' website describes the promise of its approach: "[O]ur model is poised to become fully self-funded at a country level within five years of country launch. Thus, unlike other social programs, Living Goods' required donor commitment would be for a finite period, after which the model will pay for itself."[10] Hence the operational leverage: a fixed amount of donor capital provides benefits that continue indefinitely. It wouldn't just put a Band-aid on the problem for an individual, or even fix the root cause of the problem for an individual—it improves the system in perpetuity.

The change that Living Goods hopes to create is perhaps the dream of many donors who seek to leverage their resources for the greater good. They are trying to put in place a program that permanently reduces a major problem, without the need for ongoing donor funds. Opportunities for such genuine leverage are rare. Fortunately, Living Goods is doing rigorous randomized controlled trials to robustly measure and understand the impact of their program. Results from their evaluations will be available by late 2013.

In a 1999 article "Philanthropy's New Agenda: Creating Value,"[11] Michael Porter and Mark Kramer (cofounders of FSG, a nonprofit consulting organization) assert that donors—foundations in particular—are not using all the tools at their disposal to further their missions. The article defines "creating value" as when donations and other activities "generate social benefits that go beyond the mere purchasing power of their grants,"[12] and it describes four broad ways to do this:

1. Select the best grantees.
2. Signal other funders as to what are the best grantees. This creates more value by drawing even more funds to the best charities.
3. Improve the performance of grant recipients. This creates even greater value by improving the use of all funds used by the recipient charities.
4. Advance the state of knowledge and practice in an entire sector. This creates even greater value by improving the use of all funds used in the field.[13]

The last three of these represent forms of leverage—ways to make a donation have a disproportionately large impact. Though the article is over a decade old, it continues to be frequently cited as a seminal piece on effective philanthropy.

While the validity of the basic principles is self-evident, the implementation of them is more challenging in practice than on paper. As examples of improving performance of grant recipients, Porter and Kramer point to several restricted grants, such as hiring consultants to teach an organization how to improve its fundraising or funding technology improvements. But as described in chapter 11, restricted grants have less value to charities, as they cannot be spent in the areas the organizations believe they are needed in most. The charities themselves may not believe these restricted grants will improve their performance as well, compared to what they could do with the same amount of unrestricted money.

As examples of advancing the state of knowledge in an entire sector, Porter and Kramer promote grants to support research activities. But it's important to realize that many research activities fail to provide any useful results or only advance current practices by very small increments. While it is certainly possible that researching new or better areas could have a greater impact than implementing the best existing solutions, they overstate the case for research by generalizing such a wide swath of activities as providing a benefit of ">1,000x" that of individual grants.

This is not to imply that Porter and Kramer's ideas are wrong, but just that they are not easy to implement well. Leveraged impact opportunities can be tremendous boosts to impact and are worthwhile to consider, but oversimplification can lead to poor decisions. Matching gift challenges, from either private sources like with Duke, or from public sources as with

New Leaders, can be an effective way to increase impact by leveraging other people's money, but it's important for donors to consider the ripple effects on the sources of matching funds. In the case of New Leaders, the matching funds provide a direct positive impact on the program by increasing its scale, but an indirect, negative ripple effect on the public because the matching funds come from the government. In the case of the matching challenge for the Duke Law School, the challenge could result in a meaningful increase in donations to the Annual Fund because it was specifically targeted at those who hadn't donated the prior year. Further, these new donors might start a pattern of annual giving to Duke that will continue in future years, even without a match. Even if the match only influences donors to reallocate their giving within a fixed giving budget but not increase their total giving—which may be atypical for individual donors, though very common for foundations—there would still be an impact if the reallocation was viewed as positive.

There are a different set of questions for operational leverage opportunities like Living Goods. Even if Living Goods' testing proves that its donors did develop a sustainable solution that actually improves health care, donors still have to ask questions before giving them more money. Can the results of their program in Uganda be replicated in other countries? What other funders do they have and what will be the impact of additional incremental donations?

14

Ten Smart Approaches That Work

My father used to say, "You can spend a lot of time making money. The tough time comes when you have to give it away properly." How to give something back, that's the tough part in life.

—Lee Iacocca[1]

Smart Approach 1: When deciding where to give, don't be afraid to make subjective comparisons of very different options to assess trade-offs and determine which you think would have the greatest impact.

Imagine walking into a giant philanthropy convention. Across a large room, there are donors everywhere you turn—individual donors, corporate donors, and foundations—and many, many nonprofit organizations that improve the world in so many different ways. Positive energy is flowing everywhere you look.

You turn to your left and see a booth of people that provides mentoring for children at risk of joining gangs. To your right is a group that does Alzheimer's research. An environmental group is in front of you, and behind you is a group that runs refugee camps in war-torn areas. And there are more and more of these different groups everywhere. All of the people you meet are passionate about what they do, and all seem to do such good things.

You think about what causes you want to support. The environment or the elderly? The third world or your neighborhood's third-grade children? Malaria or muscular dystrophy?

Many people specifically dislike such comparisons because they are forced to decide not only what causes they support, but which ones they don't (at least not financially). These are tough decisions, and most people love to decide who to help, but hate to decide who *not* to help. Of course, the reality is that these decisions are related. Helping people is supposed to feel good, but this line of reasoning makes you see who you are not helping. With limited resources and so many worthy causes, it makes it apparent that you are not helping a lot more people than you are helping.

You see a booth for an organization that helps sick children right next to one for an organization that supports the arts. When presented like this, a do-bester's immediate reaction may be to wonder how anyone could recommend that even a dime go to supporting the arts when there are sick children in need of help. Is it really that black-and-white? In discussing the rationale for donating to the arts instead of other causes, some people believe there are important ripple effects that may often be forgotten in simplistic analyses:

> Tommer Peterson, the Deputy Director of Grantmakers in the Arts, cautions donors from viewing arts funding as an either/or decision. "Pitting cultural organizations against social needs is missing the big picture. Arts and culture enrich our spirit, increase our understanding of both differences and similarities, while enhancing our spirit and core democratic values."
>
> Still not convinced? Even the most results-oriented funder would be interested to know that there is a plethora of studies documenting the impact and exposure of the arts ranging from enhanced physical and mental well-being, improved academic performance, violence prevention and creative problem solving, as well as creating a more accepting and inclusive society.[2]

Peterson rightly suggests that causes focusing on cultural issues are not necessarily inferior to those supporting social needs—both improve our quality of life, though in very different ways. But he is wrong when asserting that they should not be pitted against each other. They are pitted against each other because donor resources are limited. Donors should ask the tough questions about who to help, how, and why—the arts, sick children, or other options—and the answers may not be simple or obvious. Everybody will have their own views on how to assess the trade-offs, and those trade-offs should be addressed head on.

While some may be skeptical of whether arts-related causes are among the most effective at improving the world, the goal of this book is not to convince you of this. If you rigorously consider the issues and believe that donating to a particular arts charity will have a stronger positive impact on the world than other charitable opportunities, then you should give to that charity. But if you have only thought about it enough to know that it will do good, but not enough to have confidence that it is better than other opportunities, then my goal is to convince you to think harder about how important it is to have a strongly positive impact on the world, rather than just a moderately positive impact. Not all good causes are equally good; making an effort to identify the best causes is worthwhile, although not easy.

Economists describe this with the term "opportunity cost," which is defined as "the opportunities forgone in the choice of one expenditure over others."[3] The opportunity cost of donating to one place is not using the money for whatever is your next best alternative. That may be spending it on yourself or saving it, but for many people, it is donating elsewhere. That is, the opportunity cost of giving to the arts may be not giving to education, health care, the environment, or a different cause. Thinking about deciding where to give in these terms forces comparisons that require critical thinking and prioritization—both of which are necessary for do-besters.

One idea that causes inefficient giving is the premise that it is impossible to compare extremely different causes. How can one compare supporting a homeless shelter to medical research to environmental protection? It isn't simple or clear-cut, but by virtue of giving to an organization, a donor is stating a view on the merits of that organization relative to others. While it is difficult to make clear comparisons of saving lives to more diverse areas like economic empowerment and environmental protection, do-bester donors must make subjective judgments on this. Even more subjective judgments have to be made to compare the relative benefits of improving the quality of life to saving lives. And there will be further challenges in choosing between implementing known solutions (e.g., administering vaccines) versus developing future solutions (e.g., researching new vaccines). There isn't a single "best" cause, but that doesn't mean you should give up in frustration. You've come to the reality that it is hard to do a really good job helping people, an important realization that is necessary to become a do-bester.

Do-besters will disagree among themselves, and this diversity of opinion will result in a diversity of nonprofits. Nevertheless, donors with do-bester mentalities are more likely to gravitate toward the most effective causes. Pretending comparisons can't be made doesn't stop them from being made; it just sweeps the criteria under the rug. The real issue donors face—though it may not be easy—is that the opportunity cost of giving to one cause is often not giving to another. Donors should not be afraid to compare the relative merits of very different options when choosing where to give.

Smart Approach 2: Focus your philanthropy where you think it matters most.

It is challenging to compare the relative impacts of charities that work to improve the world in very different ways, and everybody will have their own views on this, but that should not stop donors from addressing the issue directly. Unfortunately, one common approach attempts to evade the issue. The approach starts with the fact that there are many causes that need support, and donors have a variety of different options on where to give. Some do-gooders will use this fact to justify donating their money to a lot of different causes. They may describe it as "diversification," noting that this philosophy on giving can be derived from principles similar to those used in investing. But this isn't a good analogy because of the differences between philanthropy and investing.

Do-besters think in terms of how their giving helps others, not as a "personal" portfolio they own. This means they consider how their contributions fit into the total portfolio of the world's philanthropy, and they do what provides the most incremental improvement to that. The portfolio of the world's philanthropy is already very diversified regardless of what any individual does—even the Gates Foundation's gifts of a few billion dollars a year are just a small percentage of the $300 billion of donations in the United States alone.[4] The charitable sector includes causes and organizations across the globe—literally thousands of different causes and over a million nonprofit organizations.

While the many types of nonprofits play important roles, this fact alone is not sufficient to suggest that individual donors should spread their contributions around. Though it is true that the world needs diverse nonprofits, do-besters know that the options are not equally impactful. The donor's question should start by noting that there already exist many diverse causes being funded by other donors, then try to understand which cause(s) could create the greatest incremental impact with additional funding. Do-besters acknowledge the importance of prioritization.

Do-besters fill in the gaps, giving to the causes and organizations that are exceptionally strong and make great impacts with a small amount of incremental funding. Filling these gaps may appear to be a "concentrated" philanthropic strategy when looking at the choices of an individual donor, but it is actually making the philanthropic sector better diversified by rebalancing the overall pool of donated funds into the hands of those who are underfunded relative to what they could do with the money. Do-besters don't have to diversify their giving. They focus their giving on only the small number of organizations and causes they believe make the best use of those funds.

Smart Approach 3: Focus on the marginal impact of your donation when evaluating philanthropic options.

Although do-bester strategies generally involve concentration, there are practical limits to how far that approach should be extended. If the Gates Foundation gave its entire multi-billion dollar annual giving budget to any single organization, that organization couldn't use it as effectively as it had used prior donations—it simply couldn't hire and train good people fast enough or increase the scale of its programs with the same quality as in the past. There would be diminishing marginal impacts of donating above the level at which an organization can manage to use the funds. While concentrating your philanthropy is generally good, there are practical limitations such that this approach shouldn't be taken to the extreme.

As a real-world example, consider VillageReach, which we discussed in chapter 8 as GiveWell's number-one recommended charity for most of 2009–2011. GiveWell removed them from their list of recommended charities in late 2011. Interestingly, it was neither because GiveWell lost conviction in VillageReach's ability to improve the world nor because GiveWell had found other charities it thought were better than VillageReach. Instead, it was because GiveWell believed that VillageReach's short-term funding needs had been met, and the incremental donations it might receive due to GiveWell's recommendation would not influence its activities over the next year, if not longer. GiveWell cofounder Holden Karnofsky described the rationale: "This is not a 'demotion' of VillageReach; rather, it reflects our success in directing enough funding to it to close its short-term gap."[5]

More broadly, it's important for donors to consider the marginal impact of their donation when evaluating philanthropic options. This is often different from looking at the "average" impact of all donations to a program or organization. In the case of VillageReach, GiveWell believed there would be diminishing marginal returns to incremental donations—either because their impact would be substantially delayed or because it might not be needed at all to fund VillageReach's best programs (depending on whether other donors ultimately fully funded those programs). In other cases, incremental donations may have a greater impact than the average donation. This could be because most donations were earmarked for specific programs, preventing the organization from using those funds most effectively. An additional unrestricted donation can have a greater impact by filling in the gaps. Ironically, this could be for activities like planning, design, and evaluation of programs, which is often looked upon negatively by many charity rating agencies as "overhead."

While the circumstances will differ, the principle remains that do-besters should consider the marginal impact of a donation when evaluating their philanthropic options.

Smart Approach 4: Put your money in the hands of people you believe in.

Looking at the incremental impact of a donation is always difficult, but it is especially difficult for large organizations with diverse programs. Consider the well-known global charity UNICEF. The organization works in about 150 countries and classifies its work into eight major categories:

- Education
- Emergency relief
- Immunization
- Malaria
- HIV/AIDS

- Nutrition
- Protection
- Water and sanitation[6]

Presumably, some of their program areas, geographies, and activities are more likely to have a greater impact than others. How can donors understand the impact of their donation on UNICEF's overall activities? Will it be divided among these eight categories in proportion to the allocation in UNICEF's existing budget, or will disproportionate amounts be directed to some areas? If the latter, how will that be determined and how can dobester donors get conviction that the resource allocation will be done with an eye for maximizing impact?

This is an issue for most large organizations. One way to address this is to earmark your donation, but as we discussed in chapter 11, this is not a cure-all for the challenges. Another way to address it is by only giving to organizations that implement a relatively homogenous set of projects, which would eliminate many large organizations like UNICEF from consideration. While this would primarily solve one problem, it is not obvious that it is the best solution, because there are some inherent advantages for large organizations. They typically have more scale, often more experience, and potentially more talented staff, all of which can translate into a greater ability to run impactful programs. They may also have more political and reputational clout, which can be helpful when it is necessary to partner with others to implement programs—this is especially important when working in foreign countries. In addition, they have a larger array of projects they are working on and a sizable donor base, so they have a greater menu from which to identify the most promising opportunities. Of course, the million-dollar question is to what extent do each of these large, multi-line organizations exploit these potential advantages. Are the organizations trying to allocate their budgets to the areas of greatest opportunity, and if so, are they doing a good job?

This issue exists even for smaller organizations and homogeneous programs, though to a lesser extent. Ultimately, donors only have a limited amount of control over how their gifts are used. Further, there is no way to perfectly evaluate an organization or program. There will always be uncertainty in the results or your ability to interpret those results.

Fundamentally, these concerns can be summarized into one question: How do you know your giving will be used in the manner that is expected to be most effective? The short answer is that you don't know with certainty, so you must make decisions with the best information available. Just as in business, there is no success without risk of failure, and the greatest successes were often undertaken with the risk of extreme failure. Bill Gates didn't know he would eventually become the wealthiest man in the world when he dropped out of Harvard. Muhammad Yunus didn't know that he would eventually win the Nobel Peace Prize for spreading microfinance when he loaned $27 to people in poverty. But both knew what they were doing—they took calculated risks based on incomplete knowledge of the future.

Many of the best nonprofit organizations have failed programs. In fact, all of them have failed programs. An organization doesn't become successful without taking some risks and learning from failures. This doesn't necessarily mean that donors should seek risk, but rather that they should be aware that risk is part of the landscape around their decision making.

Donors, especially those without the skills to directly evaluate programs, should make it a priority to get money into the hands of the best people, then help (but not micromanage) them implement the programs they recommend.

This can be a somewhat counterintuitive system. If you're looking to fund the best program, why not just look for the best program and organization directly? Isn't it a less direct route to look for the best people? This is certainly a fair question, and much of this book has been written about identifying the best ways for donors to direct their giving. The issue with such an approach is often a lack of transparency in the quality of charitable programs. It is difficult to measure how much good a program does, and most communications are designed to make donors feel good and open their wallets wider. Programs overseas are even harder to evaluate, simply because of cultural differences and physical distances. As a result, most donors—even many large foundations—don't have the capabilities to truly evaluate the merits of a potential donation or results of a prior donation.

But people do have the capability to evaluate other people. We know how to identify those who are phony and incompetent, and we know how to differentiate the average from the top tier. While our judgment is far from perfect, usually after a few conversations about something, someone can reasonably accurately tell whether people are experienced, thoughtful, motivated, and competent. Ask them what they are trying to do and why. Find out why they believe one particular course of action is better than other alternatives, and how they will assess progress along the way and make adjustments as they learn new things. Can they talk about failures in a way that shows that they've learned from them? Can they answer your hardest questions? While you may never be able to know exactly what is happening in the field, you should gain a lot of confidence by determining that the people making decisions are skilled and competent.

The best people and organizations are most likely to be the best qualified to find and run the best projects. And evaluating people is not done in isolation: it must include an assessment of the things they've done as a window into their values and capabilities. Further, the organizations they belong to and their specific skills will affect their capacity to produce future results. So this critical, but indirect route to finding the best charities shouldn't be used in isolation, but it is an important part of researching what charitable opportunities might be the most effective. Do-besters will put their money in the hands of people they believe in.

Smart Approach 5: Prioritize everyday developmental aid over disaster relief.

The 2004 Indian Ocean earthquake and tsunami disaster captured the world's attention as it devastated large portions of East Asia, killing over 155,000 people, injuring 500,000, and causing about 5 million to lose their homes or access to food and water.[7] About five years later, an earthquake in Haiti killed over 200,000 and left about 1.5 million people homeless.[8] There is no question that the destruction from each of these events was massive and horrific. Further, these are only two examples of the types of humanitarian disasters that seem to happen on a disturbingly regular basis, including Hurricane Katrina, the flooding in Pakistan, the famine in East Africa, and the Japanese earthquake and ensuing nuclear disaster.

Most of those killed by the disasters could not have been saved with donations, which can't arrive fast enough to save those pulled out to sea by a tsunami or crushed by a crumbling house. But there are survivors, and it is obvious from the media coverage that many of them are among the most desperate, neediest people in the world. For the Indian Ocean earthquake, the world reached out with $14 billion of humanitarian aid.[9] For Haiti, the amount pledged totaled about $9.5 billion.[10]

The logistical challenges of administering emergency aid are often massive.

Most relief groups don't have sufficient operations in the affected areas, so they must build up their operations to deliver aid in the scale needed to distribute such massive amounts of donations. Further, the local infrastructure is often destroyed, and it is difficult to work effectively without decent roads or regular electricity. There are countless uncoordinated relief efforts. For example, a year after the Haitian earthquake, there had been disproportionate resources devoted to temporary housing, but little had been allocated to removing the rubble. As a result, it remained almost impossible to travel around Port-au-Prince, which limited the effectiveness of almost all other forms of aid.[11] Even three years after the event, half the debris has yet to be removed.[12]

While many people are often driven to donate to disaster relief efforts because of the horrific images shown in the media, elsewhere in the world, 19,000 children die every day of preventable causes, mostly related to extreme poverty. Leif Wenar, chair of ethics at King's College, notes that "from a human perspective, severe poverty should be the top story in every newspaper, every newscast, and every news website, every day."[13] But the news media doesn't often cover this because unchanging conditions aren't news, so we forget that the tragedies are just as real. And more important for donors, gifts to developmental charities that focus on extreme poverty and related humanitarian issues may be more effective at helping the needy than those dedicated to disaster relief. In fact, disaster relief is known to be a less efficient form of assistance than many other forms of developmental international aid. This is not just with respect to saving lives, but also supporting education, health, and economic empowerment. It is quite ironic that after disasters, we see countless photos and video accounts in the media as well as encouragement to donate to disaster relief, with rarely a mention that most experts generally agree that donations focusing on developmental aid in non-disaster areas can be much more effective, dollar-for-dollar, at helping people. This is not to imply that the tsunami and earthquake victims should not receive any aid. Rather, they already receive a lot of aid, so when do-bester donors consider the incremental impact of their giving, additional support for disaster relief usually isn't as impactful as everyday developmental aid.[14]

Do-bester donors who feel an emotional desire to respond to terrible images of a disaster they see in the media may still want to do something. In those cases, they may consider an unrestricted donation to an organization that does both disaster relief and developmental aid. There are many of these types of organizations, especially since so many donors prefer to earmark donations for their preferred type of aid. If the donor can find a strong organization that he or she believes will allocate money with a do-bester philosophy, it may be a reasonable balance between the donor's emotional needs and a do-bester philosophy to give an organization an unrestricted gift that lets it determine the areas of greatest need. As offensive as it may be to evaluate life-and-death decisions based on financial efficiencies, it remains an important decision criterion as long as those 19,000 preventable deaths are still occurring daily. Disaster relief will remain relatively well funded from typical donors, and do-besters should focus on more efficient forms of help.

Smart Approach 6: Proactively search for your donation's recipient.

The philanthropy convention discussed in the beginning of this chapter, though imaginary, represents a very tangible reality of what donors do when deciding where to direct their efforts. With over a million nonprofit organizations in the United States alone, most do-besters will find it challenging to know where to start. The vast choices can be overwhelming. What should you do?

Most people take the easy route: they support what they know. They look for local organizations. They support health-related causes that have touched their own lives, either directly or through close friends and family. They support organizations that someone they know is involved in. They donate to the arts they cherish and the universities they attended. Or some simply donate to a subset of the organizations that ask them for money. These are the areas they already know, have interest in, and directly and personally can see how the results improve the world.

"Out of sight, out of mind" is exactly what happens to all the other causes. Certainly it is more admirable to help someone than no one, but is that really a good reason for donors to support whatever interests them and to largely ignore all of the tough questions discussed earlier in this book?

There are advantages to a system in which everyone donates to causes that have affected them personally. In addition to helping maintain motivated donors, it doesn't require complex global comparisons of expected impact. The system is also somewhat democratic in that the dollars that flow to causes are related to the number of people they impact. So we'd naturally expect that the American Heart Association would get more donations than the Illinois Support for Encounter Experiencers, which offers support for those who believe that they have had contact with UFOs and non-human intelligences.

A downside of this type of democracy, however, is that people vote with their dollars donated, so only the people with enough money to donate get to vote. That means the Harvard Business School has a pretty big advantage over a health clinic in rural Rwanda. This type of giving is very different from helping those most needy, as financially disadvantaged groups have difficulty raising funds for their causes. Further, the donations tend to be allocated according to the problems that affect people with the means to donate, which are not necessarily the most solvable. For example, the health-related illnesses that cause the most deaths (e.g., cardiovascular disease or cancer) are not the same as the ones that cause the most preventable deaths (e.g., malaria or dehydration from diarrhea). This is part of the reason why St. Jude's is better funded that the Malanje Provincial Hospital.

Another problem with starting with the donor's interests and passions is that it results in giving patterns directed where the donor has intimate life experiences—or at least has seen graphic images in the media, as with natural disasters—not necessarily those where the need is greatest or the solutions are most reachable. This is one of the reasons why donors tend to give to the universities they attended, organizations where they know someone involved, or to medical causes that affected their families. These may all be good causes, but donors are limiting their own effectiveness by not expanding the search beyond their life experiences or the organizations that have solicited them.

As a result, for most donors interested in having the greatest impact, it is imperative to proactively look for their donation's recipient. The organizations with the greatest impact are unlikely to be top of mind. Rather, donors must search for the greatest needs and potential solutions, asking critical questions, to find the organizations most worthy of donations.

Smart Approach 7: Be cautious when considering programs that appear to be designed around maximizing the donor's experience, as they are probably sacrificing impact.

Because so many donors tend to give based on what they know rather than follow Smart Approach 6, many charitable organizations seeking donations cater to this type of donor. They are perpetually trying to create awareness among donors and engage and inspire them.

For example, DonorsChoose.org allows individual teachers to write descriptions of the projects they would like funded. Those descriptions are reviewed for reasonableness and authenticity, then posted. Individual donors can browse the menu of project requests and choose the projects they want to support. DonorsChoose.org directly purchases the supplies needed and sends them to the teacher, alerting the school principal that they are on the way to minimize the possibility of fraud. The peer-to-peer nature of this structure not only imposes a significant amount of embedded costs (in both dollars and time), but also implicitly constrains the type of things donors can fund. That is, the structure of the charity can only accommodate isolated projects from individual teachers.

While structuring programs around the types of things that motivate donors can generate large amounts of donations very quickly—DonorsChoose.org grew from infancy in 2000 to generating over $30 million per year in 2010 and 2011, and topping $46 million in 2012[15]—the impact per dollar is lower. It is a worthwhile issue to consider the relative merits of greater donations with lower per-dollar impact or vice versa, but that question is more relevant for people running nonprofits. For do-bester donors, the question is about how to maximize the impact of their gifts.

DonorsChoose.org is only one of many organizations that structure their programs around the donors' emotions.

- Child sponsorship organizations send donors pictures and updates about the child.
- Some organizations make sure donors meet recipients, or at least have some interaction with them.
- Many organizations sponsor various forms of donor social events for fundraising, such as charity balls and athletic events.

All of these practices are intended to engage donors in order to keep their wallets open. And all of them have costs. These costs are both explicit, such as fundraising expenses, as well as implicit, from efficiency losses, because the organizations best at engaging donors are not necessarily those whose programs are best.

Donors must recognize these issues to balance meeting their own needs and those of the recipients. Unfortunately, most donors start the process with the deck stacked against balanced decision making. Donors tend to come from the world's wealthiest countries, and often the wealthiest communities in those countries, so their life experiences are very different from those of the neediest people in the world. Further, many of the organizations that are best at helping others may not be good at engaging donors. In fact, there may be a negative correlation between helping others and engaging donors because the most underserved causes tend to be those that wealthy donors have difficulty relating to. So donors should be aware of their own natural tendencies and be cautiously skeptical of those charities designed around enhancing their experience.

Smart Approach 8: When comparing new innovations versus scaling up proven ones, the new innovation must have the potential to be significantly better than the best existing solution.

One fundamental issue for do-besters is whether to invest in scaling up proven solutions or innovating to find the next generation of do-bester solutions. In that debate, it is often tempting for many do-besters to favor innovation. The temptation lies in the vision of leverage via innovation—the impact of a successful innovation could be massive, as others would then fund the programs that have been proven to work.

Imagine funding a research grant that results in finding a cancer treatment that, for only $10,000 per patient, would cure a significant percentage of patients, including those who were previously viewed as hopeless. Many would consider this the holy grail of cancer research—it would almost certainly be viewed as wildly successful by anyone giving to this cause. However, many researchers believe that it is already possible to save lives in the developing world for much less, likely between $200 and $2,000 per life, using the most effective solutions that already exist.[16] So even if the cancer research achieved success beyond what most people could imagine, it is still not as good as the best life-saving solution that currently exists. And that shouldn't be surprising—we already have some extremely effective (and cost-effective) solutions that are not being implemented broadly throughout the world.

Further, innovation involves a higher risk of failure. Doing something that hasn't been done before, or even introducing a tried-and-true solution to a new geography or culture, has uncertainties that increase the odds of an unsuccessful outcome. Further, for an innovation to be truly valuable, it must result in something both new and better than existing methods. While innovation should definitely be in the toolkit of any do-bester, its potential should be compared to the best available existing solution to determine if it is worth the risk.

Smart Approach 9: Balance the benefits of research and evaluation with the costs to yourself and potential recipient organizations.

It is not easy to be a do-bester. Following your passions is not enough. Evaluating the many different causes, organizations, and projects takes a tremendous amount of time and effort. There may be a temptation to overdo it.

While it makes sense to consider multiple organizations and ask for reports or evidence of impact, it's important to realize that the time and energy charities spend compiling this information diverts resources from program services. This issue is even greater when potential donors are asking for customized reports and presentations. Researching charities is not an academic exercise of seeking the "right" answer by using whatever resources are available. Rather, a balance should be sought between the additional accuracy from deeper research and the cost of that research, to both the donor as well as the organizations being researched.

There are several ways to do this. First, it is important to find an effective way to narrow down the list of potential recipients of your donations to a reasonable number of finalists. The maximum size of the list will vary by donor, depending on how large their donations may be—a billion-dollar foundation will obviously need to have a greater number of finalists (and eventual recipients) than an individual donor planning to give away $1,000. Earlier chapters have discussed ways to narrow down the lists of causes and organizations. Finding a few role models or a charity evaluator you believe in may be very helpful in this step. (I have used GiveWell for this purpose.) Exclusive use of this method makes the donor more of a follower than leader, which means the donor is less likely to become one of the seed funders for the "next big thing." This is appropriate for smaller donors with proportionately smaller research budgets. Large, institutional donors with significant evaluation capabilities may want to cast a wider net.

Once a manageable number of finalists is selected, it becomes necessary to dive deeper. Rather than asking for customized reports with all the information that you think appropriate, it may be better to ask for the off-the-shelf reports that are provided to other potential donors or for internal evaluations. Not only does this provide information about the organizations' impact, it also gives a better indication of how these organizations run their programs. Not all organizations will have such information, but organizations that monitor and measure their results should have them. Further, organizations that are seeking donations from impact-minded donors should also have them, although it's important to understand the difference between reports designed to show favorable results to donors and those that show accurate results for understanding and improving what is happening in the field.

Another strategy to streamline the research requirements is to talk with other funders or charity evaluators about the research and evaluation they have done, thus reducing the need to reinvent the wheel.

Ultimately, it will become necessary to get comfortable making decisions with a degree of uncertainty. Perfect conclusions from research and evaluations are more rare than unicorns, so donors will simply need to manage their own expectations when doing research. The benefits of research and evaluation are substantial, but they must still be compared relative to their costs in determining the most appropriate level of resources to devote to such activities.

Smart Approach 10: Don't meddle with the organizations you support, as you decided to give to them because you believe they are the best at what they do.

Although each of the first nine of the approaches in this chapter required a meaningful amount of effort or critical thinking, the final approach is the polar opposite. Once you've selected the best organizations and people for your donation, you should be confident that they are successfully applying their do-bester values to allocate your gift optimally. It's time for you to stay out of their way.

This is one of the most difficult things to do for many donors, especially those who are very knowledgeable about their chosen causes and charities. In an article titled "Letting Go," Hewlett Foundation staff members Kristi Kimball and Malka Kopell offer advice for many professional donors at foundations:

> We would probably be better off as a society if the decision makers in the nation's largest private foundations took up surfing. Why? Because surfing is about letting go, and that's what foundations must do to achieve higher impact. . . . Too often, funders insist on controlling the ways in which social problems are solved.[17]

That is, many donors want to tell the organizations they fund what programs to pursue, how to operate those programs, and how to measure and evaluate them. If these donors are willing to give enough money, they typically get their way. And even when the recipient organizations would prefer to do things differently, their desire to maintain the flow of funds often causes them to smile and thank the donor for the instructions. But are such detailed instructions necessary when donors believe in the mission, organization, and people they are supporting? Micromanaging talented, competent teams is rarely the way to deliver strong results.

That doesn't mean donors can't ask questions or that charities don't have an obligation for a certain level of donor stewardship. But this is different from donors telling charities how to run their programs or requiring them to write lengthy, customized evaluation reports. Donors should be aware of this slippery slope, as many charities have a tendency to coddle donors and spend significant efforts responding to their perceived needs and suggestions. One of the greatest gifts you can give a charity is the freedom to do what they believe is necessary to succeed, as their skill in doing that is likely what led you to choose them in the first place.

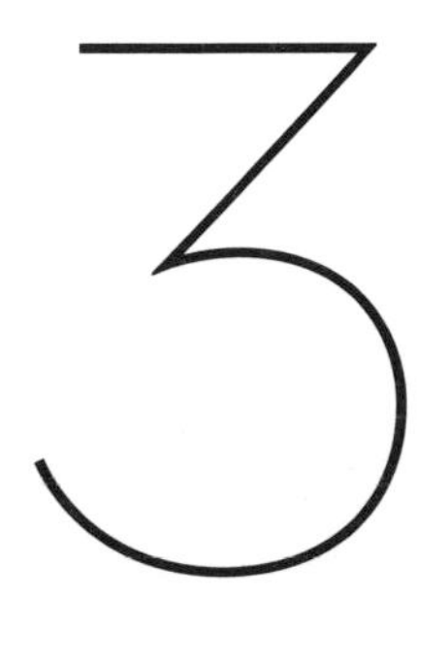

FINAL THOUGHTS

15

The Selfish Giver in All of Us

When I do good, I feel good; when I do bad, I feel bad. That's my religion.
—Abraham Lincoln[1]

Dinakar Singh and his wife, Loren Eng, found out that their daughter, Arya, had an untreatable, incurable genetic disease in 2001, when she was only nineteen months old. Arya had spinal muscular atrophy (SMA), which would cause her muscles to gradually deteriorate. Depending on the severity, the range of capabilities this disease limits almost definitely includes playing sports, probably walking, and possibly even breathing.

SMA is almost always caused by a defect in the survival motor neuron 1 (SMN1) gene that encodes the SMN protein. That protein is necessary to survive, as it is responsible for motor neurons in the spinal cord that handle muscle contraction. Fortunately, there is a "backup" gene, SMN2, that produces a limited amount of the SMN protein. This backup gene is the reason why Arya was able to live at all.[2] Some scientists believe SMN2 is a promising candidate for researching treatments, as scientists might be able to find a way to boost production of the protein through the backup gene. But because SMA is relatively rare compared with diseases like cancer and Alzheimer's, it was only receiving about $3 to $5 million per year of the government's $20 billion budget for medical research.[3]

Singh and Eng, like most parents, would do almost anything to help their child. But financially, they are not like most other parents. Singh founded and runs the hedge fund TPG-Axon Capital Management LP, reported to have $8.1 billion in assets.[4] That's not all their money, but nevertheless, it should come as no surprise that the head of a multibillion-dollar hedge fund has above average resources for philanthropy.

The couple founded the Spinal Muscular Atrophy Foundation, which had spent over $100 million by early 2013 to accelerate the development of a treatment for SMA.[5] "I was fearful and anxious that treatments would be developed, but far too late to save Arya. We didn't want to find out 25 years later that the science was really there but there isn't a drug because nobody focused on it," Singh told *Bloomberg Markets*.[6]

"I would put every penny I make from the fund into this [research] if I thought it would help the odds of a cure—in fact, I suspect we won't be far from that," Singh commented.[7] "I don't think there is a budget on your daughter's life. As long as there is a chance of doing something and we have the ability to do it, we will do it."[8]

Although the SMA Foundation has the same 501(c)(3) tax exempt status as most charities in the United States, in many ways it could be considered an extremely costly health care expense that a very wealthy couple is spending on their child. This is an example of dedicated parents and great family values. Others with SMA may be benefiting, but that could simply be a positive byproduct. This blend of philanthropy (helping others) versus consumption (medical care for a family member) is simply an extreme example of giving based on the donor's personal interests.

Most of this book has been describing a do-bester approach. To reinvent philanthropy, it is important to go a step further in accurately characterizing the philanthropic sector. There should be a clearer, more well-established distinction between approaches rooted in do-bester principles and those engineered around the donor's interests.

Recall the discussion in chapter 5 on JPMorgan Chase's corporate philanthropy program, Chase Community Giving, in which they teamed up with Facebook to allocate millions of dollars to charities selected through voting popularity contests ("crowdsourcing"). After continuing the program for a few years and giving away over $18 million to five hundred charities, in December 2011 Chase gave this program a higher public profile. They copresented the *American Giving Awards*, a two-hour prime-time special on

NBC, awarding grants totaling $2 million to five nonprofits.[9] The recipients were selected by the 3.3 million Facebook users who tagged themselves as "fans" of Chase Community Giving.

The television special had a star-studded cast, as it was hosted by Bob Costas and included performances by will.i.am and Rodney Atkins as well as appearances by Colin Farrell and Miley Cyrus. The red carpet was rolled out for both celebrities and representatives from the charities. Viewers were constantly reminded, throughout the broadcast as well as in the eight 30-second commercial spots Chase purchased, that Chase was bankrolling the donations. Sprawled along the bottom of the logo for the event were the words "presented by Chase."

Although the show appeared to be well received by most of its 1.5 million viewers,[10] a few pundits were skeptical of JPMorgan Chase's motives. *PR Watch*'s Lisa Graves described the event to the *New York Times* as a "greed-washing campaign to score P.R. points."[11]

When asked whether the show was an advertisement, an NBC spokeswoman said, "No. It's a show about charitable giving."[12] Despite this, JPMorgan Chase's head of corporate marketing, Carter Franke, was speaking about it on behalf of the company. In an interview with the *New York Times*, she noted that one of the key parties responsible for the show was Intersport, a marketing agency for Chase. When asked about whether she was concerned about large-scale negative reactions from viewers, Franke said, "Hopefully, viewers are going to see that there are some wonderful charities out there doing strong things with the help and support of Chase."[13]

Is JPMorgan Chase spinning an advertising campaign, using (abusing?) the face of charities to its own advantage? Is it incentivizing charities to run massive "get out the vote" campaigns to win their donations while singing praise of JPMorgan Chase, diverting the charities' attention from the very programs Chase claims to support? Or is the bank simply raising awareness of its own role in the community as well as bringing attention to charities and the important issues they are addressing?

The truth probably lies between the extremes. Chase probably wants its giving to have a positive impact, but the corporation's primary reason for existence is to make money for its shareholders, and it would be naïve to suggest that this does not fit into its motives. A positive image indirectly translates into higher profits. Many philanthropy gurus believe that corporate philanthropy should be aligned with corporate interests, as such a

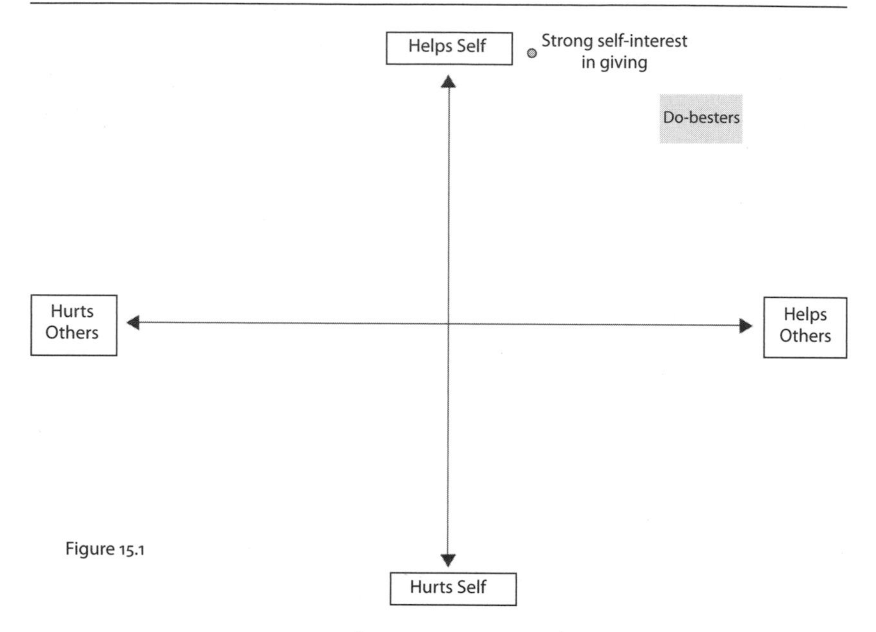

Figure 15.1

win-win situation is the best (and possibly only) way for most companies to justify continuing to give. To what extent is this truly philanthropy (helping others) versus simply doing what it takes to run a successful business? Does it matter?

Chase Community Giving has a lot in common with the philanthropy of Dinakar Singh and his wife, Loren Eng: both have a self-interest component to their giving. For Singh and Eng, it is the health of their daughter. For Chase, it is their corporate bottom line. Figure 15.1 illustrates where this kind of giving belongs on the Axis of Altruism.

Philanthropy with a self-interest component lies farther north of gifts from most other donors, both do-gooders and do-besters. What these donors have at stake is tremendously important for them. This blend of philanthropy and self-interest is like an extreme example of giving based on the donor's personal interests—the benefits to the donor are much more tangible than in the case of do-gooders donating to causes that give them the greatest emotional benefits. The self-interested donors have much more at stake than simply feeling good about helping others. It may be more accurate to characterize this as "enlightened self-interest" rather than philanthropy.

This isn't to imply that giving as enlightened self-interest is wrong. Quite the contrary—it can still help make the world a better place, so there will always be a place for this type of donor in the philanthropic landscape. But it is different from philanthropy whose primary purpose is to help others, and that is likely to reflect in the impact their donations have on the world. In the case of Singh and Eng, they choose the illness that is affecting their family, rather than considering whether focusing on other illnesses might be able to provide greater benefit to the world. In the case of Chase Community Giving, grantees are selected with a popularity contest rather than an impact assessment. Both donors are making the world a better place, just not as much as they could.

Not only do these two examples have similarities, they are only slightly different from most do-gooders, who impose impeding constraints on their giving to express their own personal interests and passions. These do-gooders focus their giving on geographic regions they like rather than the ones with the greatest need, diseases that have touched their lives rather than those with the greatest opportunities for impact, universities they have attended rather than those that could use the gifts better, and art museums rather than just about anything else. They get emotional benefits from these impeding constraints, in contrast to do-besters, who get emotional benefits primarily from knowing they are doing their best to help others. Figure 15.2 compares the do-gooders and do-besters on the Axis of Altruism.

It is not a problem when people and corporations voluntarily use their money in this way—there are many worse things they could be doing. This approach is a combination of helping others and meeting the donor's needs. The latter is not that different from consumption—spending your money on something that benefits you. There is a role for this type of self-interested giving, just as there is a role for emotional giving. In many ways, most do-gooder donors are "purchasing" the warm glow of emotions they get from giving to their favorite causes. This is much more productive for society than if they purchased a fancy car or went on an extravagant vacation that didn't help anyone else.

However, the warm glow is only possible when donors believe they are helping others. Giving to a wasteful and incompetent charity wouldn't make a donor feel good unless he didn't know it was wasteful and incompetent. Choosing to give to an average charity instead of a top-tier one is similar. Do-gooders only get the warm glow if they don't realize that they are sacrificing impact to satisfy their own emotional needs. It is ironic that donors' emotional needs are only satisfied by prioritizing helping others

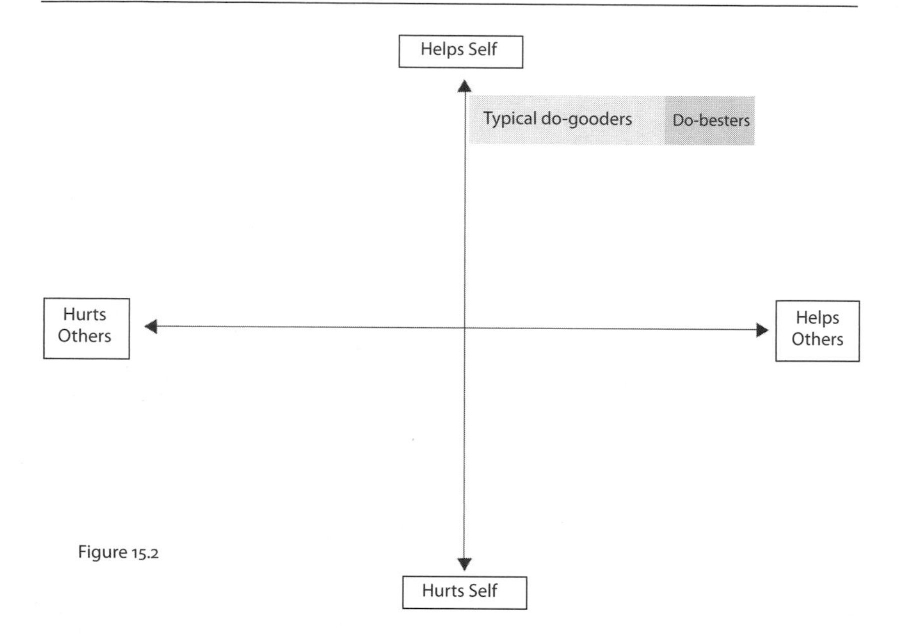

Figure 15.2

over satisfying their own emotional needs. Do-gooders may simply be do-besters who don't know any other way.

One of the reasons so many donors don't know any other way may be because society isn't intellectually honest about different styles of giving. It doesn't adequately differentiate typical donors from do-besters. Society doesn't reserve greater praise for donors who try to prioritize giving to help others over what will help the donor, nor does it tell donors that they should feel a greater emotional warm glow when their giving is focused exclusively on helping others. While one might expect this from the average person, it is fair to demand a higher standard of intellectual rigor from those deeply involved in philanthropy: major donors, foundations, academics, etc. But even they usually don't provide an intellectually honest assessment of philanthropy.

For example, the vast majority of multimillion-dollar gifts are not directed toward the most effective causes: of the ninety-five gifts over $1 million made in 2012, thirty-seven were to colleges and universities (mostly the ones the donors attended); nine were for hospitals and medical centers (not ones like the Malanje Provincial Hospital); and fifteen went to museums, libraries, arts groups, and historic preservation.[14] Yet there is minimal differentiation in the levels of public praise they receive.

As another example, after every natural disaster, expert voices in giving are quoted in newspapers across the country advocating for people to donate to relief efforts, but few ever say that disaster relief is a much less efficient way to help people than everyday developmental aid. Even the charities that focus on developmental aid don't say it, possibly because they are worried about negative publicity. And finally, as discussed throughout this book, the dominant approach recommended by "experts" in philanthropy is that donors should put significant emphasis on their personal interests and passions. (And in my own experience, they often seem confused when I suggest that there may be a different—possibly better—way.)

This lack of intellectual integrity—not differentiating do-gooders from do-besters—is a root cause for many of the aspects of philanthropy that need reinventing. The reason for this stems from a major motivation driving people to give: feeling good about helping others. For do-besters, this feeling is fully earned. But do-gooders will only get this feeling if they are deluded into thinking that their giving is primarily directed to help others—they wouldn't feel as good about their giving if they were fully aware that the impact of their giving was reduced because of their own personal motives. The lack of intellectual honesty about differentiating do-gooders from do-besters enables do-gooders to get the warm glow without actually doing very much good. Conversely, greater intellectual integrity within the philanthropy community would likely facilitate more desire among donors to shift their giving toward causes that are less personal and more impactful. In essence, many donors will give to whatever areas provide them the best warm glow, so changing the criteria for public praise and how we think about who deserves the warm glow would actually change how people donate. If we reinvent the way we think and talk about philanthropy, it is likely to cause a domino effect that changes giving itself.

Although an argument can be made that there is a moral imperative to donate like a do-bester, this book is not trying to make such an argument. It would need to be very nuanced and address not only how people give, but also how much.[15] In fact, I don't believe that most do-bester philanthropists are morally superior to do-gooders. Remember that do-besters are in the far northeastern corner of the Axis of Altruism. Just as Singh and Eng's giving can be thought of as purchasing health care for their daughter and Chase Community Giving is largely a public relations program, many do-besters are simply "consuming" the warm glow from feeling good about their giving. And many do-besters get a tremendous amount of emotional benefit from this giving. This is part of our humanity, and we should embrace it to unleash its power to improve philanthropy and make the world a better place.

Though not necessarily morally superior to do-gooders, do-besters may be intellectually superior—at least, with respect to the rigor with which they think about their giving. They are connecting their heads and hearts, so they have more passion for giving when they have conviction that their money is doing the most good.

These characteristics of do-besters are not genetically wired. Anyone who gives because of the warm glow they get when helping others should be willing to adjust their giving if they discover a way to help others more. It is in their own self-interest to maximize their emotional benefits from giving. Of course, some people donate for reasons other than the warm glow, and others will not be persuaded even if presented with a strong argument. But many will—if we reinvent philanthropy in a way that is more intellectually honest.

This means being open about the impact of donors constraining their giving to areas of personal interest. It means being willing to prioritize the various options for giving. It means thinking about all donors—from do-besters to corporate philanthropy departments—based on a fair assessment of what they are doing, why, and the likely impact of their actions on others. And it means trying to give a reasonable assessment of the relative merits of choices like donating to St. Jude and the Malanje Provincial Hospital.

This book does not provide a single, simple answer to how to give money; rather, it is meant to help donors rigorously think about the challenges in giving. While philanthropy isn't going to completely "reinvent" itself overnight, change will come one donor at a time, learning to be honest with themselves about their own giving.

16

Philanthropy Reinvented

> The test of a first rate philanthropist is the ability
> to use their head and their heart at the same time
> and still retain the ability to function.
>
> —Sean Stannard-Stockton[1]

There is a perverse system in philanthropy: the charities that survive are the ones that satisfy the donors, not necessarily the ones that are effective at their core mission. That is, and will always be, the case. Some people have told me that there's no point in trying to reinvent philanthropy—donors won't change their behavior. The reasons they've cited include the following:

- Donors and nonprofits are already doing a good job maximizing impact; there's no need for anything to be reinvented.
- The moral implications are too burdensome, appearing to require an almost superhuman level of self-control and sacrifice.
- People are too emotional; philanthropy will never be as heartless as seemingly required by the do-bester approach.
- It is too time-consuming and difficult to be a do-bester; this book doesn't present a simple step-by-step process for deciding where to give.

I don't expect there's much chance to completely reverse the practices of philanthropy that donors have been applying for decades, but I am not as cynical as the naysayers about making incremental progress. Let's consider these points one by one.

1. Donors and nonprofits are already doing a good job maximizing impact; there's no need for anything to be reinvented.

How impactful can the most effective nonprofits be relative to the typical ones? As an example, there have been several studies analyzing the cost to save a life in various places and with different interventions. Although the world's most effective charities can save a life for between $200 and $2,000, the median life-saving intervention in America costs about $2.2 million.[2] The ultra-cheap ways to save lives are funding things like mosquito nets to prevent malaria, measles immunizations, and clean water—things that typically don't get funded by donors who choose their area of giving emotionally. Most people from developed countries don't relate to these causes because we don't often know people who have died of malaria, measles, or unsanitary water. The difference between the impact of do-gooders and do-besters can be several orders of magnitude.

This is not to imply that do-besters must focus on saving lives, but simply to illustrate the relative cost-effectiveness of different causes. Comparing these to education, the environment, human rights, hunger, and other interventions is an extremely important part of the process—and one that will also yield large differences between typical charities and the most effective ones.

2. The moral implications are too burdensome, requiring an almost superhuman level of self-control and sacrifice.

Though there are certainly moral undertones to many of the issues discussed in this book, there should not be a moral imperative for philanthropists to attempt to become absolute do-besters. Nor should there be a moral imperative for people to donate every dime of their disposable income. While it is okay for people to spend their money on things other than necessities, those with more money than they need should help others. There is a lot of gray area in assessing the level of such obligations and the appropriate balance between spending on oneself and helping others.[3]

Philanthropy is one way people can fulfill their obligations to help others. Those with a do-bester approach are purely focused on maximizing the benefits of others, while those with a do-gooder approach are typically trying to balance helping others with connecting to their individual emotional passions. Giving in a way that reduces the impact to others in order for the donor to get those emotional benefits is a combination of helping others and consumption.

Ironically, a do-bester donor can actually donate less than a do-gooder donor and fulfill the same obligation to help others, because the do-bester's donations are doing more to help others. Do-gooders need to donate much more to have a comparable impact. In my experience, however, donors passionate about a do-bester philosophy tend not to use this as an excuse to donate less, but rather a reason why they choose to donate more. Regardless, the moral implications of a do-bester approach are not necessarily more burdensome than that of other approaches.

3. People are too emotional; philanthropy will never be as heartless as seemingly required by the do-bester approach

The do-bester approach may not be for every donor, but a donor doesn't have to be emotionless to subscribe to it. Most donors are not masochists. They enjoy giving money away, deriving pleasure from helping others. This is why people feel good about themselves when giving. Do-besters are no different, other than being more aware of whether and how much they are helping. A do-bester who knowingly chose to give to an "average" cause instead of a "top" cause would not get as good of a feeling. Some might actually get a bad feeling from "wasting" money. Do-besters may simply be more knowledgeable and aware versions of do-gooders. A reinvented world of philanthropy should not be about all head and no heart, but about doing a better job of focusing on what many people's hearts want to do: help others. It is not cold and calculating, but warm and smart. And ironically, it may lead to even greater emotional benefits from giving because do-besters will have more conviction in the impact of their giving, as illustrated in figure 16.1.

4. It is too time-consuming and difficult to be a do-bester; this book doesn't present a simple step-by-step process for deciding where to give.

This may be the most damning of the four criticisms, claiming that the approach this book recommends is not implementable for most donors. The reality is that it is a lot easier to donate to an average charity than it is to evaluate which charity is likely to have the greatest impact. A simple

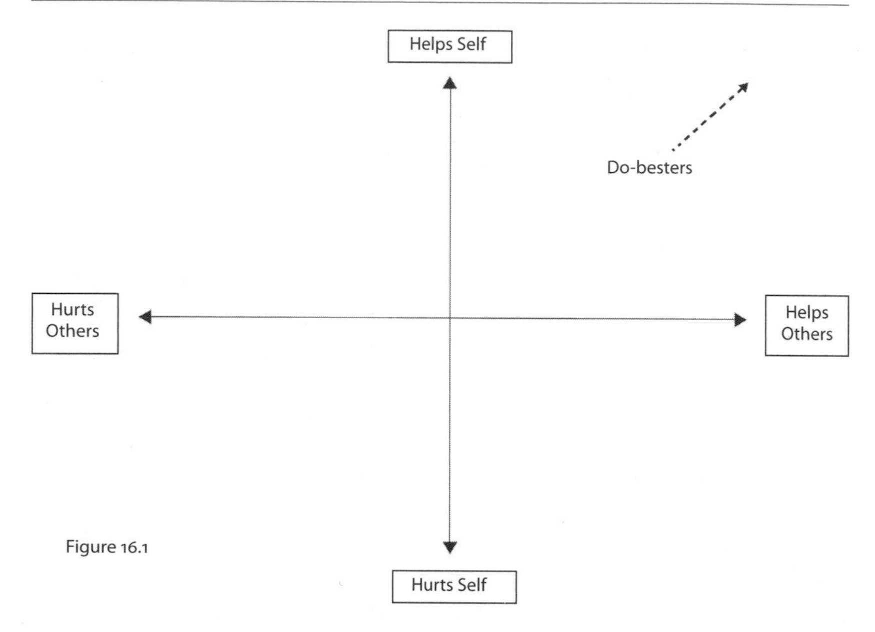

Figure 16.1

how-to manual with a step-by-step process wouldn't accurately portray the complexity of the decisions donors face. There is no single best approach, philosophy, cause, or charity. In short, a simple solution would be disingenuous. However, presenting only complex, difficult solutions is not practical. Some donors simply don't have the time or interest to dedicate to their giving. They just want their giving to be extremely impactful. For them, a simple, practical solution is needed. *The solution: Get someone else to do the hard work.*

Buffett did it by giving his money to the Gates Foundation. The choices Gates made about how to set up his foundation, who to hire, which causes to focus on, and which organizations to support represent a composite of all of his beliefs. Gates and Buffett are both thoughtful individuals. They must have agreed on many aspects of philanthropy in order for Buffett to give his life savings to the Gates Foundation, but it is unlikely that they agree on everything. While Buffett has some influence as a board member and was able to give direction about how his donation is used, ultimately he delegated so much responsibility to Gates that he almost assuredly is incorporating aspects of Gates's beliefs that he doesn't share. That is the sacrifice that Buffett made in taking the simple solution. He wanted to spend his time running Berkshire Hathaway rather than thinking about every issue in philanthropy (and due to the sheer amount of his giving, he has more issues to consider than most of us), so he adopted Gates's belief set as his own. One of the biggest problems with the simple solution is that donors can't always pick and choose the specific, shared views of whoever they get to "do the work" for them.

In Buffett's case, Gates wasn't the only option he had to get others to make decisions for him. Surely there were plenty of other foundations that would have taken his money. But he chose the one that he thought would do the best job. Similarly, GiveWell built itself around helping donors make these decisions. And many foundations publish lists of their grantees in hopes of encouraging others to give to them. So donors who want to be do-besters can limit their time commitments by making only one decision: who to piggyback.

What might the profile of the future generations of do-besters look like? To answer this, it is helpful to start with an understanding of why people enter the world of philanthropy. For most, they get into philanthropy for emotional reasons. Maybe they saw reports of the 2004 Asian tsunami, Haitian earthquake, or some other natural disaster on television. Or maybe they want to "give back" to return the favor of those who gave them a schol arship to college. Professionals in the nonprofit sector may have decided that a career of helping others would be more fulfilling than one focused on profit. Or a donor may live in an urban area and just feel uncomfortable seeing the plight of the homeless every day on their commute to work. Maybe someone's religious beliefs inspired them to help others. There are many reasons people enter the philanthropy ranks, and usually it is a decision that comes from the heart. This is how it started for me and for most of the people I know involved in philanthropy.

Greenhorns in philanthropy are unlikely to immediately adopt a do-bester approach. But as people become more experienced, their thoughts advance. They not only want to help others, but are also learning how to do it. This is often when they become more focused on the complexities of generating impact. They start to really think about where they donate and learn more about other opportunities—transitioning from all heart to a balance of head and heart. Most donors learn a lot from their initial experiences, often changing course. For example, many people transition from an emphasis on domestic poverty and health issues to a more global approach as they learn more about the most cost-effective interventions.

This is when the concept of the do-bester is something that becomes more realistic. Do-besters tend to be experienced donors and members of the nonprofit community with at least one of the following characteristics:

- **Analytical:** Those with strong analytical tendencies will have a greater comfort adopting a do-bester philosophy.
- **Morally motivated:** People who give to charity because of a belief that this is a moral obligation are also likely to believe that their giving should help people as much as possible. Though there are many reasons to be morally motivated, there may be a large concentration of this type of person in some religious groups that emphasize the importance of charity and helping others. For example, some Christians may ask what type of philanthropy Jesus would practice, with their own behavior correlating to their answer.[4]
- **Well-traveled:** People who have traveled to poor parts of poor countries often see global poverty and health through a different lens, which can translate into their approach to giving.

Although certainly not all people with one of these characteristics will gravitate toward a do-bester approach, there may be enough to start gradually reinventing the philanthropic sector.

Almost everything in philanthropy originates with donors, because they decide which organizations and projects to fund. A large group of active donors with a do-bester philosophy, even if it is far from a majority, could substantially change the philanthropic sector. My vision for reinventing philanthropy involves three major improvements over how it is practiced today.

First, there should be a general acceptance of the do-bester philosophy as legitimate. Unfortunately, that is not the case today. The dominant view of today's "best practice" in philanthropy is that donors should let their personal interests and passions dictate major decisions such as how they select causes and geographies. This view is treated as a given axiom in almost every other book on philanthropy that has been published recently.[5] Almost all of the major consulting firms for philanthropists advocate a similar perspective as the standard for how donors should think. This implicitly rejects a more issue-agnostic, utilitarian goal of trying to provide the greatest help to the greatest number of people. Though the do-bester approach is often considered void of passion or too unfocused to be implemented, neither is true. This philosophy should be accepted as a legitimate way of approaching philanthropy, at least on par with the traditional approach.

Second, there should be better information on the impact of various charitable alternatives, and nonprofits should compete for donors based on their potential for impact. More donors would demand that nonprofits demonstrate that their programs work and are cost effective, and that proof would be documented transparently on their websites. Further, more charity evaluators would exist and focus on greater impact. The watchdog organizations like Charity Navigator, CharityWatch, and the Better Business Bureau would continue their trend of focusing less on the financial aspects of the organizations they rate, and increasing their emphasis on impact. There would also be more rigorous comparisons of different causes, as we saw with projects such as the Copenhagen Consensus. Further, there should be a stronger role for charity evaluators, like GiveWell, that include more subjectivity in their evaluations. Unlike the charity rating agencies, the evaluators would emphasize deep evaluations of a small number of organizations to try to identify the best ones. More of these charity evaluators would be formed, each with its own process and philosophy, so donors could have more options to consider.[6] These organizations would even have a certain amount of competition with each other for the attention of donors. Having this support system in place would make it easier to be a do-bester.

Third, with greater acceptance of the do-bester philosophy and greater resources for those types of donors, more philanthropic funds would go to the top organizations and most cost-effective solutions. Because there is a significant amount of subjectivity in determining these organizations and causes, there would be a range of causes and organizations funded by this emerging breed of donor. But those most often viewed as having the greatest potential and likelihood of succeeding would be well funded. Further, more of the gifts would be unrestricted, as the organizations will have earned the trust of donors to make the best decisions about how to use their funding.

We've looked at a lot of different examples and issues throughout this book, from the trade-offs between donating to St. Jude versus Malanje Provencial Hospital, to Warren Buffett's delegating his philanthropic decisions to the Gates Foundation, to the volunteering efforts of Amway Global and Google. Many of these are "anti-role models": people clearly doing what do-besters don't want to do. It is easy to find flaws in other people's giving processes, and hard to find processes without flaws. That is one reason why so many within mainstream philanthropy emphasize that philanthropy is about what donors are emotionally drawn to. Since there is no single "correct" answer, they say that donors can do whatever they want and imply that their actions are equally good. This is an easy solution to a difficult problem, but its validity is questionable.

If I were the parent of a child with cancer, I'd almost certainly want my child to have access to medical care as good as what is offered at St. Jude—hopefully they wouldn't penalize my child because of this book—and I'd want no expense spared for my child. I would want the best resources to be dedicated to my child, even if that might prevent those resources from going to others. But as a donor, I may prefer to give to Malanje Provincial Hospital over St. Jude if I think Malanje Provincial can make better use of my donation to help other people's children. This is not hypocritical. My motivation and decision criteria can (and should) be very different in the role of a relatively neutral donor than someone with a vested personal interest. This is often forgotten, though it is a central difference between philanthropy and consumption.

Putting together all the pieces of the do-besters puzzle is difficult—in fact, it is impossible. It is only a dream, a vision donors can try to make progress toward, but will never truly achieve. *Reinventing Philanthropy* is not about taking the emotion out of giving or finding an objective answer to solving the world's problems. Rather, it is about channeling the emotions and intellect of donors into a framework for better solutions. And donors who genuinely understand and embrace this approach will not only do better, they'll also feel better.

Epilogue

Shortly after I graduated from college and got a full-time job, I decided to start giving some of my earnings to charity. There wasn't a particular cause or organization I was initially drawn to, it just seemed like the right thing to do. After some thinking, I decided to focus on helping underprivileged kids break the poverty cycle. In retrospect, I don't know why I thought this was a better use of my money than any other charitable options, but I did. I didn't know how to accomplish this goal, but I figured that the charities who work in this space would know. I wasn't particularly proactive about identifying the right organization; even if I wanted to be proactive, I wouldn't have known where to start looking.

One day, I received a fundraising letter from an organization that takes homeless kids off the street, provides crisis care, and helps them turn their lives around. The letter told heart-wrenching stories about kids coming from the depths of despair, and how the nuns who ran the charity would help them get on track for a better life. As I read it, my emotions went from feeling horrible for these kids to realizing that I could help with a simple donation. Both the problem and the solution were right in front of me. I had not previously heard of the organization, and I'm not Catholic, either. But I figured that nuns were good people, and they seemed to know what they were doing. So I sent them a donation of $200. It felt great.

Then I got more and more letters from them, every couple of weeks. At first, the stories in these letters reaffirmed in my mind that I was giving to the right organization. But the frequency of these letters, along with the gifts they came with—books, stationery, return address labels, key chains, religious paraphernalia—made me start to question if I gave to a charity that was as good at helping people as it was at writing letters to donors.

I realized that I didn't know anything about this organization other than what I read in the letters they sent me. As the letters continued to arrive, I started to think it was a giant fundraising machine. I began to distrust them. I wasn't sure how much of my donation was getting to the people in need or whether this organization was actually good at helping them. I felt duped or at least unconfident about whether my donations were actually doing good.

I still wanted to continue my charitable giving. Nevertheless, I decided to stop giving until I had confidence that my gifts would be used effectively. I didn't know how I would do that, so other than a few gifts to schools I attended, I didn't donate much to anyone for several years.

About three years later, I took a vacation in India. Every day, I witnessed poverty worse than anything I had ever seen at home. Among the memories that remain etched in my mind, I remember waiting for a train one day. I bought a snack of three samosas from a street vendor for ten rupees—about a quarter. After I ate two, a barefoot, ragged boy, maybe three years old, approached me with his hand out, signaling that he wanted my last samosa. As I handed it to him, he jumped for joy and ran off with it. I watched him go to a group of three or four others, presumably family members, who then methodically split up the leftovers from my snack among themselves. While in India, I also saw people urinating and defecating outside because they lived in slum neighborhoods without toilets. And I saw children so poor that the fact that they didn't own shoes was the least of their family's concerns. I had seen plenty of poor people in America, but seeing poor people in a truly poor country is an entirely different experience. I left India with greater appreciation for global causes as well as a renewed urgency to restart my charitable giving.

I still had no idea how to figure out which charities were actually doing the most good. So despite the commitment I made to myself when I returned from India, my charitable giving stalled for another year.

When the Indian Ocean tsunami struck the day after Christmas in 2004, I, like most Americans, was horrified by the images on television. I could not look myself in the mirror if I stood on the sidelines any longer. Two days after the tsunami, I gave $1,000 to a well-known international aid agency. I didn't know if their programs were better than anyone else's, but I was more comfortable taking a chance than doing nothing. Once again, I didn't know if I did good, but I *felt* good.

Charitable giving got increased media attention after the tsunami, and I discovered the charity rating agencies like Charity Navigator and the American Institute of Philanthropy (now renamed CharityWatch), which rate charities based on their financial efficiency. I was not thrilled when I discovered that the recipient of my recent $1,000 gift got a C rating, but I was very happy with the new sources of information. I selected a few A-rated charities and started reviewing their websites. I gave a few thousand dollars to three of them to make sure they would take my inquiries seriously, and I contacted them directly with additional questions. I inquired about the most effective ways to help people and how I could evaluate their organizations and others. I was surprised that none had compelling responses when I asked why they were a better recipient of my donations than anyone else. But they were unprepared for the question—all said that they aren't typically asked those types of questions. It seemed odd to me that more people ask them about the percentage of their budgets allocated to fundraising and overhead than whether their programs are actually good. That may have been naïve, as I selected my finalist organizations partially because of their "A" ratings by a charity rating agency that focused primarily on financial efficiency. Nevertheless, the information the rating agencies provided was a giant leap forward from what I previously had.

One of the organizations pointed me to a conference for donors, and I found a few books on giving. While I didn't agree with a lot of what I heard and read, it helped me clarify my own views better, perform due diligence on organizations, and have the confidence to start donating more. It took me over six years to get to that point, and I continue to learn more and improve my giving.

While this book offers plenty of criticism of less effective philanthropic practices, I will be the first to admit that my own giving past has included many of the practices this book criticizes. My giving started firmly as a do-gooder, and over time I transitioned to an aspiring do-bester. I still make mistakes and have much to learn.

Many do-gooders are actually do-besters who don't know any other way, as I was several years ago. This book is trying to challenge readers to think differently to become more effective at improving the world. Donors have to hold themselves accountable, because nobody else will. Some people may be threatened and offended by this idea, but I ask readers to accept the commentary in this book in the spirit it was intended: To improve philanthropy. To save lives. To lift people out of poverty. To make the world a better place.

Sabrina's family can interpret this book as a threat to the ideas that saved her life, or they can interpret it as an attempt to save the lives of many other children. They should take it as a plea on behalf of the parents of Domingos, whose struggle has much in common with theirs, though a less fortunate ending. Volunteers can think of this as a criticism of how they want to spend their time, or as a way to help them spend their time more effectively. Nonprofit staff can take it as a threat to their work, or they can take it as an attempt to achieve a genuine partnership between them and the donor community to try to serve the world better. Consultants can interpret it as an attack on the ideology of their work, or as a challenge to better serve the philanthropic community.

I have written this book because philanthropy needs to be reinvented, but I don't have all the answers on how it should be done. Giving is both an art and an imperfect science, and every donor should expect to make mistakes in the course of their learning processes. Readers should not feel embarrassed or ashamed of past mistakes. As you gain greater knowledge about giving, you may transition from the blissful ignorance of feeling good about giving any gift to any good cause to having a greater sense of stewardship for your giving. Better decision making is likely to come as you become more thoughtful. It is up to the collective philanthropy community to continuously strive to improve.

The vast majority of the people in the philanthropic sector are good people and they want to help others, but their efforts are not reaching their potential. This is not just an opportunity for incremental improvement, but the potential to increase impact by orders of magnitude. Most of the flaws in philanthropy are not because people don't care. Rather, it is because they don't know how to do it better. This book is intended to inform and persuade people who want to improve their giving. I wrote it not just as a call to reinvent philanthropy, but to make it better.

Notes

1. A TALE OF TWO CHILDREN

1. Bjørn Lombord, *How to Spend $50 Billion to Make the World a Better Place* (New York: Cambridge University Press, 2006), xx.

2. The patient and family's names were changed for this book.

3. Quoted from a television fundraising special called *Fighting for Life*. This quote is taken from between minutes 30 and 33.

4. See "Quick Facts about St. Jude," St. Jude, http://www.stjude.org/stjude/v/index.jsp?vgnextoid=434d1976d1e70110VgnVCM1000001e0215acRCRD&vgnextchannel=ee58ebc7a7319210VgnVCM1000001e0215acRCRD (here and thereafter, all URLs last accessed April 2013).

5. See Kathy L. Gilbert, "Malaria, Poverty Kill Children," NothingButNets.net, Mar. 23, 2007, http://www.nothingbutnets.net/blogs/malaria-poverty-kill.html; and Gilbert, "Malaria, Poverty Kill Children in Angola," United Methodist Church, Oct. 5, 2006, http://www.umc.org/site/c.gjJTJbMUIuE/b.2122873/k.174A/Malaria_poverty_kill_children_in_Angola.htm.

6. For a thoughtful discussion of many of these moral issues in philanthropy, I recommend Peter Singer's book *The Life You Can Save* (New York: Random House, 2009).

2. FAILINGS OF PHILANTHROPY

1. Quoted in "The Business of Giving" (interview with Matthew Bishop), *The Economist*, Feb. 23, 2006, http://www.economist.com/node/5517605.

2. As of August 31, 2012. Stanford University, *Stanford University Annual Financial Report for the Years Ended August 31, 2012 and 2011*, http://bondholder-information.stanford.edu/pdf/AR_FinancialReview_2012.pdf.

3. On a number of occasions, the university has directly addressed this concern by explaining that it continues to need donations because income from its endowment covers only a fraction of its operating costs. While I understand this rationale,

I find it unpersuasive. By comparison, I believe that other nonprofits are in greater need, do not have large endowments, and work in areas that may be more impactful (dollar-for-dollar) than higher education.

4. As of June 30, 2012. University of California, *Annual Endowment Report Fiscal Year Ended June 30, 2012*, http://www.ucop.edu/treasurer/_files/report/UC_Annual_Endowment_Report_FY2011-2012.pdf.

5. Leah Ingram, "The Perfect Fit," *Triumph*, Spring 2010, 13.

6. Peter Frumkin, *Strategic Giving: The Art and Science of Philanthropy* (Chicago: University of Chicago Press, 2006), 155–73.

7. "Guide to Better Giving," Philanthropedia, http://www.myphilanthropedia.org/guide_to_better_giving.

8. Joel L. Fleishman, *The Foundation: A Great American Secret: How Private Wealth Is Changing the World* (New York: PublicAffairs, 2007), 220.

9. This book often discusses philanthropy as helping people, but one could reasonably make a case that there are other important objectives, such as animal welfare or preserving the earth.

3. DO-GOODERS AND DO-BESTERS

1. Dean Karlan and Jacob Appel, *More Than Good Intentions: How a New Economics Is Helping Solve Global Poverty* (New York: Dutton, 2011), 270.

2. Definition is available at http://www.merriam-webster.com/dictionary/do-gooders.

3. Paul Brest and Hal Harvey, *Money Well Spent: A Strategic Plan for Smart Philanthropy* (New York: Bloomberg Press, 2008), xiii–xiv. (Emphasis added.)

4. "Per Student Value of University Endowments . . . or the Rich Are Even Richer Than You Thought!," *Leiter Reports: A Philosophy Blog*, July 10, 2012, http://leiterreports.typepad.com/blog/2012/07/per-student-value-of-university-endowmentsor-the-rich-are-even-richer-than-you-thought.html.

4. THE ROLE OF EMOTIONAL GIVING

1. Lucius Annaeus Seneca, *Moral Essays, Volume III: de Beneficiis*, trans. John W. Basore (Cambridge, MA: Loeb Classical Library, 2004), available at http://www.goodreads.com/quotes/86302-a-gift-consists-not-in-what-is-done-or-given.

2. Peter Frumkin, *Strategic Giving: The Art and Science of Philanthropy* (Chicago: University of Chicago Press, 2006), ix.

3. Deborah Small, George Loewenstein, and Paul Slovic, "Sympathy and Callousness: The Impact of Deliberative Thought on Donations to Identifiable and Statistical Victims," *Organizational Behavior and Human Decision Processes* 102 (2007): 143-53.

4. Ibid., 146.

5. THE PAUCITY OF HELPFUL INFORMATION

1. As posted online at The Quotations Page, http://www.quotationspage.com/quote/1135.html.

2. "Vision," To Write Love on Her Arms, http://www.twloha.com/vision/.

3. Tim Ogden, "The Worst (and Best) Way to Pick a Charity This Year"(press release), Philanthropy Action, Dec. 1, 2009, http://www.philanthropyaction.com/nc/the_worst_and_best_way_to_pick_a_charity_this_year/.

4. Stephanie Strom, "To Help Donors Choose, Web Site Alters How It Sizes Up Charities," *New York Times*, Nov. 26, 2010.

5. "Charity Navigator FY 2012 Targets Dashboard - Final" (table), Charity Navigator, https://docs.google.com/file/d/0B8LHEIgBvQJRS3Qxak56OFRHQTQ/edit.

6. "How Do We Rate Charities' Accountability and Transparency?," Charity Navigator, http://www.charitynavigator.org/index.cfm?bay=content.view&cpid=1093.

7. CharityNavigator.org, *Results Reporting Concept Note: The Third Dimension of Intelligent Giving*, Jan. 2013, http://www.charitynavigator.org/__asset__/_etc_/CN_Results_Reporting_Concept_Note.pdf.

8. "Introducing Results Reporting: The Third Dimension of Intelligent Giving." Charity Navigator, Jan. 23, 2013, http://www.charitynavigator.org/index.cfm?bay=content.view&cpid=1526.

9. CharityNavigator.org, *Results Reporting Concept Note*.

10. "Roundtable discussion with nonprofit experts," Charity Navigator (page discontinued).

11. Melissa Berman, "From Fragments to a Mosaic," *Alliance* 15, no. 3 (Sept. 2010): 24–25.

12. "Sidney Frank: Family Philanthropy," Rockefeller Philanthropy Advisors, http://rockpa.org/page.aspx?pid=340 (by permission).

13. "Your Philanthropy Roadmap," Rockefeller Philanthropy Advisors, http://www.rockpa.org/page.aspx?pid=461. (Emphasis added.)

14. Berman, "From Fragments to a Mosaic," 25.

15. Ibid., 26.

16. Holden Karnofsky, "Quick Update," *The GiveWell Blog*, Feb. 17, 2007, http://blog.givewell.org/2007/02/17/quick-update/.

17. "About GiveWell," GiveWell, http://www.givewell.org/about.

18. "Against Malaria Foundation," GiveWell, http://www.givewell.org/international/top-charities/AMF#Costperlifesaved.

19. Holden Karnofsky, "GiveWell's Annual Self-Evaluation and Plan: A Big Picture Change in Priorities," *The GiveWell Blog*, Feb. 4, 2011, http://blog.givewell.org/2011/02/04/givewells-annual-self-evaluation-and-plan-a-big-picture-change-in-priorities/.

20. Carol J. Loomis, "A Conversation with Warren Buffett," *FORTUNE*, June 25, 2006, http://money.cnn.com/2006/06/25/magazines/fortune/charity2.fortune/index.htm.

6. DEVELOPING A MISSION

1. Colin Powell, "18 Lessons in Leadership," briefing presented by Gen. Powell to the Outreach to America Program, SEARS Corporate Headquarters, Chicago,

Illinois, http://www.airpower.au.af.mil/apjinternational/apj-s/2011/2011-4/2011_4_02_powell_s_eng.pdf.

2. The Robert Wood Johnson Foundation distributed about $523 million in grants during 2008 and had approximately $7.3 billion in assets as of December 31, 2008.

3. "Our Mission," Robert Wood Johnson Foundation, http://www.rwjf.org/about/mission.jsp.

4. Paul Brest and Hal Harvey, *Money Well Spent: A Strategic Plan for Smart Philanthropy* (New York: Bloomberg Press, 2008), 2, 7.

5. Ibid., 10–11.

6. Foundations have other considerations that make the "all else being equal" statement somewhat theoretical, as giving now reduces their asset base and ability to give in the future. Acknowledging that issue, I will not address it here.

7. United Nations Department of Economic and Social Affairs, Population Division, *World Population Prospects, The 2010 Revision*, http://esa.un.org/wpp/.

7. THE MOST IMPORTANT DECISIONS

1. Elizabeth MacDonald, "The Forbes Power Women Speak," *Forbes*, Aug. 8, 2007, http://www.forbes.com/2007/08/30/women-power-speech-biz-07women-cz_em_0830speak.html.

2. Giving USA Foundation, *Giving USA: The Annual Report on Philanthropy for the year 2011* (hereafter *Giving USA 2012*) (Chicago: Giving USA Foundation, 2012), 26, available at http://www.givingusareports.org.

3. Quoted from a fundraising letter from Children's Memorial Foundation, dated September 2009. The names were changed to provide anonymity (by permission).

4. "Health," UNICEF United States Fund, http://www.unicefusa.org/work/health/ (page discontinued).

5. "The Top Ten Causes of Death," WHO Fact Sheet No. 310, Nov. 2008.

6. Joel L. Fleishman, *The Foundation: A Great American Secret; How Private Wealth Is Changing the World* (New York: PublicAffairs, 2007), 220–21.

7. "Believe in Zero," UNICEF United States Fund, http://www.unicefusa.org/campaigns/believe-in-zero/.

8. MEASURING PERFORMANCE

1. Fay Twersky, Jodi Nelson, and Amy Ratcliffe, "Actionable Measurement Guide Cover Letter," *A Guide to Actionable Measurement* (Bill and Melinda Gates Foundation, 2010), 1, http://docs.gatesfoundation.org/learning/documents/guide-to-actionable-measurement.pdf.

2. "What We Do: Build a School," Build Africa, http://www.build-africa.org/pages/about-us.html.

3. "About Us," American Association for Cancer Research, http://www.aacr.org/home/about-us.aspx.

4. "VillageReach," GiveWell, http://www.givewell.org/international/top-charities/villagereach.

5. Build Africa does list some measures of results on its homepage, http://www.build-africa.org, but the measurements are clearly not as robust as those for VillageReach.

6. Africare, *As Our 40th Anniversary Year Draws to an End, Can We Count on Your Support?* (brochure) (2010).

7. Build Africa, *Annual Review 2009*, 8, http://www.build-africa.org/data/files/ba_annual_review_09_low_spreads.pdf.

8. Ibid., 7.

9. Ehren Reed and Johanna Morariu, *State of Evaluation 2010: Evaluation Practice and Capacity in the Nonprofit Sector* (Innovation Network, Oct. 2010), http://www.innonet.org/client_docs/innonet-state-of-evaluation-2010.pdf.

10. In July 2012, GiveWell updated its assessment of VillageReach. "We now understand it is possible that factors other than VillageReach's program might have contributed to the increase in coverage rate. As a result, we have moderated the confidence we had earlier in the extent to which VillageReach's program was responsible for the increase in coverage rates. . . . AMF and SCI [the charities that replaced VillageReach as GiveWell's top recommendations] are solidly better giving opportunities than VillageReach (both now and at the time we recommended it). . . . On the other hand, we wish to emphasize another sense in which VillageReach was—and is—an outstanding giving opportunity." See Elie Hassenfeld, "Rethinking VillageReach's PilotProject," *The GiveWell Blog*, July 26, 2012, http://blog.givewell.org/2012/07/26/rethinking-villagereachs-pilot-project/.

11. "About Us," IPPNW, http://ippnw.org/about-us.html.

12. "Nobel Peace Prize Winner 1985," IPPNW, http://ippnw.org/nobel-peace-prize.html.

13. "Kraft Family, Partners HealthCare to Establish National Center for Community Health" (press release), Partners HealthCare, Jan. 10, 2011, http://www.kraftcommunityhealth.org/News-And-Events/Kraft-Center-Donation-Announcement.aspx.

14. "Against Malaria Foundation," GiveWell, http://www.givewell.org/international/top-charities/AMF; "Mass Distribution of Long-Lasting Insecticide-Treated Nets (LLINs)," GiveWell, http://givewell.org/international/technical/programs/insecticide-treated-nets.

15. "Microfinance Against Malaria: A Combined Solution," Freedom from Hunger, http://www.freedomfromhunger.org/programs/malaria.php (page discontinued).

16. Peter Boone and Simon Johnson, "Breaking Out of the Pocket: Do Health Interventions Work? Which Ones and in What Sense?" in *What Works in Development: Thinking Big and Thinking Small*, eds. Jessica Cohen and William Easterly (Washington, DC: Brookings Institution, 2009), 68.

17. Peter Boone and Zhaoguo Zhan, *Lowering Child Mortality in Poor Countries: The Power of Knowledgeable Parents* (Discussion Paper 751, London School of Economics, Centre for Economic Performance, 2006), 22, http://eprints.lse.ac.uk/19799/.

9. EXAMPLES OF DO-BESTERS

1. David Schwartz, *The Magic of Thinking Big* (New York: Fireside, 1987), 21.

2. Bjorn Lomborg, *Global Crises, Global Solutions* (New York: Cambridge University Press, 2009), back cover. This book was based on the 2008 Copenhagen Consensus project; the 2012 project only included four Nobel Prize winners.

3. "Expert Panel Findings," Copenhagen Consensus, 2012, http://www.copenhagenconsensus.com/sites/default/files/Outcome_Document_Updated_1105.pdf.

4. Ibid.

5. *Guide to Giving* (Copenhagen Consensus Center, 2010). This is the Guide to Giving for the Copenhagen Consensus' 2008 study. The version for the 2012 study had not been published as of April 27, 2013.

6. The *Guide to Giving* for the 2008 study excludes two items from the priority list, the Doha development agenda and heart attack acute management, deeming them more appropriate for policymakers than donors. It isn't obvious to me why philanthropists shouldn't allocate their resources to political lobbying of policymakers to address these two issues.

7. *Guide to Giving*, 11.

8. "Top Charities," GiveWell, http://www.givewell.org/charities/top-charities (as available in April 27, 2013).

9. "How We Fund," The Mulago Foundation, http://www.mulagofoundation.org/?q=how-we-fund.

10. "How We Think About Impact," The Mulago Foundation, http://www.mulagofoundation.org/ideas/r/how-we-think-about-impact.

11. "Aquaya: A Clear Path to Clean Water," The Mulago Foundation, http://www.mulagofoundation.org/portfolio/aquaya.

12. "PMC: Acting for Change," The Mulago Foundation, http://www.mulagofoundation.org/portfolio/population-media-center (page discontinued).

13. "Bridge International Academies: Extremely Affordable Excellence," The Mulago Foundation, http://www.mulagofoundation.org/?q=portfolio/bridge-international-academies.

14. "Mission," Skoll Foundation, http://www.skollfoundation.org/about/mission/.

15. "About," Skoll Foundation, http://www.skollfoundation.org/about/.

16. "Approach" (press kit document), Skoll Foundation, http://www.skollfoundation.org/wp-content/uploads/2011/01/Approach.pdf.

17. Rahim Kanani, "An In-depth Interview With Sally Osberg, President and CEO of the Skoll Foundation," *Huffington Post*, Mar. 22, 2011, http://www.huffingtonpost.com/rahim-kanani/an-indepth-interview-with_5_b_838033.html.

18. "Jeff Skoll Giving Pledge" (letter), The Giving Pledge, July 20, 2010, http://cms.givingpledge.org/Content/uploads/634164734995607873_Skoll_072010.pdf.

19. "We Can End Poverty 2015: Millennium Development Goals," United Nations, http://www.un.org/millenniumgoals.

20. Chris Dunford, "The Millennium Development Goals: A Dashboard for Humanity," I-Newswire, Oct. 8, 2010, http://www.i-newswire.com/the-millennium-development-goals/65377.

21. *The Millennium Development Goals Report* (New York: United Nations, 2010), http://www.un.org/millenniumgoals/pdf/MDG%20Report%202010%20En%20r15%20-low%20res%2020100615%20-.pdf.

10. CHOOSING A CHARITY

1. Dean Karlan and Jacob Appel, *More Than Good Intentions: How a New Economics Is Helping Solve Global Poverty* (New York: Dutton, 2011), 270.

2. "Programs," Freedom from Hunger, http://www.freedomfromhunger.org/programs/ (page discontinued).

3. "Freedom from Hunger," GiveWell, http://www.givewell.org/international/charities/freedom-from-hunger.

4. Chris Dunford, comment on "Guest Post from Eric Friedman," *The GiveWell Blog*, June 21, 2011, http://blog.givewell.org/2011/06/21/guest-post-from-eric-friedman/.

5. "How It Works," DonorsChoose.org, http://www.donorschoose.org/about.

11. PROJECT SELECTION (OR DECIDING NOT TO SELECT PROJECTS)

1. Peter Frumkin, *The Essence of Strategic Giving* (Chicago: University of Chicago Press, 2010), 100.

2. "Bloomberg Philanthropies Commits $50 Million to Sierra Club's Beyond Coal Campaign to Move America Toward Cleaner Energy" (press release), Sierra Club, July 21, 2011, http://action.sierraclub.org/site/MessageViewer?em_id=211461.0.

3. Michael Brune and Michael Bloomberg, "Why America Has to Get Off Coal" (opinion piece), CNN.com, July 29, 2011, http://www.cnn.com/2011/OPINION/07/29/bloomberg.brune.coal/.

4. "Bloomberg Philanthropies Commits $50 Million" (press release).

5. Brian Walsh, "'Coal Kills Every Day': Michael Bloomberg Pledges $50 Million to Fight the Coal Industry," *Time*, July 21, 2011, http://www.time.com/time/health/article/0,8599,2084476,00.html.

6. "No. 2: Michael R. Bloomberg," *Chronicle of Philanthropy*, Feb. 6, 2011, http://philanthropy.com/article/No-2-Michael-R-Bloomberg/126107/.

7. "No. 5: Michael R. Bloomberg," *Chronicle of Philanthropy*, Feb. 6, 2012, http://philanthropy.com/article/2012-Philanthropy-50-Donors/130550; Bloomberg likely would have been ranked as one of the ten most generous philanthropists in 2012, but he declined to provide sufficient information to the *Chronicle of Philanthropy* to make the list. "Why Perennial Donors Bloomberg and Gates Are Missing From the Latest Philanthropy 50," *Chronicle of Philanthropy*, Feb. 10, 2013, http://philanthropy.com/article/Why-Bloomberg-GatesOther/137171/.

8. *Foundation Giving Trends* (report) (Foundation Center, 2010). Actual percentage of unrestricted gifts is 19.2 percent.

9. *Giving USA 2012*, 26.

10. UNICEF, *Report on Regular Resources 2010* (Sept. 2011), 3–4, http://www.unicef.org/publications/index_59759.html.

11. "UNICEF's Work," *UNICEF United States Fund*, http://www.unicefusa.org/work/.

12. "Donate to Support UNICEF's Humanitarian Programs Worldwide," UNICEF United States Fund, http://www.unicefusa.org/donate/.

12. VOLUNTEERING AND OTHER WAYS OF DONATING YOURSELF

1. Shel Silverstein, "Helping," *Free to Be You and Me* (© 1972 Ms Foundation for Women, used by permission of Free to Be Foundation, www.freetobefoundation.org).

2. "Why We're Here," Kids' Food Basket, http://www.kidsfoodbasket.org/our-purpose/why-were-here.

3. Cody Switzer, "How One Corporation's Efficiency Team Improved Operations at a Charity," interview video posted on the website of the *Chronicle of Philanthropy*, July 27, 2011, http://philanthropy.com/article/A-Businesss-Gift-Improving-a/128395/.

4. Charlie Wilson, "Amway and Kids' Food Basket: Giving Back Using Lean Principles," *Managing Times* Q4 (2004): 8–9.

5. "2004 Founders' IPO Letter: From the S-1 Registration Statement," Google Investor Relations, http://investor.google.com/corporate/2004/ipo-founders-letter.html.

6. Katie Hafner, "Philanthropy Google's Way: Not the Usual," *New York Times*, Sept. 14, 2006, http://www.nytimes.com/2006/09/14/technology/14google.html?pagewanted=print.

7. "About," Google.org, http://www.google.org/about.html.

8. Stephanie Strom and Miguel Helft, "Google Finds It Hard to Reinvent Philanthropy," *New York Times*, Jan. 29, 2011, http://www.nytimes.com/2011/01/30/business/30charity.html?pagewanted=all.

9. "Expert Panel Findings," Copenhagen Consensus, 2012, http://www.copenhagenconsensus.com/sites/default/files/Outcome_Document_Updated_1105.pdf.

10. Warren Buffett, "My Philanthropic Pledge" (letter), The Giving Pledge, http://givingpledge.org/#warren_buffett.

11. Sean Coughlan, "Banking 'Can Be an Ethical Career Choice,'" *BBC News*, Nov. 21, 2011, http://www.bbc.co.uk/news/education-15820786.

12. Joseph O'Shea, "What Should I Do With My Life? An Interview with Will Crouch on the Ethics of Career Choice," *Journal of College & Character* 13, no. 1 (Feb. 2012), http://journals.naspa.org/jcc/vol13/iss1/10/ (page discontinued).

13. William Crouch, "Following in Schindler's Footsteps," *80,000 Hours Blog*, June 29, 2012, http://80000hours.org/blog/52-following-in-schindler-s-footsteps.

14. O'Shea, "What Should I Do With My Life?"

15. "Frequently Asked Questions," Clinton Global Initiative, http://www.clintonglobalinitiative.org/aboutus/faq_aboutus.asp?Section=AboutUs&PageTitle=FAQ:About Us; *Building the World We Believe in: William J. Clinton Foundation 2011 Annual*

Report (William J. Clinton Foundation, 2012), http://www.clintonfoundation.org/assets/files/reports_cf/cfAnnualReport2011.pdf.

13. LEVERAGING YOUR DONATION

1. "How to Give Away a Million Dollars," *Slate*, Nov. 10, 2006, http://www.slate.com/id/2153314/.

2. Several years after the 2006 article was published, in 2012, New Leaders' website reported that it had trained almost eight hundred school leaders in its first decade, impacting nearly a quarter of a million students. "About," New Leaders, http://www.newleaders.org/about/.

3. A fourth source is possible, though it requires a greater leap of faith. If the improvements in education ultimately result in higher income for its participants or a lower need for future government services, this may ultimately result in more income tax revenues or lower government spending needs, which could cover the program's cost.

4. "Annual Fund Matching Gift Challenge," *Duke Law News*, Apr. 6, 2011, http://www.law.duke.edu/news/story?id=6307&u=11.

5. Matt Miller, "How Billionaires Could Save the Country," *Washington Post*, Aug. 31, 2011, http://www.washingtonpost.com/opinions/the-billionaires-chance-to-save-the-country/2011/08/31/gIQAUhXtrJ_story.html.

6. Office of Management and Budget, *Fiscal Year 2012 Historical Tables: Budget of the U.S. Government*. (Washington: U.S. Government Printing Office, 2012), 23, http://www.whitehouse.gov/sites/default/files/omb/budget/fy2012/assets/hist.pdf.

7. Miller, "How Billionaires Could Save the Country." (Emphasis added.)

8. "Scaling Access to Life-Changing Products," Living Goods, http://livinggoods.org/what-we-do/our-mission/.

9. Chuck Slaughter, "Taking the 'Avon' Way to Reach 'The Last Mile,'" Living Goods, Oct. 31, 2011, http://livinggoods.org/taking-the-avon-way-to-reach-the-last-mile/ (originally published at *Huffington Post*, http://www.huffingtonpost.com/chuck-slaughter/taking-the-avon-way-to-re_b_1067840.html).

10. "Ensuring Sustainability," Living Goods, http://livinggoods.org/what-we-do/our-mission/ensuring-sustainability/.

11. Michael E. Porter and Mark R. Kramer, "Philanthropy's New Agenda: Creating Value," *Harvard Business Review* (November–December 1999): 121–30, http://www.cof.org/files/Documents/Conferences/How%20philanthropy%20can%20make%20private%20markets%20work%20for%20low-income%20neighborhoods.pdf.

12. Ibid., 123.

13. Ibid., 123–25.

14. TEN SMART APPROACHES THAT WORK

1. "Quotes," Chenango United Way, http://www.chenangouw.org/quotes.html (and several other online sources).

2. Judy Belk, "The Art of Giving: Feeding Our Minds and Souls," *Linkages Newsletter from Rockefeller Philanthropy Advisors* (Winter/Spring 2009).

3. "Opportunity cost" definition, *Answers.com*, http://www.answers.com/topic/opportunity-cost.

4. *Giving USA 2012*, 4.

5. Holden Karnofsky, "GiveWell Is Aiming to Have a New #1 Charity by December," *The GiveWell Blog*, Oct. 26, 2011, http://blog.givewell.org/2011/10/26/givewell-is-aiming-to-have-a-new-1-charity-by-december/. In July 2012, GiveWell updated its assessment of VillageReach. "We now understand it is possible that factors other than VillageReach's program might have contributed to the increase in coverage rate. As a result, we have moderated the confidence we had earlier in the extent to which VillageReach's program was responsible for the increase in coverage rates. . . . AMF and SCI [the charities that replaced VillageReach as GiveWell's top recommendations] are solidly better giving opportunities than VillageReach (both now and at the time we recommended it). . . . On the other hand, we wish to emphasize another sense in which VillageRead was—and is—an outstanding giving opportunity." See Elie Hassenfeld, "Rethinking VillageReach's Pilot Project," *The GiveWell Blog*, July 26, 2012, http://blog.givewell.org/2012/07/26/rethinking-villagereachs-pilot-project/.

6. "UNICEF's Work," UNICEF United States Fund, http://www.unicefusa.org/work/.

7. "11 Facts About the 2004 Indian Ocean Tsunami," DoSomething.org, http://www.dosomething.org/tipsandtools/11-facts-about-2004-indian-ocean-tsunami.

8. "Haiti Earthquake Recovery 3 Years Later: Where Has the Money Gone?," *Huffington Post*, Jan. 11, 2013, http://www.huffingtonpost.com/2013/01/12/haiti-earthquake-recovery-2013_n_2451267.html?utm_hp_ref=haiti-earthquake.

9. "Tsunami Five-Year Report Q&A," UNICEF, Dec. 18, 2009, http://www.unicef.org/eapro/Tsunami_Q_and_A.pdf.

10. "Haiti Earthquake Recovery 3 Years Later," *Huffington Post*.

11. Joseph Guyler Delva, "Relief Agency Slams Haiti Quake Recovery 'Quagmire,'" Reuters, Jan. 5, 2011.

12. "Haiti Earthquake Recovery 3 Years Later," *Huffington Post*.

13. Leif Wenar, "Poverty Is No Pond: Challenges for the Affluent," in *Giving Well: The Ethics of Philanthropy*, ed. Thomas Pogge, Patricia Illingworth, and Leif Wenar (Oxford: Oxford University Press, 2010), 104.

14. As an example of how disaster relief causes can be so well funded, UNICEF stopped all new fundraising initiatives for relief efforts for the East Asian tsunami on January 26, 2005 (a month after the disaster) because it estimated that all funding needs had been met. UNICEF reports that it declined some large donations afterward when suggestions of redirecting the funds were rejected by the donors. "Tsunami Five-Year Report Q&A," UNICEF.

15. "Impact," DonorsChoose.org, http://www.donorschoose.org/about/impact.html.

16. Peter Singer, *The Life You Can Save* (New York: Random House, 2009), 103.

17. Kristi Kimball and Malka Kopell, "Letting Go," *Stanford Social Innovation Review* (Spring 2011), 37–41.

15. THE SELFISH GIVER IN ALL OF US

1. Don E. Fehrenbacher and Virginia Fehrenbacher, *Recollected Words of Abraham Lincoln* (Stanford, CA: Stanford University Press, 1996), 245.

2. "About SMA: Overview," SMA Foundation, http://www.smafoundation.org/about-sma.

3. "Nightline: UpClose with Ted Koppel. 'Arya Singh'" (transcript of televised interview), SMA Foundation, Jan. 21, 2003, http://www.smafoundation.org/SMA/About-Us/Media/Stories/Stories/Nightline-UpClose-with-Ted-Koppel-Arya-Singh-.

4. Robert Langreth and Alex Nussbaum, "To Save a Child," Bloomberg Markets, Oct. 2011, 110.

5. "About Us: Overview," SMA Foundation, http://www.smafoundation.org/about-us/.

6. Ibid.

7. Robert Langreth, "For Arya," *Forbes*, Mar. 28, 2005, http://www.forbes.com/forbes/2005/0328/094.html.

8. Langreth and Nussbaum, "To Save a Child," 118.

9. "To Write Love On Her Arms Wins $1 Million Grant From Chase at First-Ever American Giving Awards" (press release), JPMorgan Chase & Co., Dec. 11, 2011, http://investor.shareholder.com/jpmorganchase/releasedetail.cfm?ReleaseID=632288.

10. Bill Gorman, "TV Ratings Saturday: 'Rudolph The Red Nosed Reindeer' Guides CBS to Victory," Zap2it, Dec. 11, 2011, http://tvbythenumbers.zap2it.com/2011/12/11/tv-ratings-saturday-rudolph-the-red-nosed-reindeer-guides-cbs-to-victory/113354/.

11. Brian Stelter, "For Chase, a TV Show to Promote Its Charity," *New York Times*, Dec. 9, 2011 (online) and Dec. 10, 2011 (in print), http://www.nytimes.com/2011/12/10/business/media/jpmorgan-is-promoting-its-charity-on-nbc-show.html?_r=2&adxnnl=1&adxnnlx=1323833008-KWis2UnK79lWFnmzlKzHrw.

12. Ibid.

13. Ibid.

14. "Gifts of $1-Million or More in 2012, by Cause," *Chronicle of Philanthropy*, Feb. 10, 2013, http://philanthropy.com/article/Gifts-of-1-million-or-More-in/137147/.

15. Peter Singer covers many of these moral issues in his book *The Life You Can Save* (New York: Random House, 2009).

16. PHILANTHROPY REINVENTED

1. Sean Stannard-Stockton, "The Test of a First Rate Philanthropist," *Tactical Philanthropy* (blog), Mar. 30, 2011, http://www.tacticalphilanthropy.com/2011/03/the-test-of-a-first-rate-philanthropist.

2. Peter Singer, *The Life You Can Save* (New York: Random House, 2009), 103.

3. For an excellent discussion of this gray area, I recommend reading Singer's *The Life You Can Save.*

4. In the interest of full disclosure, I'll note that I am not religious.

5. Examples include *Money Well Spent: A Strategic Plan for Smart Philanthropy, The Art of Giving: Where the Soul Meets a Business Plan, Give Smart: Philanthropy That Gets Results, Inspired Philanthropy: Your Step-by-Step Guide to Creating a Giving Plan and Leaving a Legacy, Giving 2.0: Transform Your Giving and Our World,* and *Give a Little: How Your Small Donations Can Transform our World* (see selected bibliography).

6. Giving What We Can is an example of an organization like this.

Selected Bibliography

Arrillaga-Andreessen, Laura. *Giving 2.0: Transform Your Giving and Our World.* San Francisco: Jossey-Bass, 2011.

Banerjee, Abhijit, and Esther Duflo. *Poor Economics: A Radical Rethinking of the Way to Fight Global Poverty*. New York: PublicAffairs, 2011.

Bishop, Matthew, and Michael Green. *Philanthrocapitalism: How Giving Can Save the World.* New York: Bloomsbury Press, 2009.

Brest, Paul, and Hal Harvey. *Money Well Spent: A Strategic Plan for Smart Philanthropy.* New York: Bloomberg Press, 2008.

Bronfman, Charles, and Jeffrey R. Solomon. *The Art of Giving: Where the Soul Meets a Business Plan.* San Francisco: Jossey-Bass, 2009.

Cohen, Jessica, and William Easterly. *What Works in Development? Thinking Big and Thinking Small.* Washington, DC: Brookings Institution Press, 2009.

Collier, Paul. *The Bottom Billion: Why the Poorest Countries Are Failing and What Can Be Done About It.* New York: Oxford University Press, 2008.

Crutchfield, Leslie R., and Heather McLeon Grant. *Forces for Good: The Six Practices of High-Impact Nonprofits.* San Francisco: Jossey-Bass, 2008.

Crutchfield, Leslie R., John V. Kania, and Mark R. Kramer. *Do More Than Give: The Six Practices of Donors Who Change the World.* San Francisco: Jossey-Bass, 2011.

Easterly, William. *The White Man's Burden: Why the West's Efforts to Aid the Rest Have Done So Much Ill and So Little Good.* New York: Penguin, 2006.

Eisenberg, Pablo. *Challenges for Nonprofits and Philanthropy: The Courage to Change.* Edited by Stacy Palmer. Lebanon, NH: University Press of New England, 2005.

Fleishman, Joel L. *The Foundation: A Great American Secret; How Private Wealth Is Changing the World.* New York: PublicAffairs, 2007.

Frumkin, Peter. *Strategic Giving: The Art and Science of Philanthropy.* Chicago: University of Chicago Press, 2006.

Goldberg, Steven H. *Billions of Drops in Millions of Buckets: Why Philanthropy Doesn't Advance Social Progress*. Hoboken, NJ: John Wiley & Sons, 2009.

Grace, Kay Sprinkel, and Alan L. Wendroff. *High Impact Philanthropy: How Donors, Boards, and Nonprofit Organizations Can Transform Communities*. Hoboken, NJ: John Wiley & Sons, 2001.

Illingworth, Patricia, Thomas Pogge, and Leif Wenar. *Giving Well: The Ethics of Philanthropy*. New York: Oxford University Press, 2011.

Jamison, Dean T., Joel G. Breman, Anthony R. Measham, George Alleyne, Mariam Claeson, David B. Evans, Prabhat Jha, Anne Mills, and Philip Musgrove. *Priorities in Health: Disease Control Priorities Companion Volume*. Washington, DC: The World Bank, 2006.

Karlan, Dean, and Jacob Appel. *More Than Good Intentions: How a New Economics Is Helping to Solve Global Poverty*. New York: Penguin Group, 2011.

Kass, Amy. *Giving Well, Doing Good: Readings for Thoughtful Philanthropists*. Bloomington: Indiana University Press, 2008.

Lomborg, Bjørn. *Global Crises, Global Solutions*. Second edition. New York: Cambridge University Press, 2009.

Lupton, Robert D. *Toxic Charity: How Churches and Charities Hurt Those They Help (And How to Reverse It)*. New York: HarperOne, 2011.

Moyo, Dambisa. *Dead Aid: Why Aid Is Not Working and How There Is a Better Way for Africa*. New York: Farrar, Straus and Giroux, 2009.

Odendahl, Teresa. *Charity Begins at Home: Generosity and Self-Interest Among the Philanthropic Elite*. New York: Basic Books, 1990.

Payton, Robert L., and Michael P. Moody. *Understanding Philanthropy: Its Meaning and Mission*. Bloomington: Indiana University Press, 2008.

Sachs, Jeffrey. *The End of Poverty: Economic Possibilities for Our Time*. New York: Penguin Books, 2006.

Singer, Peter. *The Life You Can Save*. New York: Random House, 2009.

Stern, Ken. *With Charity for All: Why Charities are Failing and a Better Way to Give*. New York: Doubleday, 2013.

Tierney, Thomas J., and Joel L. Fleishman. *Give Smart: Philanthropy That Gets Results*. New York: PublicAffairs, 2012.

Wilbur, Colburn, and Fred Setterberg. *Giving with Confidence: A Guide to Savvy Philanthropy*. Berkeley, CA: Heyday, 2012.

Index

About the Author

Eric Friedman is an individual donor who has spent several years trying to understand how to maximize the impact of his giving, including traveling to Africa to see his giving in action. He is an actuary. He graduated from Stanford University with a double major in mathematics and economics. He lives in Oak Park, Illinois.